"Too many books on preaching promote style over substance, success over faithfulness. Thankfully, *More than a Sermon* gives us a more excellent way. Dr. Webster grounds preaching in its God-given purpose by calling us to the 'why' behind the 'what,' and he instructs us in its practice by drawing from the deep well of his pastoral wisdom. Let this book teach, inspire, and challenge you as it did me!"

> E. ALCÁNTARA, professor of preaching,
ul W. Powell Endowed Chair in Preaching,
George W. Truett Theological Seminary

idents and seasoned preachers alike grow in their ability to 'rightly handle the word of truth' (2 Tim 2:15). Webster acknowledges and explores the challenges of the seemingly 'impossible' task of preaching and offers practical wisdom for proclaiming the good news."

CHASE EDGAR, church planter,
Church of the Ascension, Anderson, SC

"Weaving together personal stories with a kaleidoscope of resources from well-known preachers, pastors, and theologians, Doug Webster encourages his readers to find their God-given voice in preaching. In addition to providing practical preparation advice, Webster encourages pastors to remember their first love, Christ himself, as they approach the pulpit."

ABBY GATLIFF, pastor for student and family discipleship,
South Highland Presbyterian Church, Birmingham, AL

"The soil for preaching is as prime as ever these days. Thus, preachers of God's word must have a life-long commitment and Christlike compassion to proclaim the gospel simply, fully, and freely. In *More than a Sermon*, Doug Webster writes with the mind of a scholar and the heart of a pastor—with extensive and fruitful experience in both. He offers a compelling, theologically reasoned, and ecclesiastically-oriented approach to guide preachers in cultivating our gifts. He urges us not to reduce preaching to impressive sermons. Instead, Webster challenges us to embark on the road less traveled, preaching faithful and fruitful sermons that magnify Christ, comfort and convict, and edify the weary so that—over time, with God's help—we all may mature fully in Christ. Thank you for this timely gift!"

SAMUEL HAGOS, experience pastor,
Progressive Baptist Church, Chicago, IL

"Doug Webster taught us to look for the 'tension in the text' but an equally daunting tension lies in the calling to preach the word of the Lord in a way that convicts but also comforts, directs but also deepens, rebukes but also reminds listeners of the story of redemption. Webster uses biblical illustrations to cover that tension which the pastor typically does not feel until standing before a congregation knowing the wide variety of needs present that Sunday. The tension which teaches the preaching pastor that a sermon must be proclaimed throughout all areas of ministry and not just for thirty minutes on Sunday morning."

SHAWN RICHARDSON, pastor,
Luctor Christian Reformed Church, Prairie View, KS

"In *More than a Sermon*, Doug Webster offers a theological window of practical understanding to the homiletical adage—the faithful preacher comforts the afflicted and afflicts the comfortable. He tells readers the purpose of preaching and offers a didactic sermonic buffet of pastoral and prophetic messages designed to address the myriad of occasions requiring preachers to deliver a word from the Lord. The unbreakable tie that binds the homiletical/hermeneutical content and sermonic offerings is their focus—Christ! This book is a treasure trove for those who are serious about marrying biblical theology and homiletics. As Dr. Webster captively demonstrates, biblical theology and homiletics were intended to be joined together; therefore, let no one put them asunder!"

ROBERT SMITH JR., professor of Christian preaching,
Beeson Divinity School, Samford University, AL

MORE

— THAN A —

SERMON

The PURPOSE
and PRACTICE
of CHRISTIAN
PREACHING

MORE

— THAN A —

SERMON

The Purpose
and PRACTICE
of CHRISTIAN
PREACHING

MORE

— THAN A —

SERMON

The PURPOSE
and PRACTICE
of CHRISTIAN
PREACHING

DOUGLAS D. WEBSTER

LEXHAM PRESS

More than a Sermon: The Purpose and Practice of Christian Preaching

Copyright 2024 Douglas D. Webster

Lexham Press, 1313 Commercial St., Bellingham, WA 98225
LexhamPress.com

You may use brief quotations from this resource in presentations, articles, and books. For all other uses, please write Lexham Press for permission. Email us at permissions@lexhampress.com.

Unless otherwise noted, Scripture quotations are the author's own translation or are from the ESV® Bible (*The Holy Bible, English Standard Version*®). Copyright © 2001 by Crossway Bibles, a publishing ministry of Good News Publishers. Used by permission. All rights reserved.

Scripture quotations marked (NIV) are from the Holy Bible, NEW INTERNATIONAL VERSION®. Copyright © 1973, 1978, 1984, 2011 by Biblica, Inc. Used by permission. All rights reserved worldwide.

Scripture quotations marked (KJV) are from the King James Version. Public domain.

Scripture quotations marked (MESSAGE) are from THE MESSAGE. Copyright © by Eugene H. Peterson 1993, 1994, 1995, 1996, 2000, 2001, 2002. Used by permission of Tyndale House Publishers, Inc.

Scripture quotations marked (NRSV) are from the New Revised Standard Version Bible, copyright © 1989, National Council of the Churches of Christ in the United States of America. Used by permission. All rights reserved.

The art on the cover of the man's hand is from "Sir Francis Laking and Sir Frederick Treves. Oil painting" by Harry Herman Salomon, Wellcome images, https://commons.wikimedia.org/wiki/File:Sir_Francis_Laking_and_Sir_Frederick_Treves._Oil_painting_Wellcome_L0021980.jpg. The painting was slightly altered from its original form for this cover.

Print ISBN 9781683597520
Digital ISBN 9781683597537
Library of Congress Control Number 2023945782

Lexham Editorial: Todd Hains, Claire Brubaker, Danielle Burlaga, Mandi Newell
Cover Design: Gabe Easton
Typesetting: Abigail Stocker

23 24 25 26 27 28 29 / US / 12 11 10 9 8 7 6 5 4 3 2 1

To Beeson Pastors Who Preach

Contents

Contents

Prayers for Discernment

BLESSED LORD, who caused all Holy Scriptures to be written for our learning: Grant us so to hear them, read, mark, learn, and inwardly digest them, that by patience and the comfort of your holy Word we may embrace and ever hold fast the blessed hope of everlasting life, which you have given us in our Savior Jesus Christ; who lives and reigns with you and the Holy Spirit, one God, for ever and ever. *Amen.*

MAY YOUR LOVE abound more and more in knowledge and depth of insight, so that you may be able to discern what is best and may be pure and blameless for the day of Christ, filled with the fruit of righteousness that comes through Jesus Christ—to the glory and praise of God. (*Phil 1:9–11*)

Scripture to Sermon: Ten Steps

1. Remember that sermon preparation is a way of life, not a job description.

2. Read the passage. Pray the passage. Reread the passage.

3. Give yourself time and space to think and pray over the passage without books.

4. Study the passage in its literary, linguistic, and cultural context.

5. Put your ideas down on paper. Outline or manuscript the sermon.

6. Illustrate your sermon with people and stories.

7. Preach first to yourself. Discuss the sermon with wise and discerning friends.

8. Serve the listener. Never assume you are preaching to a captive audience.

9. Remain open to the Spirit's wisdom in developing the sermon even after you have preached it.

10. End every sermon with a focus on what Christ has done for us.

Is not my word like fire, declares the LORD,
and like a hammer that breaks the rock in pieces?

Jeremiah 23:29

A bruised reed he will not break,
and a faintly burning wick he will not quench.

Isaiah 42:3

Preface

The prophets and the apostles used a variety of metaphors to describe the impact of God's word. Jeremiah likened preaching God's word to fire burning up straw or a hammer breaking a rock. Isaiah's servant of the Lord represents the other end of the preaching spectrum: "He will not cry aloud or lift up his voice, or make it heard in the street; a bruised reed he will not break, and a faintly burning wick he will not quench" (Isa 42:2–3). The word of God is a double-edged sword, confronting and comforting, convicting and consoling, judging and saving. These two metaphors, the rock and reed, encompass the power and the wisdom of God to cover the full range of human need. The power of God's word to achieve its purposes is never in doubt, but our ability to swing the hammer that breaks hard hearts and our ability to preach so as not to break a bruised reed remains the preacher's challenge. Left to ourselves it is impossible, but in the Spirit, it is not only possible but a personal and practical necessity.

Anyone who follows the Lord Jesus Christ and seeks to communicate God's word faces the rock-and-reed challenge. For fathers and mothers, it is a daily concern. Husbands and wives, brothers and sisters, friends and coworkers need to discern when to deliver a prophetic word and when to appeal with a comforting word. Pastors ought to lead the way in showing the household of faith how to use God's word to strengthen conviction and to show compassion. There are times when we need the full armor of God, from the belt of truth to the sword of the Spirit, to do battle, and there are times when we need to clothe ourselves with "compassion, kindness, humility, meekness, and patience" (Col 3:12 NRSV; see Eph 6:13–17).

We need wisdom to preach first to ourselves and then to others so that we might "grow in the grace and knowledge of our Lord and Savior Jesus Christ" (2 Pet 3:18). By their example pastors teach us how to use God's word in God's way. The apostle Paul prayed for the believers at Philippi, a prayer that applies to us as well, that their love would "abound more and more, with knowledge and all discernment, so that you may approve what is excellent, and so be pure and blameless for the day of Christ, filled with the fruit of righteousness that comes through Jesus Christ, to the glory and praise of God" (Phil 1:9–11). This profound relationship between love and knowledge is essential in the delivery and application of God's word.

The physician who lovingly gives her patient the hard truth of a difficult diagnosis is proving the apostle's point: love and knowledge go hand in hand. The pastor is like a caring doctor informing a vulnerable patient that he has cancer. When I was eighteen an oncologist looked me in the eye and said with his hand on my knee, "I'm sorry. I have some bad news. You have non-Hodgkin's lymphoma." My doctor promised to do everything he could to help me through the ordeal, and he did. He owned my cancer as his challenge. He was devoted to my healing. He entered into my struggle as if it were his battle to fight. It is that kind of empathy and heartfelt concern that ought to characterize our delivery of God's hard truths and good news.[1]

Our deep desire to present "everyone mature in Christ" (Col 1:28) empowers us to face *the rock and reed challenge*. This involves helping believers use God's word to discern what is best so that we all may be "filled with the fruit of righteousness" (Phil 1:11). The goal for all Christ's followers is to "try to discern what is pleasing to the Lord" and "to walk in a manner worthy of the calling to which you have been called, with all humility and gentleness, with patience, bearing with one another in love, eager to maintain the unity of the Spirit in the bond of peace" (Eph 5:10; 4:1–3).

Good preaching is grounded in God's word and helps believers think for themselves, so that they are no longer "conformed to this world" but "transformed by the renewal of [their] mind" (Rom 12:2). If pastors preach the whole counsel of God, they will find the hammer that breaks the rock and the grace that protects the bruised reed. Paul exemplified both the power and the weakness we seek. He writes that we have the *divine power* "to destroy strongholds. We destroy arguments and every lofty opinion raised against the knowledge of God, and take every thought captive to obey Christ" (2 Cor 10:4–5). And we have the *divine weakness* rooted in the sufficiency of God's grace; God's power "is made perfect in weakness" (2 Cor 12:9).

The apostle Paul references the rock and reed challenge when he describes the gospel as "the aroma of Christ to God among those who are being saved," whereas to those who are perishing it smells like death (2 Cor 2:15–16). The hammer that breaks rocks proclaims the exclusive truth claim of Jesus, the Sermon on the Mount's kingdom mission, and the theology of the cross. There is no amount of positive public relations or finessing the message that will change the fact that "the word of the cross is folly to those who are perishing, but to us who are being saved it is the power of God" (1 Cor 1:18).

Jesus illustrates the rock-and-reed challenge in his dialogue with Nicodemus and the Samaritan woman (John 3–4). At the outset of Jesus's public ministry, he preached the gospel to two very different people. Nicodemus was named, and his name meant "victor." The woman at the well remained unnamed. Nicodemus was a ruler among the Jews, a member of the Sanhedrin, an orthodox Pharisee, living in Jerusalem. He inquired of Jesus at night, perhaps out of privacy concerns. He may have come out of personal interest, or he may have come out of a sense of duty. As a Pharisee, it was his vowed responsibility to evaluate Jesus's teaching. By contrast, the unnamed woman was an ordinary person living in a rural Samaritan village. She was a victim of either great loss or great lust. She may have been marginalized because of her marital status, and she belonged to the heretical sect of the Samaritans. Neither the man nor the woman would have had anything to do with each other for any number of reasons, but Jesus related to both of them in the most profound way.

These two individuals could not have been more different: Nicodemus was a self-confident, powerful Pharisee, and she was an insecure, marginalized Samaritan woman. She may have been an abused woman, a grieving widow, who was passed down from one brother to another, or else she was a promiscuous woman. In any case, she came to the well at noon to avoid others and to draw water. She had no desire to relate to anyone, especially to a Jewish man sitting by the well.

Like a blacksmith hammering on an anvil, Jesus shattered Nicodemus's self-confident religious worldview with his unexpected pronouncement, "You must be born again." But to the Samaritan woman, a bruised reed if there ever were one, Jesus humbly requested a drink of water before offering the living water of eternal life.

The apostle John narrates these two strikingly different encounters side by side in order to draw out Jesus's distinctive rock-and-reed approach to the gospel. Throughout his ministry,

Jesus met the preaching challenge. He shattered the rock of unbelief and protected the bruised reed. When God's word is taught, preached, shared, and discussed, it has the power to convict and the power to comfort. It is both prophetic and pastoral. The word preached has the power to shatter the hard-heartedness of the self-righteous and the power to comfort the insecure and brokenhearted. It confronts the oppressor and the oppressed alike with the gospel of repentance and redemption.

The hard edge of prophetic conviction remains just as relevant today as it was in Jeremiah's day. Preaching professor Jared Alcántara defines conviction "as a commitment to a cause greater than oneself for the sake of a mission greater than one's life." He then identifies five attributes that establish and sustain this gospel-inspired conviction: a personal commitment to Jesus Christ, the centrality of the Spirit's work in our lives and in our preaching, a humble submission to the stewardship of the gospel, a strategy of faithfulness and fruitfulness over worldly success, and a personal embodiment of the gospel of God's grace in our lives.[2]

The truth of the gospel shatters the ideological captivity of our late modern age. It breaks the chains that bind hearts and minds. If we preach Acts 4:12, "There is salvation in no one else, for there is no other name under heaven given among men by which we must be saved," it is like a hammer blow against the rock of unbelief. Yet the beauty of Isaiah's description of the one who does not break the bruised reed remains equally true. Jesus's great invitation still stands: "Come to me, all you who labor and are heavy laden, and I will give you rest. Take my yoke upon you, and learn from me, for I am gentle and lowly in heart, and you will find rest for your souls. For my yoke is easy and my burden is light" (Matt 11:28–30). Like Paul, we are not ashamed of the gospel because "it is the power of God for salvation to everyone who believes" (Rom 1:16). Good preaching involves both powerful exhortation and compassionate entreating.

This book explores what it means to proclaim Christ, "warning everyone and teaching everyone with all wisdom, that we may present everyone mature in Christ" (Col 1:28). I begin with the purpose of preaching. I seek to develop a fresh perspective on the importance and challenge of faithful and fruitful preaching. I follow this up with practical insights and examples of preaching Advent sermons and Lenten sermons. I offer pastoral perspectives and examples for preaching memorial service meditations and wedding sermons. I finish with practical spiritual direction on preaching in a public crisis and preaching sermons that address social and political concerns.

My aim is to stimulate an in-depth conversation on preaching. Learning how to preach faithfully and fruitfully is all about proclaiming Christ to the people we serve. It is not so much about technique and style as paying attention to the biblical text so that it shapes the content, focus, tone, and thrust of our sermons. We engage the biblical text prayerfully, theologically, linguistically, sociologically, emotionally, and politically—all of this so that we might proclaim Christ in the Spirit. Everything written here has been worked out and worked through *with people*, whether in a church or mission setting or in a seminary seminar.

Preachers preach so the people of God can preach.[3] Physical presence and personal engagement are critical to learning and genuine comprehension. Significant and edifying communication depends on being in communion with God and in community with one another. Facial expressions, tonal inflections, and body language contribute to the dialogue with both God and one another. Even in-person silence is different from silence on social media. Brothers and sisters in Christ need to be together to do this gospel work, and we need to do it in the presence of God.

Disciple making takes place in person, in community, and in worship. I cannot imagine trying to raise kids online, and I am not so sure it is all that different for growing strong disciples. Preaching and teaching God's word is vital to this soul-shaping work, but it is best done in such a way as to relate to people and invite personal interaction. Homileticians debate how many points a sermon should have, but I am not very excited about that debate. Should a sermon have one point, two points, or three points? To be honest, I do not care. All I know is that if the sermon is not pointing to Jesus Christ, it is pointless no matter how many points it has. Matthias Grünewald's famous painting of the crucifixion has John the Baptist standing to Jesus's left, holding an open book. The Bible is in his left hand, and his right hand is raised pointing to Jesus. That long, bony figure captures the essence of preaching. The sermon from an open Bible has one purpose: to point to Jesus Christ. Then, directly behind John, in the shadow of the cross, Grünewald painted faintly in the background words attributed to John, "He must increase, but I must decrease." There you have it. That is our purpose.

Preaching is a dynamic, visceral, relational activity that cannot be contained in either the study or the sanctuary. Even my body tells me that I am going to preach, hours before I preach. Preaching is a great burden and a deep joy. It is a driving passion that, even after many years, does not become any easier but grows in significance.

Part I

The Purpose of Preaching

There is a prophet within us, forever whispering that behind the seen lies the immeasurable unseen.

Frederick Douglass, *Prophet of Freedom*

Cause my mind to fear whether my heart means what I say.

Martin Kähler, *Theologe und Christ* (1926)

1

More than a Sermon

My first church job was as a janitor. I buffed floors, cut grass, cleaned windows, and vacuumed the sanctuary for a church that was not my home church. It was a lonely job because most of the time I was the only one in the building, and the pews only needed so much Lemon Pledge. The pastor was friendly and easy to please. One day he proudly showed me his 150 sermons, all neatly numbered and well organized. He kept them locked up in his office file cabinet. He informed me, "I have a sermon for every occasion." His confidence did not impress me as a boast as much as a statement of fact. I believed him. His collection of neatly outlined, generically illustrated, and well-rehearsed sermons probably covered every pastoral need he could imagine.

SERMONIC TALKS

Back then I thought preachers prepared *talks*, the purpose of which was to motivate their church members to take their faith more seriously. *Talks* were well-prepared truth packages based on the Bible, outlined in three points, with an application at the end. Through humor and anecdotes these *talks* were designed to keep people's attention and deliver a solid spiritual punch.

They were like Swanson frozen dinners or Lean Cuisine—pull off the plastic, heat them up, and serve them hot. Preachers had a reusable repertoire of these talks so that they were "ready in season and out of season" to preach "with complete patience and teaching" (2 Tim 4:2).

I did not picture myself becoming a preacher. What introverted teen wants to become a glad-handing, gregarious center of attention? The preachers in my world pretty much sounded all alike. Even in conversation, they seemed to be talking to a crowd. Their preaching voice was their conversational voice, at least when they were on the job. The pressure to be the man of the moment must have been a constant strain. Unfortunately, their artificial manner and affected tone made them seem more like salesmen than pastors or prophets. I never imagined Jeremiah acting like any of the pastors I knew. The prophet Jeremiah's message was like a hammer against rock. Preachy, never. Provocative, prophetic, powerful—always!

During my teen years, our home church pastor, whom I genuinely liked, was a shouter. When he got carried away delivering his sermon, he yelled. His face turned red, and white spittle formed around the edges of his mouth. My father, a math teacher, reasoned that there was a correlation between sermon preparation and shouting. The more the pastor prepared, the less he shouted. Sometimes when the pastor began shouting, my dad pulled out a piece of paper from his suit pocket and began working on a math problem.

I do not imagine the apostles delivered the kind of *sermonic talks* that we may be used to hearing on Sunday morning. Their powerful preaching and teaching in the household of faith contributed to a movement sweeping the Roman Empire. The gospel was turning the world upside down. House churches were springing up everywhere. It was personally and socially revolutionary. It still is, but parishioners do not get that feeling most Sunday mornings. The preacher's packaged presentation of biblical truth is like the plastic-wrapped chicken you buy at the grocery store. Sermons are usually geared to an individual spiritual consumer who wants to eat their manna on the run like an unhealthy fast-food diet.

The early church paid dearly for their faith, but we struggle to distinguish between the American dream and the kingdom of God. Shallow Christianity pays dearly, too, but it is not the high cost of discipleship; it is the high cost of compromise and complacency. The apostles showed us how to be *in* the world and *for* the world without becoming *of* the world. They believed in the real presence of the body of Christ in the fellowship of believers.

A sermonic talk is usually the religious by-product of a sentimental faith with a built-in anti-intellectual, antiscience bias. These talks do little to comfort and convict the soul. The self, whether secular or religious, remains the controlling influence, inspiring and determining what is preached and what is heard. Preachers are tempted to gear their sermons to people "who might be feeling a little lost" or "who just want to be part of something bigger than themselves"—the idea being that how I think about myself is more important than what God thinks of me. In practical terms, my felt need for affirmation overshadows my greater spiritual need for salvation. Instead of mere Christianity, we end up with a version of me-Christianity.

WE PREACH WHO WE ARE

Educator Parker Palmer insists, "We teach who we are." This is especially true of anyone who lives to proclaim the gospel. Palmer quotes from one of his students, who claims that all her bad teachers were the same: "Their words float somewhere in front of their faces, like the balloon speech in cartoons." But all her good teachers were unique. They were gripped by their subject, and they spoke with a distinctive voice. "Authority is granted," Palmer insists, "to people who are perceived as authoring their own words, their own actions, their own lives, rather than playing a scripted role at great remove from their own hearts."[4] Their *authority* comes from their own *authorship*.

What is true for teachers is true for preachers. The word of God ought to be heard, as authentic speech, voiced out of the integrity of the disciple, stripped of religious jargon and free of cliché. It is a message that issues from the preacher's heart, mind, and soul. Preaching that can be characterized as bubble speech or anecdotal babble or dry Bible information is really not preaching at all. Before we parse a verb, outline a passage, or read a commentary, we know that gospel preaching issues out of character. Phillips Brooks, in his famous Yale University lectures on preaching in 1877, defined preaching as "the bringing of truth through personality." To build on that definition, we might add that all faithful and fruitful preaching issues out of the character of the preacher. The truth of the gospel has to be lived in order to be preached. It is rooted in character, reflected in personality, and empowered by the Holy Spirit. The apostle Paul addresses this issue in one of his early pastoral letters:

> For our appeal does not spring from error or impurity or any attempt to deceive, but just as we have been approved by God to be entrusted with the gospel, so we speak, not to please man, but to please God who tests our hearts. For we never came with words of flattery, as you know, nor with a pretext for greed—God is witness. Nor did we seek glory from people. (1 Thess 2:3–6)

The willingness of Paul to raise these personal issues openly regarding motive and method emphasizes the importance he placed on holiness and wisdom. Good preaching is not a matter of technique. It comes from within, from the identity and integrity of the preacher.[5]

Saul of Tarsus was a trained Jewish theologian long before he met the risen Jesus on the road leading to Damascus and his name was changed to Paul. He grew up in a devout Jewish family and was immersed in temple and Torah. From a young age, he was dedicated to the law of God with the heroic zeal of Phinehas (Num 25:1; Ps 106:30–31). That he was taught by Gamaliel, one of the leading rabbis of his day, offers evidence that he showed promise and passion as a defender of the ancestral tradition—a future devoted leader of Israel. But none of that mattered after the blinding light of the risen Lord Jesus, the gift of the Spirit of Christ, and his commissioning to proclaim the gospel to the gentiles.

Luke says that Paul "immediately" began to proclaim Jesus "in the synagogues, saying, 'He is the Son of God'" (Acts 9:20). Paul's deep background in the Scriptures and his vision of the crucified and risen Messiah inspired his heralding of the gospel. N. T. Wright observes, "Paul's powerful, spirit-driven proclamation of Jesus as 'son of God' can hardly be called 'preaching,' if by 'preaching' we mean the sort of thing that goes on in churches week by week in our world."[6] If we were to engage in the kind of preaching that Paul did, both at the beginning of his mission and throughout its entirety, we would be announcing to the world that history has reached its climax, that God is fulfilling his promises to bless the nations through Israel, and that the crucified and risen Messiah is the Savior of the world and the King of kings and Lord of lords. The expansive reach of the gospel message embraces the totality of life. It is all encompassing, redeeming and revolutionizing every sphere of life. Paul's proclamation of the gospel was perceived as a threat to Roman rule and Jerusalem's religious authority. The power of the gospel upended every political, spiritual, and social arrangement. It was definitely not a sermonic talk.

Paul's story exemplifies an interesting development for today's disciples. Behind the scenes there is a learning curve that includes waiting and suffering, along with plenty of time to mature and grow in the grace and knowledge of the crucified and risen Lord Jesus. Luke's focus in Acts is on the emerging church, but in Paul's Letter to the Galatians the apostle quickly sketches his illuminating backstory. At some point Saul became better known by his gentile name, Paul, but we do not know exactly when that occurred. Luke traces the name change to his account of Paul's missionary work in Cyprus. But long before that there was a three-year period in which Paul called Damascus home, roughly AD 33 to 36.

We might think of this three-year period of silence for Saul in Damascus as analogous to a seminary experience of today. During that time Saul went to Arabia, a vast region that extended from the Nabatean kingdom east of Damascus all the way south to Mount Sinai in the Sinai Peninsula. F. F. Bruce speculates that Saul preached the gospel to the people of Aretas in the Nabatean kingdom.[7] N. T. Wright suggests that Saul retraced the steps of the prophet Elijah to Mount Horeb/Sinai in order to confirm God's will and the unfolding promises of God.[8]

After Paul returned to Damascus, Luke reports, he "increased all the more in strength, and confounded the Jews who lived in Damascus by proving that Jesus was the Christ" (Acts 9:22). Eventually, Saul's bold proclamation aroused his enemies, and they plotted to kill him. He escaped over a wall in a basket and fled to Jerusalem. He met the apostles at Barnabas's invitation and continued "preaching boldly in the name of the Lord" (9:28), until once again his life was threatened, and he was forced to escape. Luke reports that believers "brought him down to Caesarea and sent him off to Tarsus" (9:30).

Saul spent the next ten years, roughly 36–46, in his hometown, presumably working in the family business making tents, awnings, and other leather works. We may forget that Paul "spent most of his waking hours with his sleeves rolled up, doing hard physical work in a hot climate, and that perhaps two-thirds of the conversations he had with people about Jesus and the gospel were conducted not in a place of worship or study, not even in a private home, but in a small, cramped workshop."9

For roughly thirteen years the apostle to the gentiles flew under the radar. He was "still unknown in person to the churches of Judah," but everyone knew that the person who used to persecute those "in Christ" was now "preaching the faith he once tried to destroy" (Gal 1:22–23). For Paul, this meant that his commitment to the gospel was not the product of human origin and teaching. He owned his faith personally, not because of any person or group of people, but because he received it from Jesus Christ. His explanation echoes the prophet Jeremiah's call to preach: "But when he who had set me apart before I was born, and who called me by his grace, was pleased to reveal his Son to me, in order that I might preach him among the Gentiles, I did not immediately consult with anyone" (Gal 1:15–16; see Jer 1:5).

Pastors, who preach who they are, proclaim Christ, "warning everyone and teaching everyone with all wisdom, that [they] may present everyone mature in Christ" (Col 1:28). Like Paul, they possess faith in Jesus and the faith of Jesus as a gift from God. Their message comes from within. They may have been mentored by the likes of Tim Keller or Robert Smith Jr. or Francis Chan or John Piper or Eugene Peterson, but they are not the product of gifted preachers. Their *authority* comes from their own *authorship*. They experience the authority of God's word in their very bones, and it comes out in Jesus-like humility. Their authority is not vested in an office or in a title or in a position. Their authority comes from Jesus Christ.

Paul's three-year stint in Damascus, along with his evangelistic pilgrimage to Arabia, his intense time in Jerusalem, and his decade of hard labor in Tarsus, all contributed to his formation as a pastor-theologian, as a preacher with the heart of a pastor. Paul's apostleship is unique, but his example is compelling. In the providence of God, everything came together before and after his Damascus road experience to forge the preacher he became.

Like Paul, we tell a similar story of how God implanted his word in us. God takes our childhood experiences, our relationships, our loneliness, our education, our suffering, our successes, and all of our strengths and weaknesses and forms a pastor who lives into the gospel. The subject of our proclamation is never ourselves. Paul states it emphatically: "For what we proclaim is not ourselves, but Jesus Christ as Lord" (2 Cor 4:5). Paradoxically, "we proclaim Christ," not ourselves, but "we preach who we are," because as Paul says, "by the grace of God I am what I am, and his grace toward me was not in vain" (1 Cor 15:10). We internalize the truth of the gospel, making it impossible to preach sermonic talks. We strive "to be gospel centered, biblically tethered, exegetically proficient, theologically competent, and spiritually mature."[10] For those who strive to preach Christ, this aim is both a given and a goal.

We preach who we are, but we do not preach ourselves. Apparently, making the message about oneself was a problem in

Paul's day as it is today. He writes, "Unlike so many, we do not peddle the word of God for profit. On the contrary, in Christ we speak before God with sincerity, as those sent from God" (2 Cor 2:17 NIV). The superapostles were deceitful, dogmatic, and demanding religious professionals. They used their rhetorical skills and charismatic ways to take advantage of unsuspecting Christians (2 Cor 11:5, 13, 20).

So, we preach not ourselves, but we preach who we are. Pastors who preach, parents who nurture, friends who counsel, colleagues who explain, siblings who share, relatives who relate *all seek to proclaim Christ*, "warning everyone and teaching everyone with all wisdom, that [they] may present everyone mature in Christ" (Col 1:28). Like Paul, they are in Christ. "But by the grace of God I am what I am" (1 Cor 15:10).

The apostle Paul expresses the meaning of his mission this way: "For I resolved to know nothing among you except Jesus Christ and him crucified" (1 Cor 2:2). This basic, bedrock truth explains what Paul means when he says, "For no one can lay a foundation other than that which is laid, which is Jesus Christ" (1 Cor 3:11).

PASTORAL COMMENTARIES

Imagine yourself in a first-century household of faith praying the Psalms, studying the prophets, meditating on the Gospel narratives, and hearing the epistles for the first time. When we meditate on the biblical text, we are not far from the early church and the first generation of our brothers and sisters in Christ. Gathered around the word, we are united in Christ over the span of salvation history. We mull over the biblical text. We memorize and meditate. We pay close attention to the text. We may study the Bible in Hebrew and in Greek. If we speak another language, say Spanish or Chinese or Russian, we read the biblical text in our mother tongue. We pray out the meaning of the text. We read it for information and formation. We study how exhortation, encouragement, exposition, and explanation are all woven together in the Bible's textual weave.

Country singer Johnny Cash reportedly said, "I read the Bible to understand the commentaries." That is good advice. But if we are inclined to write commentaries off as dull and boring, it might be wise for us to reconsider. Commentaries help us poke around in the text. They cause us to pay attention. They challenge our preconceived notions and our easy familiarity with the text. We have a wealth of resources to choose from. A careful study of these commentaries will answer basic questions, stimulate fresh insights, and lead us deeper into the text. Instead of using commentaries the way we use a dictionary or an encyclopedia, sometimes it is beneficial to read commentaries cover to cover. Eugene Peterson reminds us, "Exegesis is not in the first place a specialist activity of scholars." Yes, we need the help of scholars, but exegesis is mainly about paying attention, "simply noticing and responding adequately (which is not simple!) to the demand that words make on us."[11]

Pastoral commentaries seek to draw out the meaning of the biblical text for the life of the church. They may be ancient or contemporary, but they share a common pastoral concern and a scholarly accuracy to apply the biblical text in the life of the household of faith for the purpose of genuine transformation and gospel mission. They understand the impact of revealed truth to be both personal and social, invoking concrete practical and pastoral applications. Pastoral commentaries encourage expository preaching, insightful worship, and faithful mission. They presuppose that biblical knowledge is fundamental to life-transforming wisdom. A worthwhile explanation of the text inevitably leads to practical application and worship. The purpose of all biblical information is formation in the Spirit.

New Testament scholar Esau McCaulley asks, "Where does the Bible address the hopes of Black folks, and why is this question not pressing in a community [white evangelicalism] that has historically been alienated from Black Christians?" He laments,

> I read biblical commentaries that displayed little concern for how biblical texts speak to the experience of Black believers. When there was an attempt to provide practical applications to texts, these applications were too often designed for white middle-class Christians. Others decided not to apply the text at all. Instead, scholars simply described the Jewish and Christian world of the first century. *To me, it was a sign of privilege to imprison Paul and Jesus in the first century.*[12]

McCaulley identifies the "privilege" of the academic who decides it is not her place to bring the truth of the text to bear on the real situation facing Christ's followers. This reluctance to discern the impact of God's word for today affects not only Black believers but white believers as well. The avoidance of applicable biblical meaning and action ought not to be an option, but, as Esau McCaulley observes, it is a deeply instilled habit of biblical scholarship. It is easier to live in the biblical world than it is to live biblically in the world.

Faithful biblical interpretation ought to lead to deep understanding of the text in its original context and in the life of the church today. Careful exegesis requires practical and pastoral application. If our scholarly efforts neglect this essential pastoral task, the impact of the Bible is cut off from its true purpose and where it is needed most. Sadly, good exegesis often remains outside the contemporary congregation, because those who know it best leave it to others to address the contemporary cultural situation and pastoral concerns. The ancient biblical text seldom engages the believer where it counts in the practical outworking of faithful obedience.

In the preface to his nearly thousand-page commentary on the Gospel of Luke, I. Howard Marshall writes:

> In order not to expand the commentary beyond measure I have deliberately refrained from offering an exposition of the text as Holy Scripture with a message for the contemporary world, although I believe that exegesis must lead to exposition. ... It is my hope that, although this commentary has been written as a tool for scholarly study, it will nevertheless lay a foundation for understanding the Gospel of Luke as part of the Word of God.[13]

According to Dennis Johnson, exegesis that stops short of proclamation and application leaves "the interpretative task unfinished. ... Exegesis itself is impoverished when specialization and professional pressures in the academy inculcate into the faculty and students a model of biblical interpretation that aborts the process short of application, depriving it of its sweetest fruit."[14] Exegesis without exposition results in knowledge without wisdom, and exposition without Christ produces religion without faith. Alcántara advises pastors to "avoid the common tendency to preach a sermon that sounds like it is a running commentary on the text. People might learn a lot about the text in its context, they might acquire new information or new understanding, but they will not hear the proclamation of the good news. If you preach the text without preaching the gospel, then you have failed at both tasks."[15]

Southern writer Flannery O'Conner insists that failure to see the Christian faith *biblically* is "*a correctable deficiency*, not *invincible ignorance*." The remedy calls for a biblical revival. A specifically Christian meaning can once again be restored if we rediscover the biblical story. O'Conner writes,

> Abstractions, formulas, laws, will not do here. We have to have stories. It takes a story to make a story. ... Our response to life is different if we have been taught only a definition of faith than it is if we have trembled with Abraham as he held the knife over Isaac. Both of these kinds of knowledge are necessary, but in the last four or five centuries we in the Church have overemphasized the abstract and consequently impoverished our imagination and our capacity for prophetic insight. ... We enjoy indulging ourselves in the logic that kills, in making categories smaller and smaller, in prescribing subjects and proscribing attitudes.[16]

We not only want to begin in the biblical story; we want to remain in the gospel story throughout our pastoral ministry. Eugene Peterson writes,

> Within this large, capacious context of the biblical story, we learn to think accurately, behave morally, preach passionately, and sing joyfully, pray honestly, obey faithfully. But we dare not abandon the story as we go off and do any or all of these things, for the minute we abandon the story we go off and reduce reality to the dimensions of our minds and feelings and experience. The moment we formulate our doctrines, draw up our moral codes, and throw ourselves into a life of discipleship and ministry apart from a continuous re-immersing in the story itself,

we walk right out of the concrete and local presence and activity of God and set up our own shop.[17]

Jesus accused the Bible scholars of his day of possessing the Scriptures but not hearing the voice of God: "The Father who sent me has himself borne witness about me. His voice you have never heard, his form you have never seen, and you do not have his word abiding in you, for you do not believe the one whom he has sent. You search the Scriptures because you think that in them you have eternal life; and it is they that bear witness about me, yet you refuse to come to me that you may have life" (John 5:37–40). Jesus said this to experts steeped in the Scriptures, who had memorized large portions of Scripture. They loved the books of Moses and studied the prophets diligently. They held the Hebrew Bible in the highest regard but failed to understand its redemptive trajectory. They did not hear the voice of God in the voice of Jesus. Instead of being transformed by the word of God, they molded the Bible into their own image, controlled it by their own ideas. Instead of participating in the drama of salvation history, they stood apart from it, detached and disengaged, cut off from the prophetic message. Ultimately, they stood against the Bible.

These first-century technicians of the text exegeted the Bible from every angle imaginable, listing and debating every possible interpretation. They deciphered and decoded the most inscrutable aspects of the text, but they did not see how it related to Jesus. A *technician* breaks down the finite text into its various parts and then puts these items on display for debate and exhibition. But according to John Wesley, the eighteenth-century founder of Methodism, a *textuary* delves into the finite text and enters into its meaning. *Textuaries* eat, digest, and metabolize the word of God so that it becomes a part of who they

are. Instead of sitting in judgment on the text, *textuaries* enter
into the ongoing story of salvation. We want to go beyond the
technique of a sermonic talk and proclaim God's word with
humility and authority, in a manner that is real and compelling, preaching that touches lives deeply and reaches hearts and
minds. This passion for Christ is very different from a passion
to perform a sermon and instinctively distinguishes between
proclamation and performance.[18]

John Stott's commentaries exemplify the integration of exegesis and exposition.[19] In the preface to his commentary on Acts,
Stott writes the following to "justify yet another volume to the
extensive library on Acts":

> If anything distinctive can be claimed about this book it
> is that, whereas all commentaries seek to elucidate the
> original meaning of the text, the commentary on Acts
> I have written is committed also to its contemporary
> application. I have tried, therefore, to address myself
> with integrity to some of the main questions which Acts
> raises for today's Christians.[20]

Dale Bruner's masterful two-volume commentary on the
Gospel of Matthew runs nearly fifteen hundred pages. It is what
a commentary should be: conversant with ancient and modern
scholarship, linguistically accurate, textually astute, theologically comprehensive, and ethically aware. Bruner's highly read-
able work is rooted in the canon of Scripture and filled with
pastoral insights, devotional reflection, and relevant application
for today's church.

Pastoral commentaries involve a developmental process that
is relational and practical. They are in dialogue with the issues
and concerns of the household of faith and what it means to
be a disciple in today's culture. New Testament scholar Frank

Thielman remarks that his commentary on Philippians was the most challenging work he ever wrote. Most university professors of biblical studies devote their time and effort "to clarifying the historical circumstances in which the biblical books are composed and showing how these circumstances help the modern reader understand the meaning of the text to its first readers." This effort seems like "a full-time job, and the work of application is usually left to the systematic theologians. A little thought reveals, however, that this arrangement is not ideal. To say what the text meant but never to say what the text means is to tie up heavy loads and to put them on people's shoulders without lifting a finger to move them. It is to apply oneself wholly to the text without applying the text wholly to one's self."[21]

The benefit of wrestling with the application of the text serves both the exegete and the church. Thielman describes the "many friends" who have helped him clarify and apply the message of Philippians: "Students who have attended my courses ... congregations who have heard my preaching, and Sunday School classes who have listened to my teaching have all imbibed much of the material in this commentary and helped me to sharpen my thinking, particularly on how to apply the letter to the modern church." But he does not stop there. The "many friends" includes colleagues, Pauline scholars, his wife, and parents. A true pastoral commentary is always the fruit of deep fellowship within the body of Christ. Perhaps no biblical commentary is complete without being sensitive to the Spirit's pedagogical process.

If the biblical text says only what it *said* in the first century without relevance to the issues and concerns of the twenty-first-century church and society, how can believers hope to benefit from the biblical message? One can read a thousand-page commentary on the book of Revelation with hardly a hint of how the text relates to our contemporary situation. Thankfully, there are some notable exceptions by scholars who seek to apply the text to today's church. Craig Keener's *NIV Application Commentary* and Joseph Mangina's *Revelation* serve the pastor well, as does Darrell Johnson in *Discipleship on the Edge* and Eugene Peterson's *Reversed Thunder*. These works address today's church, but they are often deemed "not scholarly enough" in the academy.

If all we do is debate the book's authorship and date, study the historical context, trace the sources, parse the verbs, describe the style, determine the structure, and then, if there is any time or energy left, mention a few theological implications, we are left empty-handed.[22] We evade the biblical text by confusing research with repentance, by equating the rigors of scholarship with the discipline of surrender. This may be why our enthusiasm for the truth wanes and our creativity in application wanders off. We fail to bring the message home for a church that is unknowingly "wretched, pitiable, poor, blind, and naked" (Rev 3:17). It is not enough to store up exegetical insights in commentaries and courses and to winsomely hint at a few intriguing possibilities of application. In the Spirit, the church needs the personal and social impact of God's word transforming our lives in every way.

Too many churchgoers see the Bible as a huge, undifferentiated mass of ancient material designed to inspire a devotional thought for the day, or they see it as the Good Book with secrets for success and stories of courage. Bryan Chapell writes, "For most people in our culture the Bible is an opaque book whose truths are hidden in an endless maze of difficult words, unfamiliar history, unpronounceable names, and impenetrable mysticism."[23] However, Chapell insists,

The best preachers guide in such a way that their listeners discover that the labyrinth is a myth. There are no dark passageways through twisted mazes of logic to biblical truth that require the expertise of the spiritually elite. There is only a well-worn path than anyone can follow if a preacher sheds some ordinary light along the way. … Excellent preaching makes people confident that biblical truth lies within their reach, not beyond their grasp.[24]

THE TENSION IN THE TEXT

"Text" is an old Latin word with roots in the textile industry. It comes from the root word *tex-ere*, "to weave." "Texture" literally means "the process or art of weaving."[25] Weaving a garment and weaving a sermon are linked linguistically. There is a connection between weaving strands of yarn together and weaving a message out of verbs, nouns, prepositions, and adjectives. The exegete is on a quest for the truth. We are committed to discovering what the text actually means. Like words in a love letter, the depth of meaning is not always obvious on the surface.

Every sermon runs along a fault line between the fallen human condition, in all of its personal and social complexity, and God's redemptive provision, in all of its grace and mercy. This tension in the text leads to the passion of the passage, without which sermons become repetitive and boring—lifeless. Every biblical passage deals with the clash between the mystery of God and the mess of the human condition. To the degree that we identify with Jesus, his person and his work, we live in that tension. Sermonic talks tell a clever opening story, plow through a text, make a few points, and draw a conclusion, but in the process miss the passion of the passage. Good exegesis discovers the tension in the text, and good preaching brings out the passion of the passage.

We live along some impressive, tension-building fault lines, but we are tempted to tone down, soften, and polish the sharp edges of the text to make our sermons more palatable to casual Christians. Years of sermons and Bible studies leave us little wiser when it comes to dealing with racism, fending off materialism, celebrating biblical sexuality, resisting nationalism, caring for the poor, and commending the gospel. We seem to draw a blank when it comes to knowing how the message of the prophets applies to us today or how the church ought to relate to the world. Cultural conformity and ideological captivity are like a strong ocean rip current moving us out to sea, rendering us useless.

There is a scene in the late seventies TV miniseries *Roots* that reflects that uselessness. The slave master in his study is reading his Bible for morning devotions. In the background we can hear the crack of a whip and the cries of a young slave, Kunta Kinte. He is being lashed brutally by the master's slave foreman because Kunta insists on keeping his African name. While this is going on outside, an elderly slave enters the master's study to plead with the master to stop the whipping. The master is provoked by the interruption of his Bible reading and angrily dismisses the elderly slave. The scene has a haunting effect on me. Sincere Bible study goes on seemingly oblivious to the personal tragedy of injustice. It makes me wonder what cries I am not hearing, what injustices I am not seeing.

Racist believers are a shock to the system. After all that has been preached and said about Jesus's Great Commandment and his Great Commission, how could any professing believer question their shared humanity with all people and their oneness with a believer from another race? Jesus Christ came "that he might create in himself one new man in place of the two" (Eph 2:15). A close friend, David Mensah, an African brother, along with Brenda, his Canadian-born, white wife, visited a church I pastored in southern Indiana to share their ministry in Ghana. I was shocked and saddened when some church members who studied the Bible *under my ministry* expressed their outrage over a mixed-race couple being invited to speak to the church. Yes, I know, believer and unbeliever alike are steeped in systemic sin. Deeply entrenched sin affects us all, and we need the Spirit of truth to confront our blindness. Faithful preaching faces the challenge of penetrating that seemingly impenetrable callousness, hypocrisy, and hardness of heart that resists God's truth, God's justice, and God's mercy. "Always learning but never able to come to the knowledge of the truth" is a phenomenon confronting the church (2 Tim 3:7 NIV).

There is a fault line between our expectation of an uplifting, inspiring sermon and the canonical impact of the biblical text. Søren Kierkegaard complained that "one only hears sermons which might properly end with Hurrah! rather than Amen."[26] He wrestled with the meaning of the Christian faith in the Danish state church even as we wrestle with what it means to preach the gospel in the American self-church. There is a clash between our subjective selves seeking affirmation and approval, and the truth that stands over against us, calling for confession and commitment. There is a tension between "Jesus talk" and the crucified and risen Lord Jesus Christ, living and incarnate. The tension in the text leads to the passion of the passage. That is the challenge of good preaching.

Is good preaching a rare phenomenon or the weekly norm? Thomas Oden writes,

> We know good preaching when we hear it. It touches us viscerally. It is profound, subtle mode of communication that somehow makes the transcendence of Yahweh

appear palpably immanent. It mixes courage and comfort, candor and sympathy, strength and vulnerability, in the kind of delicate blend achieved by an excellent cook. Most worshipers know that there have been rare and beautiful times when they have been privileged to hear such a word. When it happens, it is a remarkable event. It is a treasure in earthen vessels.[27]

Good preaching in the Spirit and in the fellowship of Jesus aims to do this every week.

Originality signifies a return to origins.
George Steiner, *Errata*

2

Harder & Easier
than We Imagine

Preaching is harder than we imagine. Getting up in front of people and holding their attention for twenty to thirty minutes is challenging enough, but that is only the beginning. If you compare a preaching course to a public speaking class, you are in for a surprise. At its core, preaching is not about performing or persuading; it is about the truth—the truth of God's word. It is not about the rules of rhetoric or stylized speech; it is about the gospel of the crucified and risen Messiah. As the apostle said, "Him we proclaim, warning everyone and teaching everyone with all wisdom, that we may present everyone mature in Christ" (Col 1:28).

Driving looks easy until you get behind the wheel for the first time. Then you realize that it is not nearly as easy as you thought it was. Accelerating, braking, steering, and parking look pretty simple, and you have experienced them as a passenger thousands of times, but behind the wheel everything feels different. After thirty minutes behind the wheel, you might even marvel that a vast array of humanity is allowed to drive three thousand pounds of steel at high speed. The mistaken notion of simplicity on this side of complexity surprises new drivers. But after a few weeks of driving around with an experienced driver who is a calm and patient teacher, we usually get the hang of it. We get to the simplicity on the other side of complexity. Like driving, preaching may look fairly easy to people who have never done it. Preaching is harder than it looks, but thanks to the promised Holy Spirit, we begin to discover the rhythm of preaching. I do not think preaching ever becomes easy, but with the Lord's help we can get to the simplicity on the other side of complexity.

WHAT MAKES PREACHING HARD

Preaching is challenging *spiritually* because we are compelled to live in tension with the fallen human condition and God's redemptive provision. It is provocative *intellectually* because we embrace a worldview and a metanarrative that runs contrary to our secular age. It is unsettling *socially* because thinking Christianly challenges the way the world works relationally, sexually, politically, economically, and globally. It is convicting *ethically* because Jesus's kingdom ethic calls for conduct that at times runs contrary to the world. It is disconcerting *pastorally* because it calls for true discernment and leadership in a countercultural household of faith.

If Jesus had to die for you to preach this Sunday's sermon, it's really not about the preacher's speaking skills, body language, voice inflection, sense of humor, and eye contact. These elements are important, and they need our attention, but preaching is much more about remaining true to the biblical text than it is about homiletics. We glean very little from the Bible itself on preaching style and method. In the West we emphasize sermon outlines, with their points and subpoints. We focus on attention-getting introductions, quick transitions, relatable illustrations, practical applications, and effective conclusions. All of this is important in preaching but never mentioned in the Bible. God's word is not subject to our sermonic forms, and one wonders whether our sermonizing does not sometimes get in the way of God's message.

The apostle Paul claimed that he did not speak with *eloquence* or *superior wisdom*, but judging from his letters, it would be difficult to deny that he preached with both eloquence and persuasion. Augustine addressed this issue by distinguishing between eloquence based on classical rhetorical conventions and true eloquence flowing naturally from the wisdom of God. Today we frame it differently; instead of speaking of eloquence, we speak of effectiveness, and instead of referencing a Greco-Roman classical style, we might refer to a modern TED talk. Augustine reasoned that whether Paul "was guided by the rules of eloquence" did not matter, because what he said could not have been said in a better way. Whatever skill and style Paul used to communicate was dictated by the message he was led by the Spirit to deliver. Augustine held that the biblical writers communicated with an effectiveness suitable to those "who justly claim the highest authority, and who are evidently inspired by God." He could not say whether Paul was guided by the rules of classical rhetoric, but he could definitely say that Paul's God-given wisdom was "naturally produced ... and ... accompanied by, eloquence." It was, in Augustine's words, a case of "wisdom not aiming at eloquence, yet eloquence not shrinking from wisdom."[1]

Even before Augustine's conversion to Christ, he concluded, "Fine style does not make something true, nor has a man a wise soul because he has a handsome face and well-chosen eloquence."[2] I doubt that Augustine would have recommended to pastors that they listen to Faustus, a well-known Manichaean orator, to learn how to communicate the gospel better. Nor do I imagine that if Augustine were alive today, he would encourage pastors to study late-night TV comedians to pick up preaching tips. Pastors are always seeking ways to communicate the gospel more effectively, but the real issue remains substance over style and truth over technique. Only when we grasp the truth of God's word in the power of the Spirit will preaching be more proclamation than performance.

Paul's rejection of eloquence and superior wisdom was never a rejection of finding effective ways to proclaim the gospel or the importance of honing one's preaching skills. It was, however, an emphatic denial of all forms of artificiality, manipulation, and deception. Clearly, Paul embraced careful reasoning and skillful communication. He was not a crafty, clever manipulator, but neither was he an artless, boring communicator. The proof of his effectiveness can be found in his pastoral letters. His eloquence is natural, flowing out of the passion of his heart for the truth. No wonder he stresses to Timothy, "Preach the word; be ready in season and out of season; reprove, rebuke, and exhort, with complete patience and teaching" (2 Tim 4:2).[3]

Ambrose, the bishop of Milan, introduced Augustine to the gospel through his fresh and powerful preaching. Augustine was attracted to Ambrose for two reasons, neither of which had anything to do with the thirty-one-year-old's search for truth. Augustine had already written Christianity off as a failed religion. It was Ambrose's relational kindness *and* his rhetorical skill that caught Augustine's attention. But Ambrose's preaching was such that Augustine could not ignore the power of the gospel. He admits,

> I began to like him, at first indeed not as a teacher of
> the truth, for I had absolutely no confidence in your

Church, but as a human being who was kind to me. I used to listen to him preaching to the people, not with the intention which I ought to have had, but as if testing out his oratorical skill to see whether it merited the reputation it enjoyed or whether his fluency was better or inferior than it was reported to be. I hung on his diction in rapt attention but remained bored and contemptuous of his subject-matter. My pleasure was the charm of his language.[4]

However, over time Augustine's immediate concern with Ambrose's "rhetorical technique" gave way to a gradual recognition of Ambrose's powerful preaching on salvation. Augustine concedes, "I could not separate them." It was Ambrose's ability to interpret difficult Old Testament passages in the light of Christ that impressed Augustine intellectually. Because of Ambrose's preaching, he began to see the Bible in a new light. Since reason alone was too weak to discover the truth, Augustine concluded that it was necessary for the Bible to be inspired by God. Augustine confessed to the Lord, "I now began to believe that you would never have conferred such pre-eminent authority on the scripture, now diffused through all lands, unless you had willed that it would be a means of coming to faith in you and a means of seeking to know you."[5]

If God's word is "fire in our bones" and "a hammer that breaks a rock in pieces," we will not be overly concerned about style and technique. Stage fright and an introverted personality will not get in the way of preaching the gospel. The passion to preach will come from our relationship with Christ and his truth. We will pay attention to good communicators and learn from them what we can, but our style will flow naturally from who we are and who we are gifted to be in Christ. Preaching will always be more about a passion for Christ than preparing, packaging, and performing sermons. Educator Parker Palmer insists that "good teaching [preaching] cannot be reduced to technique; good teaching comes from the identity and integrity of the teacher."[6]

There is a scene in the 1997 movie *Air Force One* that captures this truth. Harrison Ford plays the president of the United States. He has flown to Moscow to give a congratulatory speech at a state dinner at the Kremlin. Every word and phrase of his speech has been carefully crafted, debated, and vetted by the White House staff and the State Department. But when he gets up to address the dignitaries gathered in the banquet hall, the president pushes his notes aside, ignores the teleprompter, and to the surprise of his advisers goes off script. He delivers a bold pledge to change American foreign policy. Everyone can hear the determination in his voice. He promises to never again allow America's political self-interest to deter him from doing what is morally right. Everyone at the banquet knew that they were hearing a unique and significant message, not the usual political rhetoric. Good preaching is authentic speech issuing from the heart and mind of the person. It is not a stylized, scripted performance; it is at all points true—true to God's word, true to the person speaking, and true to the situation. The word of God ought to be heard, as authentic speech, voiced out of the integrity of the disciple, and stripped of religious jargon and cliché. It is a message that issues from the preacher's heart, mind, and soul.

The great Reformer Martin Luther saw preaching and preachers in a battle for people's souls. His big question was, "How will the devil be defeated by preaching the word of God this week?" His namesake, Martin Luther King Jr., writes in his "Letter from a Birmingham Jail" about the early church's willingness to suffer for what they believed. King writes,

> There was a time when the church was very power-ful—in the time when the early Christians rejoiced at being deemed worthy to suffer for what they believed. In those days the church was not merely a *thermometer* that recorded the ideas and principles of popular opin-ion; it was a *thermostat* that transformed the mores of society. Whenever the early Christians entered a town, the people in power became disturbed and immediately sought to convict the Christians for being "disturbers of the peace" and "outside agitators." But the Christians pressed on, in the conviction that they were a "colony of heaven," called to obey God rather than man. Small in number, they were big in commitment.[7]

Preaching that is cartoon-bubble speech or anecdotal babble or informational data is really not preaching at all.

A GOOD KIND OF HARD

Preaching is a good kind of hard when we preach the whole counsel of God, when we are committed to preaching the bib-lical text humbly and honestly, when we are willing to open our hearts, stick our necks out, and preach the truth in love. Maybe too many pastors are tempted to sacrifice the truth of God's word for positive vibes from the congregation. They do not want to ruffle any feathers, as the cliché goes. The book of Revelation may be the devil's favorite book since pastors avoid preaching it because they do not want to stir up con-troversy.[8] Pastors are intimidated by popular end-time sce-narios fostered by the Left Behind series and a tradition of dispensational thinking. I know pastors who claim that if they preached Revelation the way they believe it should be preached, they might lose their jobs. Coming from well-respected pastors, this admission is pretty sad, even shocking. Fanciful interpretations of the rapture and tribulation are left to stand uncontested in the church because pastors know that faithful preaching on the apostle John's canonical climax will stir up a hornets' nest of trouble.

Writing from his home in Copenhagen in 1846, Søren Kierkegaard gave a whimsical account of how he became an author. He concealed his passion for his prophetic vocation in his musings on a quiet Sunday afternoon. On one level he claimed life was all very haphazard, but on another level, he believed it was profoundly providential. Kierkegaard's point: one never knows the moment when life makes up its mind, when your will and God's will collide. As it happened, he was seated in his usual spot at an outdoor café drinking his coffee when he chanced to contemplate his career. His train of thought was unexpected and unprompted by any particular concern. "Although never lazy," he thought, "all my activity nevertheless was like a glittering inactivity, a kind of occupation for which I still have a great partiality, and for which perhaps I even have a little genius." The power holding him back from achieving much of anything important was admittedly a comfortable case of indolence. He was lazy.

While sipping his coffee in this idyllic setting, he thought to himself that he was on the way to becoming an old man, "without being anything, and without really undertaking to do anything." He reflected on the many "heralded" individuals and "the many benefactors of the age" who knew "how to benefit mankind by making life easier and easier." They improved transportation, set up communication systems, and contributed to "compendiums and short recitals of everything worth knowing." He reflected on "the true benefactors of the age who make spiritual existence in virtue of thought easier and easier, yet more and more significant."

His reflections led him to ask himself, "And what are you doing?" Suddenly the thought crossed his mind, "You must do something, but inasmuch as with your limited capacities it will be impossible to make anything easier than it has become, you must, with the same humanitarian enthusiasm as the others, undertake to make something harder."[9]

Kierkegaard's tongue-in-cheek account intentionally masks his unique prophetic calling to reveal the dangers of Christianity without Christ. To call his task heroic would be to invite his displeasure, if not his disdain. Nevertheless, we remember Kierkegaard's attack against Christendom because it remains relevant in our own twenty-first-century situation. He often wrote under the cover of op-ed pieces and pseudonyms because he did not want to draw attention to himself. His sardonic quest to make life harder was directed to those who wanted to blend Christianity with the world and make it easy. The proponents of cultural Christianity sought to remove the offense of the gospel and the stigma of the cross. They wanted "to be Christians only up to a certain point."[10] They were admirers of Jesus but not followers of Jesus. The notion of worldly success meant more than Christian faithfulness.

"One starts with the worldly," complains Kierkegaard, and "makes oneself as comfortable as possible with everything we can scrape together in the way of worldly goods—the Christian element being stirred in with all this as an ingredient, a seasoner, which sometimes serves merely to refine the relish."[11] Kierkegaard laments that Christianity without Christ lacks any contrast to the world. "In established Christendom one becomes a Christian in the merriest possible way, without in the least becoming aware of the possibility of offence." The church is not overly lenient, Kierkegaard reasons; it is openly apostate "from the Christianity of the New Testament."[12]

The lead preacher in Copenhagen's Lutheran cathedral was Bishop Mynster. He embodied everything Kierkegaard opposed in Christless Christianity. Kierkegaard believed that gospel preaching ought to distinguish the congregation from the crowd, and the followers of Jesus from the admirers of Jesus, but Mynster's preaching was not, as Kierkegaard said, "in the character of the New Testament." Instead of being lauded as "a witness to the truth," Mynster's version of Christianity was worse "than any heresy, any schism," because he was intent on *playing* at Christianity.

> But precisely in the very same sense that the child plays soldier, it is playing Christianity to take away the danger (Christianly, "witness" and "danger" correspond), and in place of this to introduce power (to be a danger for others), worldly goods, advantages, luxurious enjoyment of the most exquisite refinements—and then to play the game that Bishop Mynster was a witness to the truth, one of the genuine witnesses to the truth, to play it with such frightful earnestness that one cannot bring the game to stop, but keeps on playing it into heaven itself, plays Bishop Mynster on into the holy chain of witnesses to the truth which stretches from the days of the Apostles to our times.[13]

Kierkegaard's prophetic condemnation of Christendom offers insights into our present situation. It seems that Flannery O'Connor's reference to the "Christ-haunted South" and Kierkegaard's "Christianity without Christ" aptly describe the form of Christianity embedded in American exceptionalism, nationalism, populism, conservativism, and postmodern progressivism. The invisible rip currents under the surface of our sunny secular age are sweeping the church out to sea. Everything is diminished and diluted. The church is reduced to a crowd in need of spiritual services and chronic felt-need satisfaction. Admiration grows as costly discipleship declines. True followers of Jesus are few and far between, but there are plenty of admirers of Jesus pursuing the American dream.

Christendom preaching is convenient and popular by design. It is free from the burden of New Testament Christianity. The self, not Christ, is the key player on both sides of the pulpit. The preacher invariably begins with *himself*. He tells a long, lighthearted anecdote about himself out of a need to convince the crowd that he is human, approachable, and worth listening to. Sports, hobbies, and home life are favorite anecdotal starting points. Having established his rapport with the audience, the preacher glosses over the biblical text and tells motivational stories to promote self-improvement. The preacher's success depends on discovering the listener's existential subtext and tapping into his quest for significance and longing for approval. Or, the preacher may unpack the biblical text, pulling out every textual tidbit discovered in the pastor's sermon research. People follow along dutifully, using the outline in the bulletin to map the progress of the sermon, conscientiously filling in the blanks as if they were playing Bible bingo.

Either sermonic formula, whether the existential subtext sermon or the heavy-laden informational sermon, leads to the same familiar and pedantic conclusion. Come Monday morning or as early as Sunday afternoon, whatever hint of impact that was felt is conveniently forgotten as Christians go about their *secular* lives. Costly discipleship may be an expressed goal, but few in the crowd are devoted to the apostles' teaching and to the fellowship, to the breaking of bread and to prayer (Acts 2:42). Christendom today is not in the form of a *state* church, as it was in Kierkegaard's day, but it is in the form of a *self*-church.

This is what Kierkegaard found so depressing about Bishop Mynster's Sunday sermon in the cathedral: "If on Mondays Bishop Mynster had not with worldly shrewdness shirked the duty of assuming the logical consequence of his Sunday sermon, if he had put into effect a mode of existence and action which corresponded with the tenor of his Sunday address, instead of helping himself out with worldly shrewdness of various patterns, his life would then have taken on an entirely different aspect." Kierkegaard found it difficult to confront Mynster's preaching directly because it was couched in such "earnestness and wisdom." We might describe contemporary Christendom preaching as "endearing and witty" or "humorous and entertaining." Kierkegaard explained that it was out of respect for Mynster that he waited until his death to go public with his concerns. He wrote extensively about these issues in his books, but he did not name names until Mynster died. He explains, "I was to my sorrow convinced how weak he was. Out of consideration for him I concealed this from the contemporaries, and said it only to him personally, as emphatically as possible." After Mynster was "buried with full music," only then did Kierkegaard feel free to go public with his critique of Mynster's preaching. This was not hard for him to do because he was egged on by pastors and professors who celebrated Mynster as a great defender of the faith, as "a witness to the truth."[14]

Kierkegaard did not belabor his critique: "What I have said is short and to the point. Bishop Mynster's preaching soft-pedals, slurs over, suppresses, omits something of the most decisively Christian." What was missing and what made his preaching different from the New Testament was the absence of "the very deepest and most incurable breach with this world." For Bishop Mynster the world and the church were basically one and the same. Kierkegaard argued that there was a Christian veneer over Danish culture that justified the ways of the world and legitimized its idols. The offense of the gospel and the power of the cross were lost in an effort to accommodate Christianity to the world.

Kierkegaard was provoked to speak out because Mynster's defenders commended his preaching. They said things such as, "Bishop Mynster was not really a preacher of repentance," and, "Bishop Mynster was rather a preacher of peace." Kierkegaard responded emphatically, "All true Christian preaching is first and foremost a preaching of repentance," and it is "in the character of a preacher of peace to proclaim the doctrine of Him Who Himself said, 'I came not to bring peace but dissension.'"[15] Far from being "a witness to the truth," Mynster was "self-indulgently" at peace with the world so he could enjoy life.

Kierkegaard lamented that Denmark had a full crew of "eminently learned, talented, gifted, and humanly well-meaning" pastors, preachers, and biblical scholars, but "not one of them is in the character of the New Testament." The melody for Protestant Christianity in Denmark was sung to the tune of "Merrily we roll along, roll along, roll along" and offered the pagan assurance that everything about eternity was settled, "settled precisely in order that we might find pleasure in enjoying this life, as well as any pagan or Jew. Christianity simply does not exist."[16] Much of what Kierkegaard lamented in the 1850s fits the ethos of America. Admirers outnumber followers, and Christendom preaching sounds more like Bishop Mynster than it does the apostle Paul. New Testament Christianity is a foreign concept.

Preaching is hard because we are fighting on two fronts, the secular front and the religious front, and on both fronts we face the double threat of compromise and conceit. Disciples need wisdom to discern the difference between accommodation and assimilation on one side, and alienation and antagonism on the other. Failure means cultural captivity as either a postmodern progressive conformity to the world or as an alien alienation from the world. Sadly, both extremes represent popular Christianity.

Christendom as a grassroots civil religion identifies more with the American good life and American exceptionalism than with Jesus's Sermon on the Mount. "Bible-believing" proponents of this version of cultural Christianity are fiercely loyal to free-market capitalism and "America First" rhetoric. They feel that their American way of life is under attack by secular liberals. Resentment and fear run deep. They wrap the cross in the American flag and cherish the American dream as their one great hope. They are ready to use the weapons of the world and "fight like hell."

Christendom as a popular social-justice movement identifies with postmodern progressive causes such as LGBTQ+ rights, abortion rights, and radical pluralism. This postmodern version of Christendom prides itself on being open minded, tolerant, and *knowingly* at odds with biblical doctrines and the New Testament moral order. It freely diminishes biblical authority on virtually all matters that run counter to the prevailing cultural ethos.

Neither form of popular cultural Christianity is New Testament Christianity. The alienation and the assimilation fostered by the so-called conservative and progressive extremes of

Christendom are radically different from apostolic biblical fidelity and the social alienation experienced by the early church. Both the alien alienation of the so-called Christian right and the progressive conformity of the Christian left reflect the spirit of the times and worldly conformity.

New Testament Christianity is harder and easier than cultural Christianity in the following ways. Let's go back to Kierkegaard's fateful reflection on a quiet Sunday afternoon. There he was, sitting in a garden café all by himself, when he enthusiastically embraced his vocational calling to make something harder. The something he made harder involved his prophetic denouncement of cultural Christianity and his bold and courageous defense of New Testament Christianity. "For when all combine in every way to make everything easier," he concluded, "there remains only one possible danger, namely, that the ease becomes so great that it becomes altogether too great; then there is only one want left, though it is not yet a felt want, when people will want difficulty. ... I conceived it as my task to create difficulties everywhere."[17] To that end he dedicated himself.

If preaching is harder than we imagine, it is also easier. Jesus's "easy yoke" *easy* is radically different from Bishop Mynster's "I'm okay, you're okay" *easy*. Cultural Christianity's *easy* is disorienting, disillusioning, and ultimately self-defeating. Christianity without Christ does not line up with the New Testament, whereas Christ-centered Christianity is faithful to the whole counsel of God. Jesus's easy-yoke *easy* is true and demanding, costly and sacrificial, but it is surprisingly fulfilling and leads to genuine human flourishing. In an effort to make things easy, preachers like Mynster unwittingly make life difficult, whereas preachers who follow in the tradition of Jesus and the apostles make life unbelievably rewarding. Christendom confuses the character-building, soul-developing, brother-let-me-be-your servant easy with the pain-free, laid-back, "everyone does what is right in their own eyes" easy.[18]

Preaching is easy *personally* because giving one's life for the sake of understanding and proclaiming God's word is preeminently worthwhile, deeply satisfying, and lifesaving. After Jesus's bold teaching on "eating his flesh and drinking his blood," he asked his disciples whether they wanted to leave. Peter answered him, "Lord, to whom shall we go? You have the words of eternal life, and we have believed, and have come to know, that you are the Holy One of God" (John 6:68–69).

Preaching is easy *intellectually* because the same eternal word that created the heavens and established the earth is the enduring word that saves us and directs our steps. The Author of life is one and the same the Savior of the world. The history of nature and the history of redemption are revelations of the same God. Preachers never need to fear running out of good material. There is plenty here to celebrate creation and to explore redemption.

Preaching is easy *socially* because the word of God centers the person and the community in Christ. There is no greater relational guide for handling the complexities of life together than God's word.

Preaching is easy *ethically* because the Lord has shown us what is required of us, "to act justly and to love mercy and to walk humbly with [our] God" (Mic 6:8 NIV). By God's grace, we have clear moral guidance and empowerment to live in the way God designed us to live.

Preaching is easy *pastorally* because if we let the word of Christ dwell in us richly, we will be able to teach and admonish our brothers and sisters in Christ with all wisdom (Col 3:16).

The prophet Jeremiah and the apostle John exemplify the reality of preaching that is both harder and easier than we imagine. No other prophet shared his life and ministry as personally as Jeremiah did, and no other apostle delivered his message as compellingly as John did. Through them we are meant to see ourselves and identify with them. Their calling and their identity give shape and meaning to our calling and identity. Since I was sixteen, I have identified with Jeremiah and John. I have resonated with the prophet's call and the apostle's message. They were defined by God's word. I felt then and I still feel today that I can say with Jeremiah, "The word of the LORD came to me, saying, 'Before I formed you in the womb I knew you, and before you were born I consecrated you; I appointed you as a prophet to the nations" (Jer 1:5).

The followers of Jesus Christ can identify with Jeremiah's calling on all four counts. The Lord is not the passive object of our inquiry and debate, nor the quiet recipient of our adoration or apathy. Jeremiah's testimony flips the script. God's first-person action defined him. The word of the Lord came to him even as it comes to us. We are formed, known, sanctified, and called by the word of the Lord. Jeremiah's life did not begin with Jeremiah. It began with God, the God who created, commended, consecrated, and commissioned him. Without diminishing the uniqueness of Jeremiah's individuality and his particular place in salvation history, what was said of this prophet who lived six hundred years before Jesus is relevant for all who follow the Lord. We were all meant to hear the word of the Lord saying to us, "I created you, I understand you, and I alone can save you and give you significance."[19]

Likewise, we can identify with the apostle John, who writes, "I, John, your brother and partner in the tribulation and the kingdom and the patient endurance that are in Jesus ..." (Rev 1:9). His gospel story is our story; his work is our work. When John writes to the seven churches, he steps back and hides behind Christ. He is not offering his opinion about the churches; he is delivering Christ's message to the churches. Good preachers hide themselves behind the pulpit as they proclaim God's word. John's message is all about what Christ reveals. He introduces himself as our "brother and partner in the suffering and the kingdom and the patient endurance that are in Jesus" (Rev 1:9). He uses the first-person singular "I" seven times: "I, John ... I was in the Spirit ... I heard behind me ... I turned to see ... I saw ... When I saw him ... I fell at his feet as though dead" (Rev 1:9–17). John's entire being is defined in relationship to the action of God.

John's opening sevenfold self-description encompasses his personal identity and redemptive story. He is our brother in the family of God. His individual "I" does not stand alone. Whether he was by himself on the island of Patmos or in the company of other exiled Christians, he was never alone. In the Spirit, he was in fellowship with the Triune God and the body of Christ. Although physically removed from the seven churches, John remained their companion in the "tribulation and the kingdom and the patient endurance that are in Jesus" (Rev 1:9). Three descriptive attributes qualify John's companionship and underscore its costly nature. The fellowship of Christ's suffering and the power of the resurrection go hand in hand (Phil 3:10). Christ's rule has begun, but the experience of suffering and the need for patient endurance persists. All three attributes of companionship—the tribulation and the kingdom and the patient endurance—are inseparable and stand together. We were meant to see ourselves in John's self-description.[20]

THE PREACHING CHALLENGE

When I was a young pastor, there were times when I felt that I was only as good as my last sermon. I hit highs and lows on an emotional roller coaster that was anything but an amusement park ride. I hated the ups and downs, vacillating between feeling OK about my preaching and feeling awful about my preaching. My lack of confidence, physical weariness, and oversensitivity to people's reactions contributed to these mood swings. I have never enjoyed listening to myself preach, much less watching it. I agree with those wise pastors who say to trust in the Lord and forget about yourself. Self-forgetfulness in the Spirit, after prayer and a lot of hard work in the text, is key. Over time, as my preaching matured and I became more confident, the feelings leveled out. I became more at home in God's word, more trusting in the Spirit's work, and less self-conscious. I like the self-effacing idea of hiding behind the biblical text and taking cover behind a pulpit or a lectern or a music stand. The focus needs to be on Christ and his word.

John Chrysostom (ca. AD 347–407) is widely respected as one of the early church's greatest preachers. He gave a sobering assessment of the escalating challenge facing even mature preachers. John felt the constant pressure to improve in order to meet people's expectations. John insisted that preachers must reject their natural ambition for praise but do everything in their power to preach praiseworthy sermons. Good preachers are always getting better, while poor preachers are content to settle for mediocrity. John concludes,

> So the gifted have even harder work than the unskillful.
> For the penalty for neglect is not the same for both but
> varies in proportion to their attainments. No one would
> blame the unskillful for turning out nothing remarkable.
> But gifted speakers are pursued by frequent complaints
> from all and sundry, unless they continually surpass the
> expectation which everyone has of them.[21]

The preaching challenge hit home to Aaron as he was biking home from my preaching class one day. That night he sent me an email: "The popular methods used in most pulpits today are doable, I could totally work myself into that game. But true text-based, Spirit-inspired, Christ-centered, stay-in-the-Story preaching isn't that easy. It's demanding." He went on to describe just how demanding he thought it was, concluding, "This will require all of me—body, mind, and soul."[22] In that critical moment, Aaron realized what all good preachers realize—that preaching requires something far more than the ability to communicate. Preaching is an act of worship. We place ourselves under Jesus's easy yoke and submit to the God-breathed biblical text. In the Spirit we cultivate a passion for the truth and a love for God's word that is all-consuming. We want our personal lives and every part of our public ministry grounded in the whole counsel of God. We seek to discover the tension in the text and exegete our culture in the light of the text. We aim to edify and evangelize. We confront our culture's idols and preach the good news of Jesus Christ.

John Stott was pastor of All Souls Church in London and a global ambassador for Christ. He lived into his nineties and had an extraordinary impact on the church in the West and in developing nations. Many of us use his excellent biblical commentaries when we prepare to preach. In *Between Two Worlds: The Art of Preaching in the Twentieth Century*, Stott makes a noteworthy confession: "we preach biblically" because we are determined "to expound the Scriptures." But he admits that for many years he was entirely focused on the biblical world and made no effort to connect the Scriptures he expounded to the contemporary world. He describes conservative biblical preaching this way:

> If I were to draw a diagram of the gulf between the two worlds, and then plot our sermons on the diagram, I would have to draw a straight line which begins in the biblical world, and then goes up in the air on a straight trajectory, but never lands on the other side. For our preaching is seldom if ever earthed. It fails to build a bridge into the modern world. It is biblical, but not contemporary.
>
> I hope that in recent years I have begun to mend my ways, yet previously both my theory and my practice were to expound the biblical text and leave the application largely to the Holy Spirit. Moreover, this method is by no means as ineffective as it may sound, for two reasons. First the biblical text is itself amazingly contemporary, and secondly the Holy Spirit does use it to bring the hearers to conviction of sin, faith in Christ and growth in holiness.

Yet, Stott confesses, "It would be quite inadmissible to use the perpetual relevance of the gospel and the up-to-date ministry of the Holy Spirit as an excuse for avoiding the communication problem."[23] We have a great challenge before us to understand and explain an authoritative ancient text, the word of God, and expound its meaning and significance for our twenty-first-century world. We cannot leave the truth of Jesus in the first century; we need to bring it down to earth on the other side of the gulf in the mess and mystery of the human condition today.

Preachers face not only a personal and cultural challenge but the social challenge of great diversity. Embedded in their congregation of saints and seekers are people who listen to sermons from different spiritual and emotional places with very different needs. On any given Sunday, some need the hammer to break the rock of unbelief and disobedience, and others need great empathy and encouragement because they are bruised reeds barely standing. On the surface, this seems like an impossible task, and I imagine some pastors deal with this diversity by ignoring it altogether. They may preach a kind of generic sermon that has a little something for everyone: an amusing opening anecdote, a few biblical observations, a simple outline, and some practical points of individualistic application.

Sometimes preachers are tempted to use their congregations as an excuse for not preaching anything difficult. They default to a formulaic approach to the gospel. It saves them from the hard work of crafting and nuancing a sermon to cover difficult topics and practical concerns. The sharp edges of the faith are smoothed over, and most everything comes down to how the individual feels about their relationship with God. We have to ask why so many believers listen to weekly sermons but remain biblically illiterate and spiritually naive. The *predictable* "come to Jesus" sermon does not stand up to life's challenges of suffering and hardship, nor to the intellectual challenges of competing ideologies.

Gregory the Great (540–604) warns preachers in his *Pastoral Rule* to avoid saying "the right words too frequently ... because often the virtue of what is said is lost when it is enfeebled in the hearts of the audience since the speech was offered hastily or carelessly. This type of speech defiles the speaker because it shows that he does not know how to serve the advanced needs of his audience."[24] Søren Kierkegaard offers a similar criticism against preachers who take the great truths of the Christian faith for granted and repeat them over and over again as if there was nothing more obvious to everybody than the truth of the Incarnate One or the meaning of his sacrifice on the cross. Kierkegaard laments, "Ah, such parsons do not know what they are talking about, it is hidden from their eyes that they are doing away with Christianity. ... Direct recognizableness is precisely the characteristic of the pagan god." Selling Jesus with a Christianized mantra, said over and over again, is no different from the rhetoric of pagan religions.[25] Kierkegaard argues that such innocuous and predictable sermonic talk does more harm than good.

In letters from his Nazi prison cell, Dietrich Bonhoeffer blamed the German church's capitulation to Hitler's ideology of Aryan nationalism and anti-Semitism on *religious* speech. Long before Hitler's rants, Christianity was enmeshed in German notions of power and privilege. Preaching concealed the godlessness of the world and promoted cultural religion. Self-preservation became the church's goal, rather than the gospel of reconciliation and redemption. Bonhoeffer believed that the gospel had been co-opted by religion. He warned that preaching the grace of Christ had become a poison. Repeated exposure to religious jargon renders the hearer impenitent and callous: "One hears and yet does not hear. One receives and yet is not helped. God's forgiveness is not accepted but the person learns how to deal with himself gracefully. Forgiveness is taken into one's own hands." When a person lives in "unrecognized and undisclosed sin," "the word of grace becomes a poison." Bonhoeffer concluded that "countless Christians hear the word of grace only in this way. For them it has become a sleeping pill. The person is cheated out of a salutary life in awe of God."[26]

Pope Gregory was commended by John Calvin for his humility, resistance to worldly power, and emphasis on the responsibilities of a pastor.[27] His spiritual direction profiled the diversity of virtually all congregations in a way that is as relevant today as it was in the sixth century. Gregory insisted that we must differentiate between men and women, young and old, poor and rich, joyful and sad, the lazy and the hasty, the humble and the proud, the obstinate and the fickle, and the gluttonous and the abstinent. He identified more than thirty-seven categories and offered a paragraph or two on how pastors should address each group. By reflecting on Gregory's spiritual direction, we remind ourselves that every sermon addresses a wide variety of personality types, some of whom are intensely aware of their spiritual condition and others who are oblivious. There are believers and unbelievers alike who are at various stages of spiritual acceptance, resistance, maturity, and immaturity. Pastors become more aware of the need for different strokes for different folks. Wisdom often dictates a certain degree of nuanced telegraphing in a sermon—a bolder approach for the bold and a modest approach for the modest.

Nevertheless, even though the diversity of a congregation may be great, pastors who are most aware of this diversity are also most aware of the power and wisdom of the Holy Spirit to break rocks and protect bruised reeds. That is why there is a kind of synergy between prophetic blows and pastoral nurture in a grace-filled gospel sermon. That is why sermons end at the Communion table. It is never about trying harder; it is always about the grace of the Lord Jesus Christ, evangelizing and edifying, saving and sanctifying, comforting and challenging.

Then the LORD put out his hand and touched my mouth.
And the LORD said to me,
"Behold, I have put my words in your mouth.
See, I have set you this day over nations and over
kingdoms,|to pluck up and to break down,
to destroy and to overthrow,
to build and to plant."

Jeremiah 1:9–10

Now, brothers and sisters, I have applied these
things to myself and Apollos for your benefit, so
that you may learn from us the meaning of the
saying, "Do not go beyond what is written."

1 Corinthians 4:6 NIV

3

Compelling, Not Manipulative

David Martyn Lloyd-Jones was the pastor of Westminster Chapel in London for almost thirty years. He was known for his *logic-on-fire* biblical preaching and for his impatience with boring sermons. "There is something radically wrong with dull and boring preachers," he writes. "I would say that a 'dull preacher' is a contradiction in terms; if he is dull he is not a preacher." Lloyd-Jones illustrates his concern with a preacher who preached on Jeremiah 20:9, "If I say, 'I will not mention him, or speak any more in his name,' there is in my heart as it were a burning fire shut up in my bones, and I am weary with holding it in, and I cannot." Lloyd-Jones writes, "The good man was talking about fire as if he were sitting on an iceberg." Although he commends the preacher's preparation, Lloyd-Jones levels a stinging criticism of his delivery: "There was no zeal, no enthusiasm, no apparent concern for us as members of the congregation. His whole attitude seemed to be detached and academic and formal."[1]

THE PROBLEM OF BORING SERMONS

There is a memorable scene in *Dead Poet's Society* when the English teacher John Keating, played by Robin Williams, begins his poetry class by having his students read the introduction to their poetry textbook. As a student reads aloud the pedantic prose of "James Evans Pritchard, PhD," describing how to rank poetry, Keating plots Pritchard's rating technique on the board. The students assume that this is a typically boring introduction to another academic subject that they care little about. Suddenly Keating turns from the diagram on the chalkboard and says, "Excrement. That's what I think of James Evans Pritchard, PhD's introduction to poetry. We are not laying pipe. We are understanding poetry. I want you to rip it out, and while you are at it, rip out the whole introduction. Rip it out!" Slowly, as their shocked incredulity gives way to awareness, the students begin ripping the pages from their hardback volume of poetry. "This is a battle, a war," Keating declares, "and the casualties could be your hearts and souls."[2]

I share John Keating's perspective when I hear a preacher treat the congregation like a captive audience, taking their time and attention for granted because the subject is the Bible. *Boring sermons* unpack a passage as if it were an old dresser containing miscellaneous items of interest. *Inventory sermons* take stock of the grammatical, historical, linguistic, and theological aspects of the biblical text as if it were their job to catalog their findings. *Museum sermons* handle the text like an historical artifact, a period piece, which requires careful study. *Informational sermons* assume that because the subject of the sermon is the Bible, any Christian ought to be interested no matter how dull and insipid the sermon may be. Little effort is made to relate the text to the hearer, and then only at the end, when the listener's patience has been exhausted, the preacher asks, "What does this mean for us today?"

Dr. Cuticle, the surgeon of the fleet in Herman Melville's mid-nineteenth-century chronicle of an American Navy man-o'-war, profiles the kind of pastor we never want to be. Only Dr. Cuticle's ego outranks his position as the foremost surgeon of the fleet. His "marvelous indifference to the sufferings of his patients" and his gleeful enthusiasm for praise and respect set up the analogy. When presented with a hapless sailor suffering a seriously infected wounded leg, Dr. Cuticle welcomes the opportunity to perform an amputation with an audience of fleet surgeons who have gathered for a rare event—major surgery at sea.

Melville titles his chapter "The Operation," but for our purposes let's call it "The Sermon." Amid elaborate preparations, the operating table is set up on the deck of the ship. Sailors watch from above, and a ring of doctors encircles the venerable doctor. The surgeon of the fleet has even supplied a human skeleton, which is hung at the foot of the operating plank. He points out the thigh bone on the skeleton and marks where he will sever the limb. He then precedes to saw the limb while pontificating on the history of surgery.

Surgeon Cuticle reassures his attentive audience not to worry. Even though the patient has passed out, he will recover quickly. However, the doctor gives this assurance without even looking at the patient, whose flesh is quivering—his eyes are rolled back, and he is bleeding profusely. Dr. Cuticle is too busy commenting on his previous surgical cases to notice the condition of his dying patient. The operation completed, the patient is whisked away below deck, and Cuticle continues lecturing his junior surgeons. Moments later the ship's steward returns. "Please, sir," the steward says, "the patient is dead." Without a pause, Cuticle responds, "The body also, gentlemen, at ten precisely." He turns to his shocked audience, "I predicted that the operation might prove fatal; he was very much run down. Good morning." And with that the doctor departs.[3]

Sermons that are tone deaf, situationally unaware, and delivered without regard for the "patient" are boring for all practical purposes. Or worse, they are deadly, and pastors who preach them have something in common with Dr. Cuticle—malpractice. Solving the boring-sermon problem is not a matter of clever technique and an emotional performance. Manipulating externals and improving delivery will only get us so far. Palmer writes, "Technique is what teachers use until the real teacher arrives."[4] So what does it take for the real preacher to show up?

Building on the last chapter, the first thing to be said is that the real preacher submits to the word of God and internalizes its message. This is a matter of prayer, intellectual effort, heart-searching concern, and cultural understanding. The Holy Spirit quickens our internalization, but there is no shortcut to the transforming impact of being immersed in Scripture. Years of devotional *lectio divina,* along with careful study, faithful mentoring, and the practice of the spiritual disciplines, deepens our submission to the word of God.

Clergy who think of sermon preparation as occupying a few hours out of their week have not grasped the totality of the preaching challenge. If we are going to internalize God's word, *we have to eat it*—eat it, like three meals a day plus snacks! We have to ingest it, digest it, and absorb it. "Your words were found, and I ate them," writes the prophet Jeremiah. "And your words became to me a joy and the delight of my heart, for I am called by your name" (Jer 15:16). Ezekiel was commanded by the Lord, "Son of man, eat whatever you find here. Eat this scroll, and go, speak to the house of Israel" (Ezek 3:1). This vivid analogy of taking in God's intelligible revelation as if it were food means that everything about our life and work is guided, shaped, and empowered by the word of God. We were meant to live on the word of God, not on blog posts, popular opinion, and trending fads. Eating God's word is the perfect picture of personal engagement and participation. We cannot stand aloof or sit in judgment on the truth of God when we are eating it up![5]

A passion for the truth drives the preacher to the text and then to the pulpit, rather than the pressure of the pulpit driving the pastor to the text. If it is our passion to take every thought captive to obey Christ, and if it is our desire "to gaze upon the beauty of the LORD and to inquire in his temple," then our focus will be on the Lord rather than externals (2 Cor 10:5; Ps 27:4). Faithful and effective preachers concentrate on the text for the sake of others. Preachers who focus on themselves and their performance or seek to please people and add to their popularity will miss out on what it means to have a passion for Christ and his word. It is tempting to become absorbed in running the church, managing the staff, solving problems, and putting out fires. It is also tempting to craft sermons that are appealing, humorous, inspiring, and motivational, but have little to do with the power of God's word to shape the biblical community. American preaching spends considerable time building Jesus's fan base rather than nurturing discipleship. Real preachers know that their authority lies exclusively in the word of God, not in the power of their personality or their speaking skills.

Real preachers discover the tension in the text that leads to the passion of the passage. This discovery drives them to understand, describe, and illustrate the fallen human condition exposed in the text. From there they develop the impact of this passion for truth in a way that applies to the whole church practically, personally, and communally. Their aim is to explain and expound on God's redemptive provision in a way that is convicting, compelling, and life changing. Hype, humor, and human-interest stories do not make an otherwise boring sermon compelling. What makes a sermon compelling is the penetrating power of God's word, delivered in the Spirit with personal integrity.

We preachers need to think and sound more like Jesus and the apostles if we want to be heard. A hipster haircut, skinny jeans, street-smart jargon, and workout abs will not fix a boring sermon. Hooping may turn an otherwise dull sermon into a barn burner, but sadly the sermon may be forgotten quickly after the benediction. A witty, humorous, and conversational approach to the text may keep people entertained, but at the high cost of shifting the focus from the text to the performer.

THE PERILS OF
MANIPULATIVE SERMONS

The solution to a boring sermon is a compelling sermon, not a manipulative sermon. The apostle Paul was committed to communicating the gospel in a way that was powerful and persuasive. What he rejected was a performance-based communication that was designed to manipulate the listener. Like today's comedian or politician, the Greco-Roman orator sought to play the audience, winning the crowd over by whatever means possible. Musicians such as cellist Yo-Yo Ma or jazz trumpeter Wynton Marsalis play their instrument for all its worth. They do not play the crowd. They serve the listener. That is how it was with Paul. He sought to play the gospel for all of its worth—for all its truth and power. The gospel, not the audience, determined his communication theory. Form and content were subject to the power of the gospel. For Paul, both the substance and the style of a message had to be gospel based through and through. Everything about the sermon from design to delivery was rooted in God's word.

Duane Litfin argues that the apostle Paul made a conscious distinction between being a results-driven Greco-Roman *orator* and being an obedience-driven gospel *herald*. The gospel's form and content became an issue in the church at Corinth because a significant group of believers were apparently embarrassed by the apostle Paul's public speaking style. Litfin writes, "Both his physical appearance and his speaking itself were deficient, even contemptible, by the sophisticated standards of Greek rhetoric."[6] Paul acknowledges that this was the case when he quotes his critics: "For some say, 'His letters are weighty and forceful, but in person he is unimpressive and his speaking amounts to nothing'" (2 Cor 10:10 NIV). Apparently, these Corinthian believers were "connoisseurs of eloquence and wisdom and acutely conscious of related matters of status and esteem." They seem uninhibited in their criticism, finding "Paul's all-too-public deficiencies a painful liability."[7]

The Corinthian situation provides an apostolic case study in communication theory. Paul defines and illustrates the form and content of good preaching. He sets up a definite contrast between worldly wisdom and popular forms of communication on one side, and the preaching of the gospel on the other. The wisdom of the world, whether it be Jewish or Greek, is set in contrast to the gospel of Jesus Christ. For Paul, the bottom line is this: "It pleased God through the folly of what we preach to save those who believe" (1 Cor 1:21). As a herald of the gospel, Paul was neither "results-driven" nor "audience-driven." Instead, he was "assignment-driven" and "obedience-driven" (see 1 Cor 4:2).[8]

Litfin lays out the apostle's defense of his preaching strategy. Paul did not want anyone looking back and feeling that they were manipulated or coerced into yielding to the gospel. This is why he disavows worldly wisdom and eloquence, "lest the cross of Christ be emptied of its power" (1 Cor 1:17). "When I came to you," Paul emphasizes, "I did not come ... with lofty speech or wisdom. For I decided to know nothing among you except Jesus Christ and him crucified" (2:1–2). In fact, Paul sincerely thought that "self-confident rhetorical assertion" was a huge distraction because it shifted attention away from Christ to the speaker.

New Testament scholar Tony Thiselton writes, "Paul's 'authority' lay *not in smooth, competent, impressive, powers of articulation,* but in a faithful and sensitive *proclaiming* rendered operative *not by the applause of the audience, but by the authority of God."* He continues, "Paul wants to let *truth* speak for itself, *not to manipulate rhetoric to sway his audience by appeal to opinions."*[9] Paul is not shy about admitting that he came to them "in weakness and in fear and much trembling" (1 Cor 2:3), even if the socially elite found Paul's admission embarrassing.

The form and content of the gospel were countercultural in the first century. The *substance* of Paul's message, the *style* of his delivery, and the *strategy* of his preaching were all counterintuitive in the Greco-Roman culture, and, we should add, in the twenty-first century. Instead of clever rhetoric, Paul was clear; instead of ingratiating diplomacy, Paul was dynamic. He went for the jugular. "For I decided to know nothing among you except Jesus Christ and him crucified" (1 Cor 2:2). This basic, bedrock truth explains what Paul means when he says, "For no one can lay a foundation other than that which is laid, which is Jesus Christ" (3:11).

Some readers may feel that Paul's resolve to know nothing but Christ crucified in Corinth was in reaction to his attempt to explain the gospel to the Athenian intelligentsia (Acts 17:16–34). Instead of debating and dialoguing as he did in Athens, he simply gave the simple plan of salvation to the Corinthians. However, there is no evidence for concluding that Paul was dumbing down the gospel. His message to believers in Corinth indicates that he had no intention of reducing the gospel to a mere "come to Jesus" slogan.

On the contrary, Paul saw the relevance of the cross of Christ in every conceivable sphere of the believer's life. For Paul the cross of Jesus was the basis for unity in the body of Christ. To those who are ready to divide up and follow their favorite leader, Paul asks, "Was Paul crucified for you? Or were you baptized in the name of Paul?" (1 Cor 1:13). To those who are proud of their tolerance of sexual immorality in the church, Paul calls for immediate church discipline, because "Christ, our Passover lamb, has been sacrificed" (5:7). He commands, "Flee from sexual immorality" because of the cross. "You are not your own, for you were bought with a price. So glorify God in your body" (6:18–20). He counsels believers to experience their freedom in Christ, regardless of their social circumstances, because of the cross. "You were bought with a price; do not become bondservants of men" (7:23). He advises believers to refrain from eating meat that was offered to idols if it might cause a new believer to stumble. Or else, "by your knowledge this weak person is destroyed, the brother for whom Christ died" (8:11).

Paul centers the worship life of the church in terms of the cross. "The cup of blessing that we bless, is it not a participation in the blood of Christ? The bread that we break, is it not a participation in the body of Christ?" (1 Cor 10:16). He warns believers against using their social positions and wealth to humiliate other believers. "For anyone who eats and drinks without discerning the body eats and drinks judgment on himself" (11:29). To those who question the reality of the bodily resurrection, Paul affirms that the saving work of Christ on the cross depends on the risen Lord Jesus. "For I delivered to you as of first importance what I also received: that Christ died for our sins in accordance with the Scriptures, that he was buried, that he was raised on the third day in accordance with the Scriptures, and that he appeared to Cephas, then to the twelve" (15:3–5).

In the midst of every problem, every issue, and every conflict affecting the church at Corinth, Paul brings the believers back to the finished work of Christ on the cross. Paul subsumes everything under the cross, even death itself. "The sting of death is sin, and the power of sin is the law. But thanks be to God, who gives us the victory through our Lord Jesus Christ" (1 Cor 15:56–57). Paul was resolved to make the crucified and risen Lord the sum and substance of his proclamation, admonition, and teaching.

Paul continues to hammer out his communication theory: "My speech and my message were not in plausible words of wisdom, but in demonstration of the Spirit and of power, so that your faith might not rest in the wisdom of men but in the power of God" (1 Cor 2:4–5; see 2:13). Paul was convinced, and he wanted all believers to be convinced that the power of the gospel must not be obscured by or attributed to human wisdom. Thiselton writes, "It seems clear that Paul determines to let truth speak for itself, confident in the power of the Holy Spirit of God to bring this truth home to the hearts, minds, and wills of the hearers. But the price is a renunciation of the status of rhetorician."[10] The style and strategies of the orator were impressive and yielded worldly success, but for the gospel herald they were a temptation leading to failure.

Paul refers to his philosophy of preaching in 2 Corinthians as a matter of "simplicity and godly sincerity" (2 Cor 1:12). "For we are not, like so many," Paul insists, "peddlers of God's word, but as men of sincerity, as commissioned by God, in the sight of

God we speak in Christ" (2:17). Paul and his fellow missionaries renounce "disgraceful, underhanded ways," reject the use of deception and manipulation, and refuse to "tamper with God's word." Instead, they set forth the truth of the gospel plainly, appealing to "everyone's conscience in the sight of God" (4:2). They hold the treasure of the gospel "in jars of clay, to show that the surpassing power belongs to God and not to us" (4:7). They fight hard for the gospel, but they do not wage war with the weapons of the world. Paul insists, "For the weapons of our warfare are not of the flesh but have divine power to destroy strongholds" (10:3–4).

Paul's persistent effort to distance the preaching of the gospel from the styles and strategies of worldly wisdom and cultural expectations challenges today's preachers to follow his bold and sincere example. If his preaching was anything like his writing, then it is reasonable to conclude that his preaching was clear, compelling, and convicting. He did not use the truth of the gospel as an excuse to bully, manipulate, deceive, or distort the truth. He refused to participate in "the Jesus business" and rejected outright selling Jesus. He was not into marketing to felt needs or rebranding to make the gospel more appealing. He would have had little patience with the spiritual consumer who wanted to be entertained and affirmed. Paul's ministry was characterized by "simplicity, innocence, sincerity, and transparency." Litfin continues, "Eschewing any attempt to make himself look impressive, he merely placarded the truth before the consciences of his listeners. His ministry was not only from God; it was conducted with an open face before God."[11]

Psychologist William McQuire suggests that there are five key steps in influencing human attitude: attention, comprehension, yielding, retention, and action. Litfin, citing McQuire, argues that the goal of Christian preaching is attention and

comprehension, *not* yielding. The power to persuade belongs
to the Holy Spirit (Zech 4:6; Ps 127:1). Litfin writes,

> The traditional approach to homiletics seems to suggest
> that the goal of preaching is the third step, yielding; that
> is, the preacher's goal is to induce the listener to yield
> to (and ultimately to act upon) a particular value, atti-
> tude, or belief. I suggest that the preacher's goal should
> not be viewed as the yielding step at all but simply the
> previous step, *comprehension*.[12]

Preachers are responsible for delivering the message of God
with clarity, conviction, and grace. The listener's response is
the preacher's *prayerful* concern rather than the preacher's
responsibility. We can make a gospel appeal to people, but
we cannot decide for them. The preacher is called to proclaim
Christ, admonishing and teaching everyone with all wisdom so
that they might present everyone fully mature (Col 1:28). Litfin
acknowledges that this involves "urging, entreating, exhorting, or beseeching" listeners to follow Christ. Litfin affirms:
"The very essence of the gospel is invitation."[13] This is consistent with Luke's report of Peter *exhorting* and *pleading* with
his Pentecost audience (Acts 2:40) and Luke's account of Paul
imploring and *appealing* to the Corinthians to be reconciled to
God (2 Cor 5:20).

Litfin's case for Paul as *herald* rather than *orator* is persuasive.
The evidence for Paul's communication theory based on his
own words is irrefutable. But we should understand that Paul's
deep concern to communicate the gospel without coercion, dis-
tortion, manipulation, and embellishment is in its own right
persuasive. Paul shunned any hint of artificiality, entertainment,
and grandstanding. That in itself is incredibly persuasive and
constitutes a true and necessary kind of gospel persuasion.

We have no hint that Paul played the audience, but he did a phenomenal job of playing God's word to its maximum effect. The gospel in the hands of Paul was like a well-made violin in the hands of a skilled violinist. This lightweight, fragile piece of finely crafted spruce and maple can fill a concert hall with music. What the violin is to music, the gospel is to life, and Paul could play it with profound sensitivity and skill.

Paul never preached for results, but he did preach for impact. He never bypassed the brain to move the heart. He never set people up to manipulate them. He never bullied or beguiled them with interminable invitations to "come to Jesus." Yet Paul expected gospel communicators to be persuasive and listeners to be persuaded by the gospel. Anyone who is "warning everyone and teaching everyone with all wisdom" is humbly seeking to persuade (Col 1:28). This nonmanipulative persuasion is not about making people's decisions for them, but neither is it only informative speech. It is a witness that entreats, exhorts, and calls for a decision.

Paul, the gospel communicator, went beyond comprehension. Like Jesus, he challenged listeners to embrace the truth of the gospel and decide for Christ. He anticipated the listener's willingness to yield, and he helped the listener define what it meant to accept or reject the truth of Christ. Like his Lord, he entrusted the whole communication process—attention, comprehension, yielding, retention, and action—to the sovereignty of God (John 6:37, 44; 12:49–50).

Paul based his effort to persuade on his fear of the Lord. His communication theory was not subject to the Corinthian crowd or the Athenian elite. It was subject to the judgment of God: "For we must all appear before the judgment seat of Christ." This leads Paul to say, "Therefore, knowing the fear of the Lord, we persuade others" (2 Cor 5:10–11). "Fear of the Lord" is a "bound phrase," meaning that the four words cannot be defined separately but bear a singular meaning. Bruce Waltke calls it "the quintessential rubric, which expresses in a nutshell the basic grammar that holds the covenant community together."[14] "Fear of the Lord" marks the way of life consistent with Paul's challenge to "work out your own salvation with fear and trembling, for it is God who works in you, both to will and to work for his good pleasure" (Phil 2:12–13).

Paul's understanding of persuasion was linked to his missionary effort to convince Jews and Greeks to accept God's salvation. Ralph Martin writes, "[Paul] tries to persuade men and women that Christ is the means of salvation, and he attempts to persuade them of his purity of motive."[15] No one who writes the following is shy about persuasion: "I have great sorrow and unceasing anguish in my heart. For I could wish that I myself were cursed and cut off from Christ for the sake of my brothers and sisters, my kinsmen according to the flesh" (Rom 9:2–3). What could be more persuasive than a person's pure passion for Christ, delivered unadulterated by ego and eccentricities, uninhibited by fear of human reaction and rejection, unencumbered by prejudice and pride, and unhindered by duplicity and deception?

A COMPELLING SERMON

If anyone speaks, they should do so as one
who speaks the very words of God.

1 Peter 4:11 NIV

Preaching ought to look easier than it actually is. Good preachers make it seem as if preaching comes naturally. What is hidden is all the hard work and intense prayer. My father's tools and workbench were in the basement of our home. When he was working on a new cabinet, he created a lot of sawdust, but none of the sawdust made it upstairs to the kitchen and the living room. Likewise, the listener benefits from the fruit of the preacher's labor without being constantly reminded of the effort involved in the finished sermon. This is also true for musicians. We do not listen to hours upon hours of practice time. We listen to a polished, well-rehearsed performance. Correctly handling the word of truth is never an end in itself. The work is fundamentally personal, having to do with our relationship to the Lord. God's word is our unique tool for being and becoming in Christ.

Poor preaching can be used mightily by the Spirit of Christ to preach the gospel and make disciples. It happens every Sunday, but that is no excuse for poor preaching. We can be thankful, however, that "God in his ordinary providence makes use of means, yet is free to work without, above and against them, at his pleasure"—and for his glory![16] Yet how much better when the preacher is standing on the fault line between the mystery of God and the mess of the human condition and preaches the word of God in the Spirit. Good preaching requires discernment, hard work, and much prayer. We want to pay attention prayerfully and thoughtfully to God's overarching salvation history, the original intention of the passage, the context of the text, and the people to whom one is preaching. Diligence, devotion, and discernment will result in "the intelligible interpretation and transmission of Christian faith through concepts and means that are tailor-made and custom-fit to the needs of a particular community."[17]

Gary Millar and Phil Campbell explore what it takes to preach a compelling sermon in *Saving Eutychus: How to Preach God's Word and Keep People Awake*. In short, what it takes is not complicated, but that does not mean it is easy. The basics are knowable. The issue is whether we are willing to do them. Millar and Campbell insist on prayer. The biblical text drives pastors to preach, and preaching drives pastors to prayer. We pray for ourselves, for our listeners, and for our world. We need to pray for our preaching and encourage our brothers and sisters in Christ to pray for our preaching.[18] The authors say that the best way to preach to the heart is through expository preaching. If we allow the Bible to set the agenda, and if the message of our sermon equals the message of the text, then the word of God will affect hearts and lives. Their emphasis is consistent with Bryan Chapell's encouragement, "Expository preaching does not merely obligate preachers to explain what the Bible says; it obligates them to explain what the Bible means in the lives of people today."[19]

Millar and Campbell insist that we ought to aim for preaching that is natural and conversational rather than technical and scholarly. Clarity is key: "Being comprehensible, without being condescending. Being simple without being simplistic."[20] Pacing is important. Illustrations and stories help people absorb the message. The authors suggest writing out the biblical text longhand as an exercise in discovering the big idea of the text. If we want "the freshly-squeezed essence of the passage," we have to study, read, pray, meditate, reflect, and then repeat. Note repeated words and phrases. Figure out the logic of the text. Question easy assumptions and preconceived ideas.[21]

Millar and Campbell stress the theme of the next chapter here: gospel-centered, whole-counsel-of-God preaching. They emphasize the importance of preaching Christ from the entire Bible. "So our aim," they write, "is to preach in a way that is shaped by biblical theology. This requires doing the hard work of hermeneutics and biblical theology and then crafting a message that conveys the big idea of the passage in a clear and engaging way so that our listeners can apply God's truth to their lives." Finally, they offer helpful practical advice on sermon delivery. They challenge us to consider how our volume, pitch, and pace help people hear and understand our sermons. They emphasize the importance of agile transitions, purposeful delivery, and heartfelt convictions.[22]

A good sermon has substance to inform, eloquence to engage, and intensity to persuade. The preaching pastor is three in one—part professor, part poet, and part prophet. The preacher seeks to be heard intelligently, willingly, and obediently. Augustine held that verbal skills should be learned quickly so that a person could get on with the real work of understanding the Bible: "For those with acute and eager minds more readily learn eloquence [effective communication] by reading and hearing the eloquent [excellent communicators] than by following the rules of eloquence [effective communication]." A preacher "will learn eloquence especially if he gains practice by writing, dictating, or speaking what he has learned according to the rule of piety and faith." He continues, "I think that there is hardly a single eloquent man [or woman] who can both speak well and think of the rules of eloquence while he is speaking."[23] Good preachers are not formed in the classroom listening to their teachers; they are formed in the church as they listen to good preaching.

AUGUSTINE ON PERSUASIVE PREACHING

Augustine believed that there was a dynamic synergy between the two aspects of preaching, *understanding* and *explaining*. He writes, "There are two things necessary to the treatment of the Scriptures: a way of discovering those things which are to be understood, and a way of teaching what we have learned."[24]

We cannot explain what we do not understand, and we cannot understand what we are unwilling to explain. The more we understand, the more we will explain, and the more we explain, the more we will understand. Augustine quotes Jesus's promise, "Whoever has will be given more, and he will have an abundance" (Matt 13:12).

Neither interpretation nor explanation is an end in itself, and neither can be separated from worshiping and obeying the Holy Trinity: God the Father, Son, and Holy Spirit. According to Augustine, "Whoever thinks that he understands the divine Scriptures or any part of them so that it does not build the double love of God and of our neighbor does not understand it at all."[25]

Augustine believed that God designed the Scriptures to humble the believer, because when we begin to comprehend that the Bible is all about loving God with our whole selves and our neighbor as ourselves, we discover that we have been "enmeshed in the love of the world, or of temporal things, a love far remote from the kind of love of God and of our neighbor which Scripture itself prescribes."[26] Augustine believed that we have no other recourse than to lament our dire situation and turn to God for his grace and mercy.

Augustine also believed that only a person whose character was forged in humility, repentance, and redemption was ready to understand and teach God's word. He taught classical rhetoric for many years, but after his conversion he put little stock in the world's methods of communication. In his treatise on preaching, he wrote, "I must thwart the expectation of those who think that I shall give the rules of rhetoric here which I learned and taught in the secular schools."[27] He was skeptical of the art of rhetoric because he concluded that the rules of rhetoric were equally effective in communicating truth or falsehood. There was little benefit in mastering the world's methods of communication, but there was great benefit in writing and speaking what one "learned according to the rule of piety and faith."[28]

Even so, Augustine did not minimize the effort necessary to effectively and faithfully preach God's word. The "expositor and teacher of the Divine Scripture, the defender of right faith and the enemy of error, should both teach the good and uproot the evil." This "labor of words," as he called it, was meant to win over the opposition, inspire the careless, and teach the ignorant. But if the preacher finds his listeners pleasantly indifferent and docile, then he must double down and work that much harder to communicate effectively, "in order that those things which are doubtful may be made certain." Augustine says, "If those who hear are to be moved rather than taught, so that they may not be sluggish in putting what they know into practice and so that they may fully accept those things which they acknowledge to be true, there is need for greater powers of speaking." Augustine suggested earnest appeals and reprimands, exhortations and rebukes—whatever method of communication "necessary to move minds must be used."[29]

*Our teaching needs to become more like
our preaching and our preaching needs
to become more like our teaching.*

Gordon Fee

*Te totum applica ad textum:
rem totum applica ad te*

*Apply your whole self to the text:
apply the whole text to yourself.*

Latin aphorism

4

The Whole Counsel of God

Preaching God's word in the name of Jesus is rooted in the great drama of God's ongoing redemptive story. Salvation history is his story. It bears repeating that everyone has a story, but only one story, his story, redeems our story. Increasingly, we are aware of the need to understand and to explain the whole counsel of God. We are headed in the opposite direction from the flitter of fleeting tweets. We need to set our hearts and minds on God's metanarrative.

Tim Mackie directs the Bible Project, which is guiding a new generation to read the Bible as "one unified story that leads to Jesus and has wisdom to offer the whole world." Mackie is surely right when he says, "There's something about seeing the artistic brilliance of the biblical authors drawn out before you. It anchors the ideas in your mind in a way that invites exploration and ignites the imagination."[1]

Humble students of God's word hold the finite biblical text in tension with the beauty and magnitude of infinite truth. We share the apostle's *biblically rooted* passion:

Oh, the depth of the riches and wisdom and knowledge
of God! How unsearchable are his judgments and how
inscrutable his ways!

"For who has known the mind of the Lord,
     or who has been his counselor?" [Isa 40:13]

"Or who has ever given a gift to him
     that he might be repaid?" [Job 41:11]

For from him and through him and to him are all things.
To him be glory forever! Amen. (Rom 11:33–36)

The finite biblical text has parameters—fixed canonical limits.
The message is vast, and the truth exceeds our comprehension. When I was a young pastor, I wondered whether I would
eventually run out of good material. I do not worry about that
anymore. In fact, I would love to start preaching and pastoring
all over again. There is plenty here to work with for seventy
times seven lifetimes. We will never exhaust it, but the Bible
has only so many pages—1,005 in my Bible. We have to find
ways to grasp this finite text if we expect to proclaim its infinite
meaning. Beautiful music relies on twelve pitches. The artist
works with a palette of five primary colors. The periodic table
is made up of ninety-two natural elements. The English language uses twenty-six letters. The Bible is knowable: its literary
forms are recognizable, its history is manageable, and its revelation of God is comprehensible. The truth we never would
have imagined or invented has been revealed.[2]

THE CANONICAL SCOPE

Open up your Bible to the table of contents, and you will see
sixty-six books listed in order of their purpose and genre.[3] The
first five books are commonly known as the books of Moses

and are foundational to the rest of the Bible. They tell the story of God's creation of the world, from the cosmos to the first human couple, and from the nations to the covenant people of Israel. God conceives, redeems, identifies, and gathers a people for himself to be a blessing to the nations. Twelve history books follow, from Joshua to Esther, charting the course of this tiny, beleaguered people through Israel's early history. Then, the Wisdom Books explore the human experience in relationship to God and each other: Job, Psalms, Proverbs, Ecclesiastes, and Song of Songs. The rest of the Old Testament is made up of prophets, sixteen of them, from Isaiah to Malachi. The prophets are confrontational. Their job is to declare the judgment of God against all sin and rebellion and the salvation of God for all those who turn to God in humility, repentance, and faith. The tension in the text is between judgment and salvation—between the fallen human condition and God's redemptive provision.

The New Testament consists of five stories, twenty-one letters, and one visionary poetic epic. The four Gospels place Jesus in the context of all that has gone before. He is the culmination and climax of all the Law and the Prophets. Everything points to him. They tell the story of Jesus in the street language of the day. Matthew, Mark, Luke, and John use the Jesus way to communicate his personal encounters, parables, miracles, and messages. They take us to the cross and the empty tomb. Acts tells us the story of Christ and the early church. Luke picks up the narrative of the risen Lord Jesus and describes how the church grew from Jerusalem to Rome. The twenty-one letters give apostolic shape to the emerging mission of God. All their theology is practical. Nothing is esoteric and abstract. Everything involves the day-to-day life of the church. Sin and salvation, worship and judgment, mission and love get worked out in the real world. No one is playing church or going through the motions. The apostle John's Revelation brings the canon to an end. In the Spirit, he orchestrates a powerful symphony of countervailing tensions, worship and judgment, judgment and worship.

To our human imagination, space is limitless. When we begin talking about so many light years to the nearest star, we lose track of time. But human history is not like cosmic space. Day-to-day living is still framed the same old-fashioned way from sunrise to sunset to sunrise. Twenty-four hours in a day, 365 days in a year, ten years in a decade, one hundred years in a century, one thousand years in a millennium, and before you know it you have counted up human history. Time frames human history on planet earth in parameters we can understand. Think of it this way: my grandfather lived to ninety-three. Just twenty or so generations of people who lived like my grandfather to a ripe old age, and we are back to the time of Christ's resurrection. Biblical history, which is to say human history, has a knowable timeline. It is not a black hole of limitless time, even if we may feel that way in history class.

Only Genesis 1–11 covers a span of time too long for us to take in. Dating the cosmos is anyone's guess, because we cannot calculate the time lapse in Genesis 1. For all we know, it may have been billions of years. Adam begins human history, but Abraham is our historical key for dating, somewhere around 2000 to 1800 BC. Three generations of patriarchs—Isaac, Jacob, and Joseph—cover two hundred years in Canaan, followed by 430 years of bondage in Egypt. Moses and the exodus date somewhere around 1450 BC. Forty years of wilderness wanderings precedes Joshua's conquest of Canaan in 1400 BC. The history of the judges from Othniel to Samson covers another four hundred years. David, the great grandson of Ruth, was fully established on the throne of Israel by 1000 BC. Following his son Solomon's reign, Israel was divided into two kingdoms in 931 BC, Jeroboam in the north and Rehoboam in the south.

From the divided kingdom to the fall of Jerusalem in 586, we have two long lists of thirty-eight kings split between Samaria and Judah. During this time, the major players are the prophets, along with Ezra, Esther, and Nehemiah. Listed in chronological order, they appear as follows: Joel, Jonah, Amos, Hosea, Isaiah, Micah, Habakkuk, Zephaniah, Jeremiah, Ezekiel, Daniel, Ezra (1–10), Haggai, Zechariah, Ezra (6–19), Esther, Nehemiah, and Malachi. Between Malachi's prophecy of the coming Lord (Mal 3:1) and its fulfillment in Jesus (Matt 11:10) stands another four hundred years, remarkable for their canonical silence. The main contours of this timeline are easy to remember, even if it is difficult to remember the names of the kings and the order of the prophets. At times the line of salvation history seems to grow perilously thin, but the theology of God's promise and provision remains constant.

The chronology of the New Testament is altogether different. Five Gospel narratives, twenty-one letters, and one visionary poem were all written in the first century. Mark may have been the first Gospel account, followed by Matthew, Luke-Acts, and John. The fourfold Gospel story covers the span of Jesus's life, concentrating on the three years of his public ministry. What is surprising is that a third of the Gospels is devoted to the week of his passion, death, and resurrection. The span of salvation history stretching thousands of years narrows down to this one week in time that is absolutely pivotal for all that preceded and all that follows. The apostle Paul was probably the first to put pen to paper when he wrote Thessalonians in the early 50s, followed by Galatians, 1 Corinthians, Philippians, 2 Corinthians, Romans, Colossians, Ephesians, 1 Timothy, Titus, and 2 Timothy. Paul's letters span a little over a decade, assuming that Paul died in Rome sometime in the mid- to late 60s.

Presumably, the book of Hebrews was written in the 60s, prior to the destruction of the temple in AD 70, since the book seems to assume the Levitical priesthood was going strong. James may have written his letter shortly before his martyrdom in AD 62. Peter's two letters were probably written shortly before the Neronian persecution in AD 64. Jude may have been written between 66 and 70. The letters of John and the book of Revelation may date from the 90s. In the space of forty years, we have our New Testament, a finite text with infinite meaning. We cannot help but think of the real incarnation of our Lord every time we open the Bible. The Word became flesh, entered our neighborhood, and chose the limitations of human language and history to make known his grace and truth.

REDEMPTIVE HISTORY

Over the years I have made five trips to northern Ghana to train pastors. On one of the early trips, the plan was for me to study the Pastoral Epistles with a group of about thirty bivocational rural pastors for a week. Many of these pastors and preachers were hardworking farmers and fishermen who took a week off from their regular work to study the word of God intensively. To get ready for this trip, I preached through Timothy and Titus in my home church. I felt comfortable with the material and well-prepared. But on the long flight over, I became concerned that my approach to Paul's letters was too Western and that I did not have enough understanding of Ghanian culture to make the necessary pastoral applications. When we landed in Ghana, I was in a quandary as to what I should do.

The next day, a day before the teaching sessions were to begin, mission director David Mensah and I, along with our families, visited the Muslim chief in a nearby village. The whole village turned out for the festive occasion. Young men danced with all their might to the pounding beat of drums, and the women sang. We were greeted by a wiry old man who took center stage in the proceedings. He was a storyteller, known as the tribal linguist. His responsibility was to tell the story of the tribe. In Janga the tribal linguist or poet was the most interesting person to observe. To the delight of the gathered crowd, he danced his way from the chief to our visiting delegation, transforming protocol into a memorable event. Everyone could tell that he thoroughly enjoyed the art of communication, and he had everybody's attention. He used his poetic flair, personal charisma, and passion to proclaim the history of his people.[4]

Our encounter that morning with the energetic and charismatic tribal linguist gave me the perspective I needed for the coming week's pastoral training. The next day we began with Genesis and spent five hours a day for five days working through the Bible from cover to cover. I encouraged these dedicated pastors, men and women, to be God's tribal linguists, telling the story of God's salvation history. I discovered in Ghana what I should have known all along: that there is great power in grasping salvation history from Genesis to Revelation. When I came home to San Diego, I determined to share the drama of God's redemptive story with our congregation. Over several years I preached Christ from Genesis to Malachi.

Janga's tribal linguist is a picture to me of what the followers of the Lord Jesus are to become. We are God's linguists. To use Paul's words, our task is to "guard what has been entrusted to [our] care." We are to "turn away from godless chatter and the opposing ideas of what is falsely called knowledge" (1 Tim 6:20 NIV). We are to do our best to present ourselves to God as true craftsmen, who do not need to be ashamed and who correctly handle the word of truth (2 Tim 2:15). Jude urges us "to contend for the faith that was once for all entrusted to the saints" (Jude 3). The analogy seemed to work well for the African pastors, who readily embraced the idea of being God's linguists.

Like the Janga linguist, we are born into our responsibility—"For you have been born again, not of perishable seed, but of imperishable, through the living and enduring word of God." Peter continues with a word from the prophet Isaiah: "All people are like grass, and all their glory is like the flowers of the field; the grass withers and the flowers fall, but the word of the Lord endures forever" (1 Pet 1:24–25 NIV). When the people of Janga see their tribal linguist, they see so much more than a little old man. They see the pride of their history, the meaning of their tradition, and the joy of their culture. Is this not how it should be with us? God meant for our lives to embody the gospel message, so that when people see us, they see Christ.

The ministry of the word requires that we comprehend more deeply the drama of God's great salvation history. This is an approach to the Bible that I would have benefited from at the beginning of my formal theological education. Like so many Bible and theology students, I started out by taking language studies and courses in theology and hermeneutics. I enjoyed classes that delved into background of the text and explored the latest critical studies. I studied works by famous biblical scholars and theologians, and did research on higher criticism, form criticism, and the historical-grammatical method of biblical interpretation. I found these courses and my professors fascinating. In fact, there was very little in the graduate school curriculum that I did not enjoy or imagine myself teaching someday. I liked it all: biblical and historical theology, church history, evangelism, and missions.

But something was missing in my theological education and ministry preparation that I was not aware of until years later. I spent several years studying theological German and Latin and exploring every facet of Latin American liberation theology. I read Augustine for the better part of an academic year and sat under brilliant scholars, but I could not have explained to you the importance of the prophet Zechariah or the impact of Isaiah. I knew the trends of modern theology better than I knew God's salvation history.

I grew up in a home that practiced the spiritual disciplines and encouraged a devotional life. For family devotions we read from *The Daily Bread* and a short passage of Scripture that the devotional guide recommended. In my personal devotions I read Oswald Chambers and kept a journal of my daily Bible reading. Thanks to my parents, who lived out the kingdom lifestyle long before it was called that in popular evangelicalism, I was nurtured and instructed in a home that embraced God's word. But I still did not have a sense of the big picture of salvation history. Much of the Old Testament was foreign to me, like the old and forgotten stuff that got stored in our attic. I heard a zillion evangelistic messages at our church, but almost nothing from the biblical prophets.

During my junior high years, our pastor focused almost exclusively on the apostle Paul, but it was preaching through the narrow lens of our subculture rather than the great drama of salvation history. I knew a lot about "getting saved" but not a whole lot about the comprehensive meaning of salvation. Looking back, I sense that my family had an intuitive grasp of the message of the prophets and Jesus's kingdom ethic, but I did not see how it all fit together. I had pieces of the puzzle, but not the big picture. Except for a few well-known psalms, the riches of the Bible's wisdom literature was lost to me. Biblical books such as Leviticus or Numbers were basically ignored or, when thought about at all, regarded as anachronisms for New Testament Christians. Forays into confusing books such as Ezekiel or Daniel were usually for the sake of discovering a devotional thought for the day. I used the book of Revelation to fuel my curiosity more than to deepen my courage.

Although good in themselves, my devotional experience of the word and my graduate theological education conspired to conceal my ignorance of the sweep and drama of salvation history. My experience and my scholarship produced an unintended and hidden deficiency—a trained incapacity to see the big picture and feel the drama of God's story. My well-intentioned devotional subjectivity and specialized expertise had unwittingly obscured the gospel story. I was left with a piecemeal understanding of the Bible, and at the time it did not bother me that large portions of the Bible remained relatively unknown to me. What I was missing was a coherent understanding of the compelling unity of the word of God.

Comprehending the fullness of the redemptive story is imperative for learning how to preach the truth. No matter how much preachers attend to the clarity of their thoughts and the effectiveness of their style, if the driving force of God's truth is not shaping their message, then they are bound to fail, even if their sermons are well-received. Students come to divinity school to learn how to tell the gospel story from cover to cover, but this is where we often disappoint them. By focusing on prolegomena and technical issues at the expense of the big picture, seminaries have a way of exhausting students and preventing them from understanding the scope of God's work. Good teachers know this and guard against it. They defy the scribal propensity to overwhelm students with the complexities and intricacies of scholarly opinions. Their primary purpose is positive: to guide students in the powerful story of God's revelation. Their goal is not to debunk students of their intellectual naivete. There is a place for careful explanation, where interpretations are weighed, scholarly debates reviewed, and the latest research cited, but spiritual formation works best when the flow of salvation history is understood.

Wisdom dictates that we first hear the story before dissecting the text. By the time many divinity students plow through the scholarly introduction of a biblical book, including authorship, sources, date, setting, redaction criticism, exegetical problems, and all the accumulated debunked theories attached to the text, they have lost the intellectual and spiritual energy to hear the story, much less proclaim it. These academic questions and concerns can be important, but their priority should be reversed. Begin with the story, revel in the truth, and when that storied truth is internalized in the soul, turn to the textual technicalities and complexities. Students find it difficult to proclaim what they have been trained to see as problematic.

To use an analogy, seminary professors are trying to teach advanced auto mechanics to people who have not learned how to drive. Textual experts need to be careful with the biblical story. Their love of grammar and syntax may cause them to miss the tone and texture, and especially the truth, of this real-life story. Scholars can exegete a biblical passage and pastors can work up sermons but never really tell the story and embrace the message. Thousands gather every Sunday to hear what they have heard many times before. There is a large and appreciative market of religious consumers who want to be given a recital of familiar truths. The impact of this kind of preaching is bigger auditoriums, filled with strangers who rarely fellowship beyond their familiar cliques. Consequently, it is becoming more difficult to distinguish between what is done for spiritual growth and what is done for public relations.

Years ago, when I was on the staff of a megachurch, the pastoral team, seven of us, met once a week for breakfast. The designated refrain for the anecdotes and jokes that we thought good enough for prime-time preaching was "That'll preach!" We rarely discussed the text, but we were always on the lookout for what might hold the attention of a restless audience. Sermons were often built on a humorous anecdote or an emotional story, with the text added later. What was missing in our preaching was a sense of "Thus says the Lord."

What we do not want to preach is religious bubble speech, sermonic, cliched jargon. Listening to us, people have the right to ask whether preachers are not themselves bored with the text. We do so much talking, it seems, without really preaching. I picture the prophet Jeremiah sitting in the congregation with a scowl on his face waiting for us to get to the word of God. Instead of dumbing down the gospel story and editing the canon for what we find relevant, we ought to let *salvation history* and the *intensity of the text* shine through in all of its complexity and mystery. The truth of God revealed to us in the Bible and through salvation history deserves our careful attention.

It is ironic that as our culture becomes more sophisticated in its methods of communication, it insists on a simplistic message. As the speed of communications increased, so also did our apparent impatience with the message itself. But it is here that we have to resist the reduction of the gospel to sound bites and insist on comprehending the whole counsel of God. I cannot help but believe that there are many people who long for a passionate, in-depth proclamation of God's story from Genesis to Revelation.

I believe pastors have a *cover-to-cover* responsibility and a *tension-in-the-text* obligation to teach and preach the whole counsel of God. A great deal of preaching tends to rely on incidental, anecdotal material. Preachers can unwittingly interrupt God's story with their own human-interest stories and doctrinal expositions. It is time we concentrate on that compelling, convicting, life-saving, redemptive story.

STORIED TRUTH

Easter 2020 was celebrated in the midst of a global Covid-19 pandemic, with no vaccine on the horizon. Believers sheltered at home because we were under attack by a microbial enemy. The very real fear was that a potentially deadly virus might spread as we greeted one another or sang, "Christ the Lord Is Risen Today." The invisible killing machine that attacked its victims at random forced a worldwide lockdown. We worshiped at home and celebrated the risen Lord around the kitchen table, remembering that "where two or three are gathered in my name, there I am among them" (Matt 18:20). My sermon text that Easter was Luke 24.

Two disciples were walking the seven miles from Jerusalem to their home in Emmaus when "Jesus himself came up and walked along with them" (Luke 24:15 NIV). Only one of the disciples, Cleopas, is named. The two travelers may have been friends or possibly a husband and wife. We do not know. A married couple makes sense because the journey ends in a home at the table.

When I was in high school, my pastor, Frank Wuest, gave me a framed Scripture verse that had hung on his wall in China, where he served for many years as a missionary. It read, "Jesus himself drew near and went with them" (Luke 24:15 KJV). He gave me the calligraphy when I was in the hospital for three weeks. I placed it in the hospital room for all to see. For years it hung in my study, until I gave it to a good friend who went to China as a medical missionary. What does it mean in the midst of a pandemic to focus on the line "Jesus himself drew near and went with them"? Does it not mean that even in the midst of a pandemic we are in the company of the risen Lord, and we embrace the hope of the resurrection? We do not walk alone.

When Jesus joined the two disciples on the way, they were preoccupied and distracted. They may have been distraught. They were engaged in an intense conversation about the events that had gone on in Jerusalem. For whatever reason, they did not recognize Jesus. Luke says, "They were kept from recognizing him" (Luke 24:16 NIV). In that moment Jesus was intent on his anonymity. He came to them in humility, without a hint of glory. The hidden God remained hidden. He intersected with their lives without interrupting either their pace or their dialogue. He asked them, "What are you discussing together as you walk along?" (24:17 NIV). The question stopped them dead in their tracks: "They stood still, their faces downcast" (24:17 NIV). One wonders whether they were so absorbed in the trauma of the last few days that they did not even bother to get a good look at the stranger who joined them on the way. Jesus drew near and went with them, but they did not recognize him.

In the throes of a pandemic, we were tempted to do the same thing. The presence of God may go unrecognized. The temptation was to fixate on the upsetting news and to dwell on the uncertainty to the point that we failed to recognize the gifts of God and the comfort of his presence. As was the case for the Emmaus-bound disciples, our confusion and heartache obscured the presence of the risen Lord. Jesus's question invoked their grief and discouragement. They were shocked at the stranger's ignorance: "Are you the only one visiting

Jerusalem who does not know the things that have happened there in these days?" (24:18 NIV). Jesus replied, "What things?" (24:19 NIV). This question triggered a response, and out poured their heartbreaking news of grief and dismay.

In humility, Jesus listened. Luke implies that their response was important to Jesus. He records more of their conversation in this narrative than Jesus's words. Parker Palmer observes, "People do not willingly return to a conversation that diminishes them." Palmer likens the soul to a wild animal—"tough, resilient, and yet shy." We have to approach the soul with care. We cannot confront the soul head-on and get very far. We are reminded of the challenge to preach in a way that smashes rocks without breaking bruised reeds. A startled soul escapes for its life. "When we go crashing through the woods shouting for it to come out so we can help it, the soul will stay in hiding."[5] But if we are willing to follow Jesus's strategy of humility and meekness, we will carry on a real conversation with people. We will get past their defenses and care for their souls.

The conversation along the way reveals that the two disciples were upset on several levels. They were directionless. Their hopes and expectations, based on Jesus, were dashed, and the established religious hierarchy and Roman authorities were responsible for his crucifixion and their grief. They could not retreat to Jesus, nor could they return to Judaism. They had no spiritual home to return to. They spoke of Jesus in the past tense. He "*was* a prophet," and "We *had hoped* that he *was* the one who was going to redeem Israel" (Luke 24:19, 21 NIV). Without Jesus, they had neither a future nor an identity. On top of all their grief and confusion, they heard deeply unsettling news, reported by some of their friends, that the tomb was empty. The women saw a vision of angels, who said he was alive. These two Emmaus-bound disciples did not know what to believe. There was confirmation that the tomb was empty, but no one had seen Jesus. They were disillusioned, distraught, and profoundly bewildered.

Their state of confusion may help us to identify with this generation of *unbelieving believers*. We can link these two bewildered disciples on the road to Emmaus with believers today. Emerging adulthood is marked by intense identity exploration and confusion.[6] Studies indicate that there is a major disconnect between what young people are taught in church and in the home and what they remember and embrace in their twenties and thirties. Jeffrey Arnett writes, "The most interesting and surprising feature of emerging adults' religious beliefs is how little relationship there is between the religious training they received throughout childhood and the religious beliefs they hold at the time they reach emerging adulthood. ... Evidently something changes between adolescence and emerging adulthood that dissolves the link between the religious beliefs of parents and the beliefs of their children."[7]

The Oscar-winning movie *Slumdog Millionaire* illustrates the new epistemology of people in their twenties. Jamal Malik is a street kid (or "slum dog") who has landed an appearance on India's version of the hit TV game show *Who Wants to Be a Millionaire?* Jamal exceeds expectations on the show, and the producers alert the police after they become suspicious that he knows too much. The young contestant is subsequently arrested and interrogated by the police. As the interrogation proceeds, Jamal's story is told through harrowing flashbacks that show the terrible poverty of Mumbai and help to explain how he knew the answers to the show's questions. Everything he knows he remembers from his personal experience. He has no formal education, but as fate would have it, the miscellaneous and haphazard collection of information that he has acquired along life's perilous journey is just what he needs to answer the random questions on the game show.

Book knowledge provides nothing useful for Jamal. Life is a pluralistic junkyard with thoughts, ideologies, and random facts lying all around. In the moment, Jamal seems to gather these up, because who knows when they may be useful. He cobbles together a worldview out of street-savvy survival skills and his relational drive to be reunited with his childhood sweetheart and his brother. All of his knowledge is based on personal experience. The world of teaming masses, abject poverty, drug lords, and game-show hype swirls around him. Jamal only appears to be dull; his blank demeanor serves as a cover. He is careful to give nothing away. But he illustrates well the new epistemology: it is not what you are taught or what you study that counts. It is your ability to adapt to an ever-changing, life-threatening world, and knowing what you need to know to survive the crisis and take advantage of a few lucky breaks along the way.

The disillusionment felt by the two disciples needed to be expressed before it could be addressed. And this may be a necessary first step if people are to move from being admirers of Jesus to being followers of Jesus. Søren Kierkegaard believed that the life of Jesus, "from beginning to end, was calculated only to procure *followers*, and calculated to make *admirers* impossible." Kierkegaard said of Jesus: "His life was *the Truth*, which constitutes precisely the relationship in which admiration is untruth. ... But when *the truth*, true to itself in being the truth, little by little, more and more definitely, unfolds itself as the truth, the moment comes when no admirer can hold out with it, a moment when it shakes admirers from it as the storm shakes the worm-eaten fruit from the tree."[8]

Added to the grief and confusion of these two bewildered disciples was the unsettling news of the empty tomb. They recounted to Jesus the witness of the women and the negative report of the disciples that "they did not see Jesus." With that, Jesus pivoted the conversation from their confusion to his *explanation*. Jesus's tone is forceful and authoritative. He said, "So thickheaded! So slow-hearted! Why can't you simply believe all that the prophets said? Don't you see that these things had to happen, that the Messiah had to suffer and only then enter into his glory?" (Luke 24:25 The Message). Jesus challenged their grasp of revelation and reality, as if to say, "What are you thinking? Have you not read your Bibles?" He shifted their focus from the painful circumstances to the storied truth of God's word.

The pivot from lament to hope involved both *explanation* and *understanding*. The psalmist expresses it this way: "Then I said, 'I will appeal to this, to the years of the right hand of the Most High.' I will remember the deeds of the LORD; yes, I will remember your wonders of old. I will ponder all your work, and meditate on your mighty deeds'" (Ps 77:10–12). Instead of succumbing to his dark and tortured feelings, the psalmist is intent on remembering what the Lord has done. "Feelings, and feelings, and feelings," remarks C. S. Lewis. "Let me try *thinking* instead."[9] We must connect with people's existential longings, but if we fail to ground the truth that satisfies those longings in God's redemptive provision, we have betrayed both them and the gospel.

Jesus appealed to their cognitive understanding and emotional embrace of revelation. In that seven-mile walk from Jerusalem to Emmaus, Jesus told the story of salvation history. "And beginning with Moses and all the Prophets, he *explained* to them what was said in all the Scriptures concerning himself" (Luke 24:27 NIV). I wish we had Jesus's explanation verbatim, but even if we did, it would not add anything to what we already know from God's word. What a wonderful experience it must have been for these two disciples to hear Jesus explain "all the Scriptures concerning himself."

In our praying imagination, Jesus begins with the innocence of Abel, the first sacrificial lamb, followed by Abraham's costly experience on Mount Moriah with knife in hand standing over Isaac. Jesus quotes Job's cry, "I know that my Redeemer lives, and that in the end he will stand on the earth. And after my skin has been destroyed, yet in my flesh I will see God" (Job 19:25–26 NIV). He references Israel's Passover lamb and describes Moses raising the serpent in the wilderness. He recalls David's prayer, "My God, my God, why have you forsaken me?" (Ps 22:1 NIV). Jesus emphasizes Isaiah's picture of the suffering servant, Daniel's vision of the victorious Son of Man, and Zechariah's humble king, who is the unappreciated Shepherd and the mourned martyr. "Beginning with Moses and all the Prophets" takes in the whole account of Christ from Genesis to Malachi (Luke 24:27 NIV).

In the time it took to walk to Emmaus, "he opened their minds so they could understand the Scriptures" (Luke 24:45 NIV). He gave them an explanation that led to an exclamation: "Were not our hearts burning within us while he talked with us on the road and opened the Scriptures to us?" (Luke 24:32 NIV). You know good preaching when you hear it. It touches you viscerally. That is what happened to these two disciples, but they still did not know they were in the presence of the risen Lord Jesus.

TEXT TO TABLE

When they reached Emmaus, Jesus made it seem as if he were going to continue on. The two disciples "urged him strongly, 'Stay with us'" (Luke 24:29 NIV). They invited Jesus into their home. Jesus's teaching was so compelling that they did not want it to stop. The moment of recognition came at the table, when Jesus took bread, gave thanks, broke it, and began to give it to them. Having "eaten" the word of God, their eyes were opened to the presence of God. They recognized him.

The eucharistic table is the altar call for the preached text. Every sermon should move from the pulpit to the table smoothly. The word proclaimed is the word remembered, internalized, and eaten as food for the soul. The words of institution, "This is my body broken for you," and, "This cup is the new covenant that I pour out with my blood," signify the whole body of revealed truth. They include the whole counsel of God from Genesis to Revelation. Eucharistic sermons end with four simple action verbs: take, thank, break, and give. As we partake of the bread and the cup, we participate in Christ receiving, thanking, sacrificing, and giving. The mission of God begins and ends at this table in fellowship with the crucified and risen Lord Jesus Christ. All evangelistic sermons are eucharistic sermons. Good sermons bring us to the table of the Lord.

It was only after Jesus left them that they began to realize how compelling and transforming their encounter with the risen Lord had been. Once again, the past tense is used. "*Were not our hearts burning within us while he talked with us on the road and opened the Scriptures to us?*" Jesus draws near to us as he did with the two disciples, *unexpectedly*. He engages us as he did with them, *humbly*. He listens to us as he did to them, *intently*. He explains the word of God to us as he did to them, *authoritatively*. Jesus is no longer the stranger. He is our Savior. We are not admirers of Jesus; we are followers. He is no longer in the past tense, *religiously*; he is the risen Lord in the present tense *eternally*.

Preaching the whole counsel of God is a household-of-faith commitment, not a preacher-only commitment. It is the responsibility of pastors to challenge all believers to grasp God's overarching redemptive story and to understand the contours of God's metanarrative. We want all believers to pray the Psalms, to understand the impact of the prophets, to appreciate the distinctive features of the Gospel accounts, and to grasp the apostles' spiritual direction to the household of faith. We want every aspect of the life of the church affected by the whole counsel of God. This includes personal and family devotions, as well as Bible study groups and community groups. It affects the way we worship and pray for one another. Embracing the whole counsel of God permeates and informs the life of the church. The whole-counsel-of-God curriculum takes its direction from pastors but affects youth ministry, student ministry, Sunday School classes, and small groups.

*[Ministers] should imitate the faithfulness of Christ
in his ministry, in speaking whatsoever God had
commanded him, and declaring the whole counsel of
God. They should imitate him with the manner of his
preaching; who taught not as the scribes, but with
authority, boldly, zealously, and fervently; insisting
chiefly on the most important things in religion.*

Jonathan Edwards, *Sermons on the Matthean Parables*

*Take heed to yourselves, lest your example contradict
your doctrine … lest you unsay with your lives, what
you say with your tongues. … We must study as
hard how to live well, as how to preach well.*

Richard Baxter, *The Reformed Pastor*

*Right down to his final illness he preached the word
of God in the church uninterruptedly, zealously, and
courageously, and with soundness of mind and judgment.*

Possidius on the life of Augustine

5

A Lifelong Commitment

The Bible is not a massive mountain of inscrutable material that preachers chip away at over time. The purpose of preaching is not to break up the Bible into smaller and smaller pieces, into more manageable informational packets. We are not unpacking the biblical text to satisfy our intellectual curiosity. Nor are we mining the biblical text for nuggets of truth. The purpose of preaching is not to remove layers of biblical sentiment in order to expose the listener's existential subtext. There is a better analogy for preaching than mining a rock quarry or unpacking a suitcase.

German Lutheran pastor-theologian Helmut Thielicke resisted Nazism and biblical higher criticism. Remarkably, he found in Charles Haddon Spurgeon, the self-educated Victorian Baptist London preacher, his preaching soulmate. He found so much to emulate in Spurgeon that he wrote about him. He attributed Spurgeon's remarkable nearly forty-year preaching ministry in the same pulpit to his "childlike candor of a preacher who could 'listen like a disciple.'"[1] Thielicke believed that Spurgeon's secret was the *gift of charismatic hearing*.

Preaching the whole counsel of God is more like studying the works of art in a world-renowned gallery filled with a stunning variety of exceptional paintings. The monumental task of sorting, detailing, and unpacking biblical truth fits the rock-quarry analogy. But the art-gallery analogy inspires understanding and reflection from the young novice and to the expert art critic. We revel in the beauty and depth of truth—the truth that shapes the mind, moves the heart, and reaches into our soul.

AN ESSENTIAL GOAL

Tim Patrick and Andrew Reid challenge "all vocational pastors" to "set themselves the goal of preaching through the entire Bible over a thirty-five-year period." Explicitly, this means "preaching through every biblical book from start to finish as a coherent whole. And that means every chapter of every book, and every verse of every chapter—the whole lot!" They admit that the thirty-five-year period "is a little arbitrary," but what they hope is that pastors will endeavor to lead their congregations over the span of their ministry career in the whole counsel of God.[2]

Preaching the whole counsel of God is an essential goal for the church, but a preaching strategy or methodology that insists on "every chapter of every book, and every verse of every chapter" flattens the biblical text, focuses attention on details, fosters an unrealistic time frame for accomplishment, and fails to follow the Bible's own models of exposition.[3] Verse-by-verse analysis belabors textual details, and unnecessarily extends and exhausts the interpretative process. The verse-by-verse approach tends to foster detailed expositions and minimize pastoral application. The biblical scholar may emphasize a verse-by-verse or line-by-line Bible-study method, but pastor-theologians need to see the essence of the whole biblical book and preach from the DNA of the biblical book. The purpose of preaching is not to render a detailed analysis of the text as much as it is to expound its meaning for shaping the Christian life today.

The goal of preaching the whole counsel of God is for all believers to live with their eyes fixed on Jesus. Believers need a grasp of God's redemptive plan through Israel's kings and prophets, but a verse-by-verse journey through Kings and Chronicles may actually miss the point. The variations and emphases of the apostle Paul's thirteen letters are important for all mature believers to understand, but not an analysis that belabors detailed differences between Paul's letters. The goal is not Bible knowledge as such but growing in the grace and knowledge of the Lord Jesus Christ. A verse-by-verse methodology may inadvertently compete *against* the whole counsel of God.

Preaching the whole counsel of God is a lifetime commitment. The point of preaching is not checking off the biblical books that we have preached as much as it is living into the wisdom of God as revealed in the Bible. We gather up the grand sweep of God's revelation, not for mechanical analysis but for living a life worthy of the calling we have received. Bryan Chapell is surely right when he says the job of good preachers is to open up the Bible and encourage the household of faith to be devoted to the apostles' teaching (Acts 2:42). "There are no dark passageways through twisted mazes of logic to biblical truth that require the expertise of the spiritually elite. There is only a well-worn path that anyone can follow if the preacher will shed some ordinary light along the way," Chapell rightly emphasizes. "Excellent preaching makes people confident that biblical truth lies within their reach, not beyond their grasp."[4]

If preaching the whole counsel of God means spending a year of Sunday sermons in Genesis or two years in Romans, I am afraid the focus shifts from the dynamic of the message to the details of the text. There is a difference between preaching the Bible exhaustively and preaching the life-changing gospel message passionately. I do not imagine the apostle Paul would be impressed with a pastor who spent three years expounding and expositing the book of Romans. Verse-by-verse exposition can digress into detailed word studies, or it can offer theological overviews from a single verse. It is easy to get bogged down in detail analysis and unnecessary repetition. It is also tempting to teach the whole Bible under the pretense of studying Romans. Chapell writes that pastors "should delight to proclaim truth as expansively and as powerfully as God grants [them] the gifts to do so. All preachers simply need to make sure that what they preach will communicate and not complicate the truths of God."[5]

BIBLICAL FUSION

The *internal testimony* of *how* Jesus and the apostles interpreted the gospel in the flow of biblical theology and salvation history is important for our preaching today. On his seven-mile journey to Emmaus, Jesus summed up the meaning of the crucified and risen Messiah "beginning with Moses and all the Prophets" (Luke 24:27). Within hours he went through it again with a larger group of disciples in the upper room, saying, "These are my words that I spoke to you while I was still with you, that everything written about me in the Law of Moses and the Prophets and the Psalms must be fulfilled" (24:44).

The biblical models of whole-counsel-of-God preaching offered by Jesus and the apostles are as compelling as they are practical. It makes sense for pastors to learn from the Bible's internal examples of how the prophets and apostles used the Bible. Four biblical examples of whole-counsel-of-God preaching are given below: Stephen's sermon before the Sanhedrin, Asaph's Psalm 78, the preacher's sixty-minute sermon in

Hebrews, and the apostles' interpretation of Psalm 110. Instead of thinking the Bible into pieces, each sermon ought to fuse the whole counsel of God. Consider these remarkable examples of biblical fusion.

STEPHEN'S ACTS 7 SERMON EXEMPLIFIES WHOLE-COUNSEL-OF GOD-PREACHING

When Stephen was hauled before the Sanhedrin to give an account of his gospel preaching, he gave a sweeping account of salvation history. His strategy was to recite two major themes: First, Israel consistently rebelled against the revelation of God. Stephen laid out their faithlessness. Second, "the Most High does not dwell in houses made by human hands" (Acts 7:48). Stephen made his case against religion and ritual. He built his case for Christ by highlighting four epochs in salvation history that revolve around four principal characters: Abraham, Joseph, Moses, and David. In his message, Stephen emphasized four key truths and an underlying theme.

The God of glory comes to us in unexpected ways. Just as God came to pagan Abraham out of nowhere, while Abraham was still in Mesopotamia, he comes to us. God called Abraham to leave his country and his people: "Go out from your land and from your kindred and go into the land that I will show you" (Acts 7:3). God did not offer a health-and-wealth gospel but instead a gospel of grace and redemption. God told Abraham "that his offspring would be sojourners in a land belonging to others, who would enslave them and afflict them four hundred years" (7:6). From this brief synopsis of salvation history, stretching from the call of Abraham to the exodus, we learn that the descendants of Abraham do nothing to earn their salvation. Yahweh intervenes on their behalf, judging the oppressors and leading them into the promised land to worship God.

The God of glory seals his covenant in an unusual way. Stephen emphasized a second important truth when he rooted the identity of God's people in their personal relationship with God, rather than in the land or their ethnicity. The truth of their identity was symbolized in the act of circumcision (Gen 17:11; Exod 4:24–26). No one was born a Jew. One had to be initiated through the rite of circumcision, which was an act of faith in Yahweh's promise. What kind of God would do this? The Lord said to Abraham that this act of circumcision was going to be a sign that he own them, that their little lives were being caught up in his grander purposes. In circumcision the foreskin of the male organ is pulled back and cut, exposing the most vulnerable, sensitive part of the male anatomy. Circumcision makes what was private and secret become personal and public. God got intimate with the descendants of Abraham. Stephen's message emphasized that circumcision underscored a personal and intimate relationship with God.

The God of glory makes himself known in the most unlikely places. Throughout his message Stephen makes it clear that the sojourner God did his major redemptive work outside the promised land. He called Abraham out of Mesopotamia, and he called the children of Abraham out of Egypt. For emphasis, "Egypt" or "Egyptian" is mentioned some seventeen times. The living God of the Bible is not a localized deity, invented by a tribe and tied to a place. Yahweh is Lord of the nations, who rescues his people in the foreign land of oppression. We all need to come out of Egypt. We have all lived in the far country far too long. We all need to be rescued and delivered. A theme running through Stephen's message is that the God of Abraham, Isaac, and Jacob can turn anyplace, even a wilderness, into holy ground. The living God is not limited to sacred places and religious rituals. God can use a burning bush to get our attention and call us into his redemptive service. This thought brings us to Moses.

The God of glory chooses an uncommon person to fulfill his will and reveal his glory. Following Abraham and Joseph, Stephen turns his attention to Moses, who occupies a major place in his message. The first thing Stephen says about Moses gives us a clue as to how he is going to present Moses. He was "no ordinary child." He received a unique upbringing and training. He had a unique passion for his people and justice. And he spent forty years in the wilderness before God unexpectedly called him into service. Stephen's point is that how God used Moses was a model for how God sent and used the Messiah. Moses was a forerunner of the Christ. Stephen summarizes the essence of Moses's message when he tells of how Moses said to the Israelites, "God will send you a prophet like me from your own people." Interestingly, when Stephen speaks of Moses being "in the assembly in the desert," he uses the same word translated elsewhere in Acts as "church." Moses was in the church in the desert, receiving "living words to pass on to us" (Acts 7:38 NIV).

Stephen's extemporaneous witness emphasizes the call of God in unexpected ways, the sealing of his covenant through unusual means, the revelation of God's redemption in the most unlikely places, and the choice of Moses to fulfill his will and reveal his glory. His five-minute message may have been compressed by Luke, but it also may be one of the most verbatim speeches we have in Acts. It is much more than a highlight reel or a movie trailer. The quick pace and broad-brush approach capture the sweep of salvation history. It is an example of powerful preaching that takes into account the details of revelation and draws them together into a compelling and persuasive message.

ASAPH'S PSALM 78 IS AN EXCELLENT
EXAMPLE OF BIBLICAL INTERTEXTUALITY

Israel's worship leader introduces this epic psalm as a parable wrapped in history. He uses the five-hundred-year history of Israel from the exodus to King David to prove two things: the covenant faithfulness of Yahweh and the hardhearted, stubborn rebelliousness of Israel.[6] Psalm 78 sounds more like a sermon preached at the city gate by a prophet than a song sung by the chief musician. Asaph warns the people not to follow in the footsteps of their ancestors. Israel's worship leader levels a scathing rebuke against those who refuse to remember the Lord's unforgettable and miraculous acts of redemption: "Again and again they put God to the test; they vexed the Holy One of Israel. They did not remember his power—the day he redeemed them from the oppressor" (Ps 78:41–42 NIV).

The Israelites played out a sad history of faithlessness, first in the wilderness and then in the promised land (78:8, 17, 22, 36, 56, 58). The apostles drew on Psalms 78 and 95 to warn the early church against drifting away from so great a salvation. Paul was concerned that history would repeat itself. He writes, "Now these things happened to them as an example, but they were written down for our instruction, on whom the end of the ages has come. Therefore, let anyone who thinks that he stands take heed lest he fall" (1 Cor 10:11–12; see Heb 3:1–4:11).

Psalm 78 tells an epic story in two overlapping parts. Part 1 is the story of the exodus and Israel's wilderness rebellion (Ps 78:9–40). Part 2 repeats the story of the exodus, with an emphasis on the plagues, followed by Israel's apostasy in the promised land (78:41–72). Both parts end with a description of Israel's rebellious ancestors as a warning to all believers. Yet through it all God remains faithful to his people. Asaph's pedagogical strategy is pastoral and prophetic. He seeks to warn believers against falling away, even as he seeks to encourage believers to remain faithful (78:1–8).

THE BOOK OF HEBREWS EXEMPLIFIES
PREACHING THE OLD TESTAMENT

This sixty-minute sermon shows how the entire Old Testament is centered in Jesus Christ. The preacher begins by citing seven Old Testament texts in his prologue. At first glance it may seem like he is stringing verses together in rapid succession and using the Bible to prooftext his point. But the pastor is not thumbing through his Bible (the OT Septuagint) looking for a line here or a line there to bolster his case. On the contrary, he is preaching from the whole Bible, drawing out these prophetic lines to represent the whole counsel of God. His eloquent citation of seven scriptural declarations in defense of the deity and exaltation of the Son confirms the rhetorical power of these texts to synthesize exegetical reasoning and to express the whole counsel of God succinctly. He is not preaching against the grain of Scripture; he is preaching with the grain.

The pastor's selection process conveys in lucid brevity the power of the Son's exaltation and enthronement. None of these verses is isolated from the whole counsel of God or pulled out of the context of its revelational meaning. They are grouped together more like a string of priceless pearls. They serve "to highlight the necessary interpenetration of exegesis and dogmatics."[7] The preacher is not merely listing points or compiling excerpts. He is orchestrating a crescendo of symphonic meaning leading to the truth.

Like the DNA code of a living cell, Hebrews' overture contains the themes for the entire sermon. The pastor goes on to develop at length how God's revelation in the past "through the prophets at many times and in various ways" (Heb 1:1 NIV) is fulfilled in the Son of God. He preaches the Psalms and tells the story of Moses and Joshua and the Israelites in the wilderness. He explores the significance of Abraham, Melchizedek, Aaron's priesthood, and the new covenant. He draws out the significance of the tabernacle, the priestly order, and the sacrificial system. He does all of this to underscore the finality and fulfillment of Jesus Christ, the mediator of the new covenant, who "having been offered once to bear the sins of many, will appear a second time, not to deal with sin but to save those who are eagerly waiting for him" (Heb 9:28). The preacher makes the case for the better priesthood, the better covenant, the better tabernacle, the better sacrifice, and the better future.

The reader senses that the pastor never meant to interrupt the flow of his exposition with a detailed analysis of the Aaronic priesthood or the tabernacle sacrificial system. He never would have envisioned an extended exposition of the book of Leviticus. That is not to say that a detailed exposition of Leviticus is not important, but it is to say that the message of Leviticus can be summed up beautifully. We should pay attention to the pastor's advice when he says, "Of these things we cannot now speak in detail" (Heb 9:5). The force of the sermon should not be interrupted by distracting digressions into tabernacle furniture, priestly offerings, the location of the golden altar of incense, and legal technicalities surrounding wills. When we ignore the example of the preacher in Hebrews and do our own thing, we interrupt the synergy of exposition and exhortation. We miss the thrust of the message. It is like watching a movie with a lot of commercial interruptions or listening to a soundtrack at a slower speed. The pastor never imagined that Hebrews would be an excuse for a yearlong, detailed exposition of Exodus or Leviticus. A certain kind of curiosity or fascination becomes engrossed in the details of the tabernacle and the sacrificial system at the expense of hearing the message intended by the preacher. We want to remain true to the sermon's expository momentum and heed the pastor's exhortation (Heb 10:19–39). To do that, we have to keep up with the pastor's fast-paced tempo.

We honor the original meaning and method of Hebrews by recognizing the momentum of the pastor's argument. We want to track his fast-paced exposition to his equally powerful exhortation. Faithful exposition avoids getting bogged down in mind-teasing details. This expository section is largely illustrative, culminating in the exhortation to "hold fast the confession of our hope without wavering, for he who promised is faithful" (Heb 10:23).

PSALM 110 CAPTURES AND COMPRESSES THE HIDDEN WHOLENESS OF GOD'S WORD

"All Scripture is breathed out by God and profitable for teaching, for reproof, for correction, and for training in righteousness," but not all Scripture is used and emphasized in the same way (2 Tim 3:16). Over the course of a long pastoral ministry, it makes perfect sense that we preach certain biblical texts over and over again in order for pastor and congregation alike to get their bearings. This is different from preaching from a canon within a canon. We need the whole counsel of God as we keep coming back to the Sermon on the Mount or Psalm 73 or Romans 8. This is the beauty of preaching God's word; the Spirit has made sure that the DNA of the entire Bible is contained in each and every text. No matter how deep we dig down into the word, we can always look to the crucified and risen Messiah. Jesus and the apostles kept coming back to Psalm 110 for a reason. They boldly grasped Psalm 110 as messianic prophecy.

In seven short verses, the psalm comprehends the eschatological consummation of salvation history. The psalmist includes the ascension ("Sit at my right hand until I make your enemies a footstool for your feet," 110:1 NIV), the militancy of Jesus Christ ("The LORD will extend your mighty scepter from Zion," 110:2 NIV), the church age ("Your troops will be willing on your day of battle," 110:3 NIV), the sacerdotal royal priesthood ("You are a priest forever, in the order of Melchizedek," 110:4 NIV), the final judgment ("He will judge the nations, heaping up the dead and crushing the rulers of the whole earth," 110:6 NIV), and the incarnation ("He will drink from the brook along the way, and so he will lift his head high," 110:7 NIV). The sweeping impact of the shared work of the Triune God, Father, Son, and Spirit, is deftly sketched in bold strokes on the canvas of our praying imagination. Spirit-inspired finite words reveal infinite truth. Martin Luther writes: "This beautiful psalm is the very core and quintessence of the whole Scripture. No other psalm prophesies as abundantly and completely about Christ. It portrays the Lord and his entire Kingdom, and is full of comfort for Christians."[8]

The apostles learned from Jesus how the Old Testament worked. He was the first to draw their attention to a radical new interpretation of Psalm 110. Toward the end of his public ministry, Jesus quotes Psalm 110:1 in the temple courts (Matt 22:41–45; Mark 12:35–37; Luke 20:41–44). Jesus asks the Pharisees, "What do you think about the Christ? Whose son is he?" They reply, "The son of David." Jesus responds, "How is it then that David, in the Spirit, calls him 'Lord'?" Jesus quotes from the psalm, "The Lord said to my Lord: 'Sit at my right hand until I put your enemies under your feet.'" Jesus leverages this break with tradition (the father being superior to the son) and asks a question, "If then David calls him 'Lord,' how is he his son?" Matthew reports, "And no one was able to answer him a word, nor from that day did anyone dare to ask him any more questions" (Matt 22:41–46).

Jesus implied that someone was destined to come after King David who was greater than David. Moreover, Jesus left the distinct impression that he was that someone. This conversation came back into focus when Jesus was arrested and brought before the Sanhedrin. The high priest asks him pointedly, "I adjure you by the living God, tell us if you are the Christ, the Son of God." Jesus replies, "You have said so. But I tell you, from now on you will see the Son of Man seated at the right hand of the Power and coming on the clouds of heaven" (Matt 26:63–64; Ps 110:1; Dan 7:13).

Psalm 110 became critical in shaping the apostolic understanding of Jesus. The apostles quote Psalm 110 twenty-four times in the New Testament to testify about the Son, "who was descended from David according to the flesh and was declared to be the Son of God in power according to the Spirit of holiness by his resurrection from the dead, Jesus Christ our Lord" (Rom 1:3–4).

The dynamic purpose of the Psalms as a whole and Psalm 110 in particular, according to Bruce Waltke and James Houston, is "to inspire and to promote the faith of Christians that Jesus is the Christ, the Son of God."[9] The majestic tone of David's Spirit-inspired prophecy draws the believer into a future that is now present and into a reality that is still unfolding. The ascended Lord Jesus sits enthroned at the right hand of the Father. The metaphoric language describes the indescribable majesty and power of the Triune God (Rev 4:1–11). The ascension of Christ is preceded by his atoning sacrifice: "He is the radiance of the glory of God and the exact imprint of his nature, and he upholds the universe by the word of his power. After making purification for sins, he sat down at the right hand of the Majesty on high" (Heb 1:3).

Psalm 110 was Peter's go-to text when he preached at Pentecost, saying,

> This Jesus God raised up, and of that we all are witnesses. Being therefore exalted at the right hand of God and having received from the Father the promise of the Holy Spirit, he has poured out this that you yourselves are seeing and hearing. For David did not ascend into the heavens [but Jesus did!]. ... Let all the house of Israel therefore know for certain that God has made him both Lord and Christ, this Jesus whom you crucified. (Acts 2:32–34, 36)

Peter refers to Psalm 110:1 when he defends the gospel of Jesus Christ before the same Sanhedrin that weeks before accused Jesus of blasphemy for making a similar reference (Matt 26:64). Peter declares, "God exalted him at his right hand as Leader and Savior, to give repentance to Israel and forgiveness of sins" (Acts 5:31; see 1 Pet 3:22).

The author of Hebrews brings his sevenfold sequence of Old Testament messianic prophecies to a climax with Psalm 110:1 (Heb 1:5–13). The author chooses angels, the highest created beings, to contrast the utterly incomparable relationship between the Father and the Son. Each of his carefully selected Old Testament references bears up under closer scrutiny as an inspired testimony to the supremacy of the Son. In the pastor's chain of quotations, each line is linked to form "a direct verbal prophecy concerning the perpetual nature of the Son's reign, having been explicitly fulfilled ... in the exaltation of Jesus to the right hand of God."[10]

The apostle Paul draws on Psalm 110:1 when he speaks of the crucified and risen Christ Jesus seated at the right hand of God interceding for us (Rom 8:34); and when he encourages believers to set their hearts on things above, "where Christ is, seated at the right hand of God" (Col 3:1); and when he speaks of "the immeasurable greatness of his power" because it was the same power that God exerted "when he raised him from the dead and seated him at his right hand in the heavenly places" (Eph 1:19–20).

The art-gallery analogy versus the rock quarry invites a comprehensive approach to whole-counsel-of-God preaching. In the quarry, laborers need the right tools and a good work ethic. But in the gallery, art lovers need understanding, insight, and passion. Preaching is a labor of love that requires prayer and Christ-centeredness. Biblical fusion calls for a preacher who is a pastor-poet-theologian rather than a textual technician. Instead of mining for interesting details or crafting a brilliant sermon, we are striving for the meaning and impact of the gospel in the light of the whole counsel of God. The purpose of preaching is not so much to convey a body of knowledge, as important as that may be, as it is to grow and nurture the body of Christ. We take our preaching cue from the Lord Jesus, along with Stephen, Asaph, the author of Hebrews, and the psalmist. The goal of preaching the whole counsel of God calls for life-on-life discipleship over a lifetime.

All the parts of preaching can be taught: exegesis,
language, metaphor, development, delivery. What is
hard to teach is how to put them all together, so that
what is true is also beautiful, and evocative, and alive.

Barbara Brown Taylor, *The Preaching Life*

One thing I have always said about evangelicals is
that they know how to rightly divide the word of God,
but they don't know how to put it back together.

John Perkins, *With Justice for All*

Preachers preach so that the congregation will preach.

Robert Smith Jr., *Doctrine That Dances*

6

Life-on-Life Discipleship

Pastors who truly preach, *preach* the whole counsel of God. They have a passion for Christ, and they preach who they are in the Spirit of Christ. Their message comes from within. They preach Christ from the Old Testament. They preach Christ from the Psalms. They preach Christ from the prophets. They preach *Christ*. They love the biblical text, and they love people. They hold to God's word with conviction, and they show compassion to all people. Their sermons possess the character of "Thus says the Lord." They preach gospel sermons that edify and evangelize. They preach cost-of-discipleship sermons that comfort and challenge. They preach to the community and then to the individual.[1] They pray. They seek to attract and grow followers of Jesus, not admirers. They aim to be faithful and fruitful. They refuse to pander, flatter, entertain, bully, or manipulate. They strive to preach Christ with warmth, intensity, sensitivity, boldness, and care.

"Go therefore and make disciples of all nations, baptizing them in the name of the Father and of the Son and of the Holy Spirit, teaching them to observe all that I have commanded you" (Matt 28:19–20). Jesus's Great Commission requires a form of communication that is relational, real, and relaxed. Dale Bruner suggests that the verb "to disciple" is prosaic. It suggests spending time with people, patiently nurturing them in gospel truth, helping them understand and embrace what it means to follow the Lord Jesus. Jesus's implied preaching strategy, as well as his personal example, tones down the rhetoric, cuts out the hype, and engages people thoughtfully. To "preach and teach in a discipling way" says, "I am ready and willing to meet with you to talk with you more personally about life with Jesus."[2]

Pastors who preach are immersed in the word of God as if everything about *their* life depended on it, because it does. They are filled with the Spirit, and their spirituality is biblical. It is real. Their private and public life are one in Christ, and they practice a long obedience in the same direction. They feed the household of faith with true food. They embrace the work ethic of a farmer, the conviction of a prophet, the concern of a parent, and the passion of a poet. They preach and teach so others will preach and teach. They are focused on the ministry of word and sacrament, and along with other coworkers they shepherd the household of faith. They share preaching responsibility with others so that the body of Christ may be built up in Christ. Some disciples preach from the pulpit, some from the kitchen table, and some from the office. But all who are in Christ *preach.*

"YOU KNOW ME"

"For I did not shrink from declaring to you the whole counsel of God. Pay careful attention to yourselves and to all the flock, in which the Holy Spirit has made you overseers, to care for the church of God, which he obtained with his own blood" (Acts 20:27–28). The apostle Paul's farewell to the Ephesian elders captures the logos, ethos, and pathos of a faithful and effective pastoral preaching ministry. Luke's compressed version of Paul's parting testimony to his Ephesian coworkers demonstrates the synergy of these three elements in the apostle's gospel-centered, word-saturated life. In every way and at every turn Paul's logos logic, kingdom character, and personal passion for Christ are on full display.

After two and half years in Ephesus, Paul felt the need to return to Jerusalem before setting out for Rome. Luke's high-impact visual collage of Paul at work is followed by the apostle's farewell to the Ephesian elders (Acts 19:1–20:38). Luke's portrayal of the emerging church in Acts causes us to examine ourselves and our church to see whether we are rooted exclusively in the name of the Lord Jesus, capable of arguing persuasively for the kingdom of God, willing to follow the Spirit's lead, ready to absorb the world's resistance, and eager to encourage our brothers and sisters in Christ everywhere. Paul's message to the leaders of the church of Ephesus is one of the most powerful descriptions of true spiritual leadership found in the New Testament.

Paul was on the move and eager to get to Jerusalem before Pentecost. His stopover in Miletus gave him one last opportunity to relate to the leaders of the church of Ephesus. To save time, a two- to three-day journey on foot, he asked the elders to meet him in Miletus. We do not know how large a delegation came, but there appears to be no hierarchy among them, and they are referred to by different names that mean the same thing, including "elders" (a word borrowed from the Jewish synagogue), "overseers" (a word borrowed from their Greek context), and "shepherds" (a word that captures pastoral ministry).[3] Paul addressed them as a pastoral team with shared leadership responsibilities. His message was as personal and as passionate as anything Paul had ever spoken, and it was completely in character with his letters to the churches. Although

Paul's address only takes about three minutes to deliver, we imagine Paul spending at least a full day with his coworkers.[4]

The *validity* of his testimony was based on the fact that he was not telling them anything that they did not already know. Three times he appealed to their memory to confirm his testimony: "*You yourselves know* how I lived among you the whole time from the first day that I set foot in Asia . . . . [*You know*] how I did not shrink from declaring to you anything that was profitable, and teaching you in public and from house to house. . . . *You yourselves know* that these hands ministered to my necessities and to those who were with me" (Acts 20:18, 20, 34). They could vouch for him. They knew Paul. They knew that what he was telling them was the truth. This kind of ethical credibility is not rooted in an office or in a position. It is established over time. For the sake of the gospel Paul had proved himself selfless, courageous, and hardworking.

The *intensity* of his testimony, his pathos, can be felt in his unqualified and unconditional commitment. The *allness* character of the Great Commission is reflected in Paul's all-out-commitment to the gospel. The five "all"s of the Great Commission—all authority, all nations, all God, all commands, and all days—are evident in Paul's total commitment. He measured faithfulness in at least five different ways. He was faithful *the whole time* he was with them. He never stopped warning them *night and day* with tears. He served the Lord with *all humility*. He did not hesitate to preach *anything* that would be helpful to them, and he insisted on proclaiming the *whole* will of God. Furthermore, he taught anywhere and everywhere, whether publicly or house to house. His ministry was all-embracing, reaching out to both Jews and Greeks, and he was innocent of the blood of all people because he had never hesitated to proclaim the gospel. He was not only invested mentally, emotionally, and physically, but he even provided for his own means. "In *all things* I have shown you that by working hard in this way we must help the weak" (Acts 20:35).

The *meaning* of his logos testimony was rooted in the gospel. After all Paul said and did, he still refused to take the gospel for granted. He never tired of speaking of Christ and his cross. Even in his farewell address to this pastoral team, he reiterates the gospel. His opening paragraph concludes that he has declared "both to Jews and to Greeks of repentance toward God and of faith in our Lord Jesus Christ" (Acts 20:21). He refers to his responsibility to testify to the gospel of God's grace. He speaks of being innocent of the blood of all people because he never refused to proclaim the whole will of God. He reminds the Ephesian shepherds that Jesus bought the church of God with his own blood, and he commits to them the word of God's grace. For Paul the way of salvation meant a totally transformed way of living. Eternal salvation and ministering to the weak and the poor were inseparable dimensions of the gospel.

The *power* of his testimony can be found in Paul's passion for Christ. Everything in Paul's perspective is God-centered, from his opening statement on serving the Lord with great humility to "Now I commend you to God and to the word of his grace" (Acts 20:19, 32). His Trinitarian understanding of God pervades his thinking: "Pay careful attention to yourselves and to all the flock, in which the Holy Spirit has made you overseers, to care for the church of God, which he obtained with his own blood" (Acts 20:28). Paul felt "compelled by the Spirit" to challenge them to be faithful to the whole counsel of God. In the middle of his address to the Ephesian elders he opened up and shared his heart: "I do not account my life of any value nor as precious to myself, if only I may finish my course and the ministry that I received from the Lord Jesus, to testify to the gospel of the grace of God" (Acts 20:24). We hear echoes here of what Paul wrote to the church at Philippi, when he says, "For to me to live is Christ, and to die is gain" (Phil 1:21).

The *realism* of his testimony was rooted in his biblical understanding of evil. Paul was not an optimist, but neither was he a pessimist. He refused to underestimate the power of evil. He warned the elders, "I know that after my departure fierce wolves will come in among you, not sparing the flock; and from among your own selves will arise men speaking twisted things, to draw away the disciples after them. Therefore, be alert" (Acts 20:29–31). Paul saw dangers from without and dangers from within. The church then and now is engaged in a spiritual battle that requires two uniforms. On the one hand, we must put on the full armor of God: the belt of truth, the flak jacket of righteousness, the protective armor of faith, the helmet of salvation, and the sword of the Spirit (Eph 6:10–18). On the other hand, we must clothe ourselves with compassion, kindness, humility, gentleness, and patience (Col 3:12–14). We need to be both vigilant for the truth and caring for the weak, humble about ourselves and confident in the truth of the word of God.

Paul cannot be accused of boasting here. The nature and character of his commitment was rooted in Christ and fundamentally unattractive to the world. Those who follow Paul's example today will not be held in high regard in either secular or religious circles. The kind of humility that he claimed was actually despised by the world. His life was hardly the picture of success in either Greek or Jewish culture. If anything, he was considered a fool for Christ.

Yet the model of courageous pastoral ministry exemplified by Paul is necessary today. We are meant to identify with Paul's vision for ministry and share not only his passion but his method and character. He had a vision of reaching out to all people with the gospel of grace and the whole counsel of God. All those who follow Christ share that vision. His primary virtue was "great humility with tears," rather than a great ego with drive. Instead of accruing power for himself and thinking that the future of the church rested on his strategic plan and personal enthusiasm, Paul kept giving away responsibility. He entrusted the destiny of the church to the sovereign will of God, to the power of the Holy Spirit, and in the name of the Lord Jesus.

Paul teamed up with an amazing variety of people to carry on the mission. Instead of projecting success, Paul followed Jesus's path to the cross. Risk taking did not involve jeopardizing his reputation by overextending the church financially; it meant risking his life. What Paul accomplished for Christ and his kingdom could never be confused with personal ambition. His all-out commitment to Jesus Christ meant selfless work, personal sacrifice, and constant danger. Paul invited his coworkers to kneel and pray for the grace and humility to serve the Lord wholeheartedly: to be self-sacrificing, led by the Spirit, committed to the whole counsel of God, hardworking on behalf of the poor and weak, all-embracing of others for the sake of the gospel, and faithful to the end. We say "Amen" to that!

With that said and prayed through, we should emphasize that Paul's testimony is doable. His apostolic responsibility in salvation history is unique, but his life and ministry are there for our encouragement and emulation. We may not have enemies plotting our death, although many Christians face severe persecution, but we can still serve the Lord with great humility and tears. We may risk our standard of living, our popularity, and our professional success for the sake of the gospel. We

need not hesitate, nor should we be intimidated by denomina-
tional loyalties, political ideologies, or powerful personalities in
the church from preaching the whole counsel of God. Nothing
should stand in the way of proclaiming the truth of God's word.
We may not be self-supporting as Paul was, but that should only
encourage us to work tirelessly for the cause of Christ.

PREACHING'S UNIFIED
FIELD THEORY

Preaching that meets the rock-and-reed challenge is both prophetic and priestly. It is preaching that addresses the individual
and the community. Good preaching knows how to integrate
personal experience with stay-in-the-story preaching. "You
must risk telling your own story," writes Thomas Oden, "not
as an end in itself, but rather as a sharply focused lens through
which the whole Christian story is refracted." Good preaching knows how to evangelize and edify in the same sermon
by delivering a clear evangelical witness while deepening the
household of faith through spiritual formation. It is "more than
rational demonstration or logical argument" because it reaches
into the soul of the individual and the heart of the community
with the life-changing, community-building gospel of Jesus
Christ.[5] Good preaching issues out of the holistic character of
the preacher, who combines gift and responsibility, style and
substance, text and context into a sermon that speaks to the
mind and moves the heart.

The real preacher is not just a good communicator, accurate
Bible interpreter, and faithful pastor. Good preaching pervades
every aspect of the preacher's life in a unified field theory of
spirituality and ethics. Preaching alone, no matter how good,
requires a personal delivery that is holistic. A divided life just
does not work. We have to be all in.

This is the *all* that must not be evaded but embraced by all who desire to please God, because God's holy claim rests equally on all. As Kierkegaard says,

> It makes no difference at all, God be praised, how great or how small the task may be. In relation to the highest of all this simply does not matter when it comes to being willing to do all. Oh, how great is the mercy of the Eternal toward us! All the ruinous quarreling and comparison which swells up and injures, which sighs and envies, the Eternal does not recognize. ... The demand upon each is exactly the same: to be willing to do all.[6]

It is not whether we do this or that, but whether we do all that God calls us to do. *We* put a certain premium on certain jobs and roles, but God does not.

This is the *all* that makes the all-important distinction between temporal and eternal achievements. In an effort "to accomplish all the more for the Good," the clever person evades the purity of God and the exclusiveness of his truth.[7] In their cleverness, people refuse to sell all and buy into the single investment that is priceless. They have yet to understand Jesus when he told the parable of the hidden treasure: "The kingdom of heaven is like treasure hidden in a field, which a man found and covered up. Then in his joy he goes and sells all that he has and buys that field" (Matt 13:44).

This is the *all* that believes that Jesus accomplished *all* on the cross. Judging from a worldly perspective, Jesus's life ended in tragic failure. His crucifixion was a political accident that might have turned out otherwise, an ironic twist of fate. If he had only been more politically astute and opportunistic, he might have capitalized on his popularity. This is how the worldly order judges the Crucified One, but "a distinction must be made between the momentary and the eternal view of the thing." From the perspective of the moment, all was lost, hopelessly lost. Yet eternally understood, Jesus "had in the same moment accomplished all, and on that account said, with eternity's wisdom, 'It is finished.'"[8]

This is the *all* that is willing to *suffer all* for God. Suffering reveals the purity of heart that wills one thing in truth. True sufferers realize that they better understand the purposes of God by experiencing pain and suffering than observing success and achievement. There is no whining, no deceitful evasion, no disappointment with God, and no acceptance of deliverance on the world's terms, "because to take one's suffering to heart is to be weaned from the temporal order, and from cleverness and from excuses, and from clever men and women and from anecdotes about this and that, in order to find rest in the blessed trustworthiness of the Eternal."[9] Real sufferers take up their cross and follow Jesus. Their passion is to know Christ and "the power of his resurrection" and to "share his sufferings, becoming like him in his death, that by any means possible" they may "attain the resurrection from the dead" (Phil 3:10–11).

This is the *all* of covenant love (as opposed to a contractual obligation) that is grandly inclusive of all we are and will be. The pure in heart pledge themselves in an all-encompassing, timeless commitment. "As long as our lives should last" is the bottom line of a costly vow that carries us all the way to eternity. The purity of heart that wills one thing covenants to love Christ and serve him, worship and cherish him in prosperity and in adversity, in sorrow and in happiness, in sickness and in health, and forsaking all others, be united to him for all eternity.

This is the *all* that knows no limits. "There is a time for everything, and a season for every activity under the heavens"

(Eccl 3:1 NIV) but this is the one thing for all time and the one thing on which everything else depends for time and eternity (Ps 27:4). This is the *all* that gives light to our vision of God. Without it we are in darkness, but with it everything is brought into the light. May Kierkegaard's prayer be our prayer:

> Father in Heaven! What are we without You! What is all this human knowledge, vast accumulation though it be, but a chipped fragment if we do not know You! What is all this striving, even if it could rule the world, but a half-finished work if we do not know You: You the One, who art one thing and who art all!
>
> So may You give to the intellect, wisdom to comprehend that one thing; to the heart, sincerity to receive this understanding; to the will, purity that wills one thing. In prosperity may You grant perseverance to will one thing; amid distractions, concentration to will one thing; in suffering, patience to will one thing. Oh, You who gives both the beginning and the completion, may You early, at the dawn of the day, give to the young person the resolution to will one thing. As the day wanes, may You give to the old person a renewed remembrance of his first resolution, that the first may be like the last, the last like the first, in possession of a life that has willed only one thing.[10]

The very nature of God's word supports this unified field theory. Sixty-six books and multiple authors written over time, but what is so striking is the consistency and character of the profile of the people of God. Jesus's Sermon on the Mount, his upper-room discourse, Paul's letters, the Psalms—they all cohere into a meaningful, holistic pattern of logos logic, kingdom character, and pathos passion. The Bible opposes the divided life and centers every aspect of our being and living in Christ.

A PREACHING STRATEGY

The goal of preaching may at times feel like getting through Sunday morning without embarrassing oneself or the Lord (not that the Lord can be embarrassed, but that is how we may feel!). On Sunday morning before leaving my study, I kneel and pray, "Lord, help me." Sometimes I say more, but everything is covered in that prayer. I know the apostle Paul never felt that he was just putting in time and appealing to religious consumers. On those weekends when he was almost stoned to death, he must have taken solace in that he was not preaching his opinions and in his own strength. The call, the gift, the responsibility, and the challenge to proclaim Christ came from above. It came from the Incarnate One himself, God in person, who gave Paul the grace to preach. God gave Paul not only the grace to preach, but the command and strategy to preach as well.

> To equip the saints for the work of ministry, for building up the body of Christ, until we all attain to the unity of the faith and of the knowledge of the Son of God, to [full maturity], to the measure of the stature of the fullness of Christ, so that we may no longer be children, tossed to and fro by the waves and carried about by every wind of doctrine, by human cunning, by craftiness in deceitful schemes. Rather, speaking the truth in love, we are to grow up in every way into him who is the head, into Christ, from whom the whole body, joined and held together by every joint with which it is equipped, when each part is working properly, makes the body grow so that it builds itself up in love. (Eph 4:12–16)

The word preached became the way to grow strong Christians, not because it was the only way, but because it was the chosen way. John Calvin observes, "We see that God, who might perfect his people in a moment, chooses not to bring them to maturity in any other way than by the education of the Church." Therefore, God might have used angels or no means at all, but instead he chose humans and the "ordinary method of teaching" to convey his truth, "that he may thus allure us to himself, instead of driving us away by his thunder."[11] God declared his own love and humility toward us by choosing people like us "to be interpreters of his secret will; in short, to represent his own person." The method and the means not only demonstrate the humility of God but require our humility as well. Calvin calls it "a most excellent and useful training in humility."

We might think that, having described preachers as the mouthpiece of God, "doing God's work by their lips," Calvin would emphasize the exalted status of the preacher, but he does just the opposite. By divine design, we learn humility by having to listen to God's word through people like ourselves, "or, it may be, our inferiors in worth." Calvin goes on to say, "When a feeble man, sprung from the dust, speaks in the name of God, we give the best proof of our piety and obedience, by listening with docility to his servant, though not in any respect our superior. Accordingly, he hides the treasure of his heavenly wisdom in frail earthen vessels (2 Cor 4:7), that he may have a more certain proof of the estimation in which it is held by us."[12] We should not take this as an excuse for boring sermons. It is rather the recognition of the slow, humble, mentoring process of maturity that God chose. God chose to communicate his word through the ordinary method of teaching, based on the humility of sincere believers, who receive God's word from people like ourselves ("or, it may be, our inferiors in worth").

The saints who are equipped "for works of service" are those who allow the word of God to train and condition them "for every good work." Because they have a hunger and thirst for righteousness, they feed on God's word. Because they have been called to be salt and light in the midst of decay and darkness, they have a need for the life and light of the word of God. The equipping process takes two sincere people: an honest, humble teacher who is submissive to the Bible and capable of communicating its truth effectively and faithfully, and a sincere saint who is ready to do works of service so that the body of Christ may be built up. After many years of preaching, I have concluded that those who see themselves as missionaries in the marketplace or in the classroom or in their families are those who get the most out of the Sunday morning message. Salt-and-light Christians have a hunger for the word of God, and they profit from this equipping ministry.

The diversity of gifts contributes to the unity of the body, not its division. Paul never intended to reduce the bulk of church members to "the rank of mere consumers of spiritual gifts."[13] Nor was his emphasis on teaching gifts meant to produce a division between pastors and people. The responsibility to build up the body of believers belongs to the people as a whole, not to pastors in particular. Paul assumes two important principles: a team-ministry approach for teaching God's word and an every-member-ministry approach to building up the church. No single person is responsible for teaching the word of God. Christ gives his church a variety of people to minister the word: apostles, prophets, evangelists, pastors, and teachers. The ministry of the word is indispensable, but never independent from the full-orbed work of the gospel. Strong Bible teaching invariably produces well-equipped servants who demonstrate "the manifold wisdom of God" and the multidimensional love of Christ.

If we think unity can be achieved through any other means than Christ and his word, we are mistaken. In the absence of this maturity, Christians remain as weak and as vulnerable as infants. Paul concludes this section with a set of contrasts. Those who do not "reach unity in the faith and in the knowledge of the Son of God and become mature, attaining to the whole measure of the fullness of Christ," remain like "infants, tossed back and forth by the waves" (Eph 4:13–14 NIV). If our growth in Christ is stymied, we will remain as vulnerable as a baby in a raging sea. Paul pictures the immature Christian tossed around "by human cunning, by craftiness in deceitful schemes" (Eph 4:14).

Instead of being held together and built up, they are tossed around and broken down. Instead of being equipped by apostles, prophets, evangelists, pastors, and teachers, they are confused and manipulated by imposters—spiritual con artists who prey on unstable believers. Instead of "speaking the truth in love," these schemers use tricks and gimmicks and deceit to sway unsuspecting believers. But it is God's will and Paul's preaching strategy that "we are to grow up in every way into him who is the head, into Christ, from whom the whole body, joined and held together by every joint with which it is equipped, when each part is working properly, makes the body grow so that it builds itself up in love" (Eph 4:15–16).

Paul repeats a similar preaching strategy in his letter to the church at Colossae. His preaching is Christ-centered—"Him we proclaim"—and he preaches with the utmost diligence and devotion by "admonishing and teaching everyone with all wisdom." The purpose of his preaching is singular, "so that we may present everyone fully mature in Christ" (Col 1:28 NIV). Full maturity for everyone is not a goal often cited today, but Paul had no reservations about making it his well-publicized objective. Paul's "everyone" strategy underscores the priesthood of all believers and the unity of the body of Christ. "There is no part of Christian teaching that is to be reserved for a spiritual elite," writes F. F. Bruce. "All the truth of God is for all the people of God."[14] Peter O'Brien writes, "As a true pastor Paul will not be satisfied with anything less than full Christian maturity of every believer. There are to be no exceptions, since his aim is that each one should reach perfection [whole, complete, intact]. However, this will be fully realized only on that last day."[15] The believer's initial conversion is only the beginning in a lifelong process of maturing in Christ. Paul's telos-defined work could not be clearer: "to present everyone fully mature in Christ." What was true for Paul should be true for us. To that end Paul "strenuously" contended with "all the energy Christ so powerfully worked" in him. Or, to quote The Message, "That's what I'm working so hard at day after day, year after year, doing my best with the energy God so generously gives me" (Col 1:29).

PSALM 119'S PRAYER GUIDE

The longest psalm in Jesus's prayerbook is an extended meditation on the significance of the word of God. Each of the twenty-two stanzas of this elaborate acrostic psalm serves as a prayerful prelude for Bible study and preaching. In the torah tradition of Psalm 1 and Psalm 19, the psalmist crafted twenty-two prayers in a single psalm to deepen and develop the ways we are dependent on the word of God. Each stanza of Psalm 119 focuses our attention on God's word.

Disciples of all ages may begin here in prayer when they open the Bible. Whether you are a young parent sitting down for morning devotions or a pastor preparing a sermon, Psalm 119 gives us the words to express our heartfelt desire to understand and obey the word. To pray these eight-verse stanzas is to be reminded that we are blessed in specific ways when we come to the Bible for wisdom and direction.

Each of the twenty-two acrostic stanzas consists of eight alphabetized verses constructed around eight synonyms for God's word. These eight synonyms for the word of God are listed here in order of their occurrence: "law" (*torah*, 25×), "word" (24×), "decision" (or "judgment," 23×), "testimony" (23×), "command" (22×), "statute" (21×), "precept" (21×), "saying" (or "oracle" or "promise," 19×). All eight words are used in four stanzas (Ps 119:57–64, 73–80, 81–88, 129–36), and all the stanzas have at least six references to the word of God.[16] Furthermore, all 178 references to Scripture relate "explicitly to its Author."[17] The word is never abstracted from its personal source in God. Each word is described in relation to God: *your* commands, *your* statutes, *your* word of truth, and *your* laws.

Each eight-verse stanza calls for action. We are not passive recipients of divine revelation but active followers of God's word and God's path of devotion and obedience. We seek more than head knowledge. We want to be wise with the wisdom of God. Understanding yields to devotion, and devotion to obedience. Through meditation and study, we internalize God's word. Disciples love the word of God, and it shows in how they live. Psalm 119 is "a medley of praise, prayer and wisdom" dedicated to discerning, applying, and enjoying the wisdom of God in every aspect of life. "There is no hint of legalism. ... It breathes a spirit of devotion and celebrates the closest of relationships between the psalmist as 'your servant' and Yahweh as 'my God.'"[18]

Dietrich Bonhoeffer begins his meditation on Psalm 119 by insisting that we go beyond beginnings. "God has once and for all converted me to himself," he writes. "It is not that I have once for all converted myself to God. God has made the beginning; that is the happy certainty of faith."[19] Only the Holy Spirit has the power to convert the old creation into a new creation: "The *Creator Spiritus*, who began the world's *creation* ("the Spirit of God swept over the face of the waters," Gen 1:2), and who now begins the world's *new creation* and its definitive salvation."[20] Beatitude-based believers know that their new-creation beginning lies not in themselves but in God. We are the least likely candidates for conversion, and all of us need a miracle to believe. "Every conversion is a virgin birth."[21] The apostle John writes, "Yet to all who did receive him, to those who believed in his name, he gave the right to become children of God—children born not of natural descent, nor of human decision or a husband's will, but born of God" (John 1:12–13 NIV).

Psalm 119 weans us away from a preoccupation with the start of the Christian life and redirects our focus to finishing well. Faithfulness to the end affirms faith from the beginning. "Today we emphasize the New Birth," writes Peter Gillquist. "The ancients emphasized being faithful to the end. We moderns talk of wholeness and purposeful living; they spoke of the glories of the eternal kingdom … the emphasis in our attention has shifted from the completing of the Christian life to the beginning of it."[22] We embrace the law of God not as a burden that induces guilt but as a blessing that gives freedom. We hear Jesus say to us, "If you abide in my word, you are truly my disciples, and you will know the truth, and the truth will set you free" (John 8:31–32). To be Jesus's friend involves obeying his commands, not out of compulsion and duty but out of love and devotion. "You did not choose me," Jesus says, "but I chose you and appointed you that you should go and bear fruit" (John 15:16). Mercy, not merit, induces the desire and the gift of obedience.

FAMILY REUNIONS

Family reunions are glorious, chaotic, and exhausting affairs. We have hosted a couple with our three children and their spouses and our five grandchildren. They are always great, memorable, and loads of fun. But getting the whole family together requires a lot of planning. I am not sure an algorithm has been invented to handle coordinating schedules and choosing a date for even relatively simple families like ours. Logistics is another complexity because we are spread out all over the country and Costa Rica. Plane tickets have to be booked, and our grandchildren no longer fly free! Getting the family together is a major job, not to mention hosting and feeding our little tribe of thirteen when we are together. Virginia, my wife, is the point person behind this Herculean effort and labor of love. I am the cheerleader.

Gathering the family together helps me grasp what is involved in gathering the household of faith around the whole counsel of God. In the household of faith pastors are responsible for helping believers grow up in Christ, and that involves grasping the whole counsel of God. Family reunions, at least for our family, do not just happen. We have to be really intentional about pulling them off. Intentionality is also key when it comes to embracing the whole counsel of God in our preaching, teaching, Sunday classes, small groups, and Bible studies. Family reunions are not going to happen unless the family wants to get together, and they are not going to want to get together unless they have a good time when they are together. Timing and financial obstacles need to be managed, logistics solved, and plenty of planning thought through. Somebody cooks, somebody cleans up, and everybody pitches in. The same is true of preaching and teaching the whole counsel of God. It is a household-of-faith affair, and when it is done right, believers embrace it.

Our failure to grasp the canonical scope of any biblical truth unwittingly fosters a vulnerable naivete among sincere believers. University-bound believers are often blindsided by simple issues, such as the so-called synoptic problem (variations in the Gospel accounts), or the apostolic use of the Septuagint version of the Old Testament, or various eschatological interpretations. It is surprising but true how many believers reach seminary without a sense of the overarching history of redemption. They have spent their whole lives going to church, listening to sermons, attending youth groups and Christian camps, and yet they have never heard the metanarrative of the gospel. One of the reasons Christians are open to conspiracy theories and political propaganda is that they have not been taught how to think biblically. It takes insight to understand Jesus's use of parables, Paul's use of irony, and John's use of metaphor. It takes discernment to understand a biblical writer's literal use of figurative language and poetic expression. It takes wisdom to understand what aspects of Old Testament worship and prophetic concern ought to be replicated in the New Testament church.

Since preaching the whole counsel of God is a goal that many pastors have, I would like to suggest a strategy that aims to meet this goal over time. A good place to begin regardless of your church tradition is with the church year and the school calendar. September signals a new school year and a fresh start. We have a nearly three-month period before the first Sunday of

Advent. The four Sundays of Advent, together with Christmas and Epiphany, bring us to a new year and a third preaching period that runs until the seven weeks of Lent leading up to Easter. From Easter to Pentecost is a fifth preaching period, followed by spring and summer, which can be divided into two more preaching periods. The seasons—fall, winter, spring, and summer—can each be subdivided into two, depending on the optimum length of a preaching series.

The year divides into seven preaching periods:

1. Fall (the beginning of school)

2. Advent/Christmas

3. Winter

4. Lent/Easter

5. Pentecost

6. Spring (the end of school)

7. Summer

These seven periods in the church calendar give pastors not only a framework for sermon planning and preparation, but a flexible thematic guide. There is a start-up feel every fall because of school and work that lends itself to embarking on a new biblical study. Advent offers an opportunity to preach from Old Testament prophecies of Christ and New Testament narratives. Sometimes it works to balance Old and New Testament preaching by noting parallel biblical books. For example, four weeks in the book of Ruth followed by 1 Peter develops the theme of God's people as resident aliens and chosen outsiders, or a study in Jonah followed by Jesus's conflict with the religious leaders shows religion's resistence to the gospel. The seven Sundays of Lent provide a season of penitential preparation for believers to focus on the cross of Christ and the cost of discipleship. This emphasis on Christ's passion culminates with Easter and the celebration of Jesus's bodily resurrection. During Lent I have preached through Job, Jeremiah, Revelation, 1 Corinthians, and Matthew, all of which develop the meaning of the cross and the importance of cross-bearing discipleship, and I conclude with an Easter message that focuses on the power and hope of the resurrection. Leading up to Pentecost and beyond is a good time to study the Epistles as well as the Psalms. One year we finished our Lenten series in the book of Revelation with an Easter Sunday message on Revelation's picture of Jesus Christ, the ruling and reigning King of kings, Lord of lords. We followed that series with the book of Acts. Spring and summer provide ample time to preach from various biblical books so as to convey the wisdom of the whole counsel of God.

The rhythms of the church year and the natural flow of the seasons serve to give shape to preaching the whole counsel of God. The aim of part one has been to show that biblical preaching is more than a sermonic talk delivered once a week, even more than a well-crafted impressive sermon. It is a life-long commitment to making disciples through gospel-centered teaching and preaching. It is preaching that accepts the rock and reed challenge and seeks to respect rather than manipulate or diminish the listener. Good preaching takes in the totality of God's word, the centrality of the gospel, and the fellowship of believers. Preaching's true home is in the worshiping body of Christ. In part two we aim to show how this purpose is worked out practically over the course of the church year and in the flow of life's seasons.

Part II

The Practice of Preaching

Lord of the universe, Hope of the world, Lord of the limitless reaches of space, here on this planet you put on our flesh, vastness confined in the womb of a maid: born in our likeness you ransomed our race: Savior, we worship you, praise and adore; help us to honor you more and yet more!

Margaret Clarkson, "Lord of the Universe, Hope of the World"

If you do not hear in the message of Christmas something that must strike some as blasphemy and others as sheer fantasy, the chances are you have not heard the message for what it is.

Frederick Buechner, *A Room Called Remember*

7

*Preaching Advent &
Christmas Sermons*

Some pastors begin thinking about the four Sundays of Advent, along with Christmas Eve and Epiphany, in July. They start their preparations early because of the pressures of the fall schedule and because Advent is a significant worship event that meets the rock-and-reed challenge, especially in churches that follow the liturgical calendar and preach from the lectionary. This long-standing tradition can be a very promising spiritual discipline for the household of faith.

Advent provides an annual opportunity to explore the Old Testament promises of the coming of the Messiah.[1] Preaching Christ from the patriarchs and the prophets and the Psalms leads the church to a deeper understanding of how salvation history points to Christ on every page of the Bible. Every year is a fresh opportunity to present Jesus unembellished, free from religious trappings, holiday hype, sentimentality, and nostalgia. Preachers face the challenge of elaborating on the meaning of the incarnation. As Jesus emptied himself, God emptied the nativity of all but Jesus.[2]

Advent also encourages an informed and nuanced understanding of how the four Gospel accounts introduce Jesus, the Incarnate One. The rich variety of texts, genres, and characters inspires preachers to evangelize the seeker and edify the follower with the story of Jesus. The Lord has given us many angles to work with.

Advent is our opportunity to tell the story of Jesus. One year we gave our grandson Liam, who lives in Seattle, a Fisher-Price manger scene. We thought it was a bit pricey, so we only got the basic manger scene, which included Jesus, Mary and Joseph, and the shepherds. We did not buy the optional figures of the magi and the angels. We mailed the gift to Seattle in October, and Liam's parents thought they would let Liam see it and then put it away until closer to Christmas. Liam loved it. The Fisher-Price manger scene provided an imaginative playground for Liam, along with his two parents, who were his pastor-theologians bearing witness to faith in Christ. We have only one "stay in the story" narrative, but there are many ways to introduce and explore that narrative. Psychologist Jonathan Haidt is right: "The human mind is a story processor, not a logic processor. Everyone loves a good story; every culture bathes its children in stories."[3]

TELLING THE STORY

Sally Lloyd-Jones, well-known for *The Jesus Storybook Bible*, encourages parents and grandparents to tell the story of Jesus in the fullness of its meaning with great care. David Suchet, a British actor whom you may know as PBS's Hercule Poirot, is the voice on the audio version of *The Jesus Storybook Bible*. When interviewed over the phone from his London home, he was asked why he accepted the project. Suchet told his story of how he was converted in 1986 at the age of forty. He said that his journey to Christ was a long one. "I was dragged kicking and screaming," he explained. "I felt like Jacob, but God would not let me go."[4]

Suchet's description of various biblical scenes with genuine reverence and theological depth was impressive. He said that as an actor he imagined himself playing the apostle Paul. He remarked in passing that he had twenty-six books on the apostle lining his bookshelves in his London home. Suchet said that what he liked especially about *The Jesus Storybook Bible* was how Sally Lloyd-Jones introduced Jesus right from the beginning. Suchet quoted from Luke 24, the description of Jesus with the two disciples on the road to Emmaus: "And beginning with Moses and all the Prophets, he explained to them what was said in all the Scriptures concerning himself" (Luke 24:27 NIV), to emphasize the beginning of the story.

We have many inspired guides leading us in the truth of the crucified and risen Messiah. Matthew, Mark, Luke, and John weigh in, along with the Prophets and Psalms. We are not left to our own opinions and speculations. We are encouraged to be creative in our telling of the Jesus story, but not inventive. We have a story to tell the nations and to our children, and it is important that we do it right.

Most everyone agrees that George Frideric Handel's *Messiah* presents the gospel exceedingly well. His devotional classic prepares us for worship and guides our celebration of Christmas. Handel is a wonderful spiritual director, drawing out the depth of meaning of Old Testament prophecy. He leads us into the biblical text musically, so that we might open our ears and our heart to the voice of the Lord. One of Handel's biographers, R. A. Streatfield, claimed it was "the first instance in the history of music of an attempt to view the mighty drama of human redemption from an artistic standpoint."[5]

Handel's gift to us was born out of struggling circumstances and musical talent. When Handel wrote *Messiah* in 1741, he was a broken and defeated man, financially bankrupt and in great pain from rheumatism. In the summer of that year a friend, Charles Jennens, wrote a text (libretto) for an oratorio on the theme of redemption. It was entirely taken from Scripture. Handel told his friend it would take him about a year to complete the work. Then Handel received a commission from a group of churches in Dublin to compose a work as a benefit concert. Richard Dinwiddie writes,

> On August 22 he sat down in his little house on Brook Street in London and six days later he had completed Part I of *Messiah*. In nine more days, he had written Part II, and in another six, Part III. He took an additional three days to "fill out" the orchestration. In 24 days, he had filled 260 pages of manuscript, a phenomenal physical feat in itself. The fact that he borrowed a few tunes of his own composition as well as a few traditional tunes for themes takes nothing away from his staggering achievement.[6]

Handel begins *Messiah* with Isaiah's prophecies. His work brings us into God's large world of salvation history.

Every year pastors are tasked with leading their congregations into the one story that redeems our stories. They proclaim Christ in fresh and powerful ways. They do not write oratorios, but they do write sermons. It is a privilege to bear witness to the gospel in this way. As a catalyst for your own preparation, I offer a few suggestions on how to approach Advent and Christmas. We begin with a layout of four Advent sermons inspired by the prophets Isaiah and Malachi along with Handel's *Messiah*. Then we will explore sermon ideas from the Gospels.

GOD'S ADVENT GREETING (ISAIAH 40:1–11)

A solo tenor breaks the silence with a singular thought, "Comfort ye, comfort ye my people, comfort ye, comfort ye my people, saith your God, saith your God. Speak ye comfortably to Jerusalem, speak ye comfortably to Jerusalem, and cry unto her, that her warfare, her warfare is accomplished, that her iniquity is pardoned, that her iniquity is pardoned."

God's word comes to those who are not at home in this world. They are political exiles and spiritual refugees, but more than that, they are sinners in need of God's grace. The message is both immediate and prophetic. The prophet begins with Jerusalem, a symbol for the people of God, a symbol of the people of God that extends out universally. The price has been paid for their sins and our sins. They, as well as we, are free because of God's redeeming grace to finally fulfill God's will for their lives. *The salvation and comfort of our souls depends on receiving the mercy of God personally.* God's deep, redemptive comfort was not delivered from a distance.

The comfort declared by Isaiah and Handel is the deep comfort of God. This is the comfort of our sins forgiven. The price paid for this comfort is described in detail in Isaiah 53. This is not the momentary, feel-good comfort offered by creaturely comforts, but the enduring depth-of-soul comfort that comes from "the Father of mercies and the God of all comfort" (2 Cor 1:3).

Handel's *Messiah* begins and ends in the heavenly court. From the opening plural imperatives, "Comfort ye, comfort ye my people!" to "Worthy is the Lamb that was slain," Handel's climactic "Amen" draws attention to the glorious work of God. There is nothing here about our finding God or meriting God's favor. The emphasis is on God's gracious forgiveness of our sins through the blood of the Lamb. Handel begins where the prophet Isaiah did, with the council of the Lord. The message of comfort, spoken tenderly, "is not just expressing comfort and kindliness but is seeking to persuade, inviting to respond to love."[7]

The directive "says your God" is delivered with an emotional intensity emphasized by Handel's repetition. Three voices of revelation follow in quick succession, Isaiah's redemptive trio: the voice of expectation (Isa 40:3–5), the voice of desperation (40:6–8), and the voice of celebration (40:9). In keeping with Isaiah's prophecy, Handel begins with the hope of the gospel. The Advent message is spoken tenderly. God's Christmas greeting is consoling and comforting.

Taken together, these three voices of revelation are essential for a true perspective on life. Spiritual renewal is based on the confident expectation of God's fulfilled promises, a true understanding of the struggle of the human condition, and the celebration of the good news of Jesus Christ. For the prophet Isaiah, God's Advent greeting meant three bedrock truths: God's mercy is essential for our salvation and comfort, God's revelation is crucial for getting our bearings in a confusing and chaotic world, and God's power is the only true source for salvation and security.

GOD'S ADVENT WARNING (MALACHI 3:1–5)

The word of the Lord is emphatic. "Behold, I send my messenger, and he will prepare the way before me. And the Lord whom you seek will suddenly come to his temple; and the messenger of the covenant in whom you delight, behold, he is coming, says the LORD of hosts. But who can endure the day of his coming, and who can stand when he appears?" (Mal 3:1–2). Prophecy telescopes the first advent and the second advent. Instead of seeing twin peaks, the prophet Malachi saw one huge mountain of God's accomplishment. From a distance the prophets see one major history-consummating event. Advent and apocalypse run together.

In a quick burst, Malachi gives us the total truth, the big picture. Malachi's sober prophecy is both warning and promise. We cannot talk about Advent without Mary's song, Simeon's warning, and Joseph's retelling of the Bethlehem massacre. Truth demands that we hear the sober and somber note of judgment before the joyful melody of Isaiah 9 and God's Christmas gift.

GOD'S CHRISTMAS GIFT (ISAIAH 9:1–7)

It is easy to celebrate the *mood* of Christmas without Jesus. Sadly, many do. But it is impossible to celebrate the *meaning* of Christmas without Jesus. Sentiment defines Christmas as Santa Claus and evergreen trees, Rudolph and mistletoe, shopping and gifts. Love defines Christmas as God sending his Son. Dietrich Bonhoeffer drew a telling analogy between his incarceration and the incarnation. He wrote to his fiancée comparing life in prison to Advent: "A prison cell, in which one waits, hopes, does various unessential things, and is completely dependent on the fact that the door of freedom has to be opened *from the outside*, is not a bad picture of Advent."[8] The freedom we long for and the salvation we seek come *not* from within but from Jesus, who came that we may have life and have it to the full (John 10:10).

Handel captured the profoundly personal nature of God's Christmas gift when he repeated over and over, "For unto us a child is born, unto us a son is given." In the Messiah, God's giving is emphatic. Isaiah used four titles—Wonderful Counselor, Mighty God, Everlasting Father, and Prince of

Peace—to explain and expound on the meaning of Immanuel, God with us (Isa 9:6). The prophet makes it impossible to evade the claim that God himself is coming. The titles attributed to this child by the prophet Isaiah remind us of what the author of Hebrews wrote, "The Son is the radiance of God's glory and the exact representation of his being, sustaining all things by his powerful word" (Heb 1:3 NIV). The witness of the prophets and the apostles agree, and Christians confess that Jesus is the Wonderful Counselor, the Mighty God, the Everlasting Father, and the Prince of Peace.

We are surprised by the deep wonder, the paradox of the long-expected but never-imagined fulfillment of God's Advent. Have we been in God's great salvation history story long enough to see the wonder and wisdom of how God chose to come into human history? For those in the story there is a wonderful coherence between prophecy and promise, precedent and praxis. The Wonderful Counselor, "in whom are hidden all the treasures of wisdom and knowledge" (Col 2:3), "made himself nothing, by taking the very nature of a servant, being made in human likeness" (Phil 2:7 NIV).

Jesus is not a great man on the order of Confucius, Buddha, or Muhammad. Great personalities may be taken seriously without ever wrestling with the uniqueness of their personal identity. They are what they are by virtue of their commanding ways, historical circumstances, superior intelligence, and powerful charisma. But this is decidedly not true when it comes to Jesus. For there is no way we can read the prophets and the life of Jesus, along with the witness of the apostles, without concluding that the Bible proclaims Jesus is God. Isaiah's prophecy reveals that the baby in the manger was none other than the Mighty God. It is this paradox that has always caused both the greatest difficulty and the only reason for people to come to Christ. Advent is not about the coming of a nonconformist rabbi who eventually would die because he upset the political authorities. It is all about the coming of God in Christ, who came to save us from our sins.

Advent celebrates this truth that God, infinite in power, knowledge, and wisdom, became a man who was limited in power and knowledge and whose wisdom was the result of a real process of growth and development, not only to show his love for us but to fight for us. Advent marks God's strategic assault against evil, designed to liberate all who are held hostage by sin and death.

Throughout salvation history there have been strong indicators that God would assault the forces of evil in a unique and unexpected way. Abraham's personal agony over the possibility of sacrificing his son Isaac reveals the hidden dynamic of God himself offering his one and only Son. Job's defenseless vulnerability against Satan's onslaught indicates how the Almighty God will secure victory in the critical battle with Satan. King David's experience of feeling godforsaken captures the experience of Jesus on the cross, and Isaiah's description of the suffering servant graphically portrays the price to be paid for our redemption. "Surely he has borne our griefs and carried our sorrows; yet we esteemed him stricken, smitten by God, and afflicted. But he was wounded for our transgressions; he was crushed for our iniquities; upon him was the chastisement that brought us peace, and with his stripes we are healed" (Isa 53:4–5). The power of the powerlessness of God on the cross goes beyond empathy and identification with us in our suffering; it attacks and defeats the root cause of suffering, sin, and evil. God in Christ paid the ransom that set us free (Mark 10:45). The powerlessness of God on the cross is best understood in light of the power of God to raise Jesus from the dead.

Isaiah's prophecy attributes the fullness of God to this child who was born, this son who was given. We cannot reduce these titles to themes and abstractions. We do not celebrate the wonder and goodness of Christmas; we celebrate the one and only one whose counsel we depend on for all truth and wisdom. Christ alone has the power to save us from sin and death. These exalted names—Wonderful Counselor, Mighty God, Everlasting Father, Prince of Peace—elicit our confession, not our compliments. They invoke praise. Their meaning is irreducible, and their significance cannot be scaled down.

Yet, of all four titles, the boldest one may be Everlasting Father. There is at least an initial pause sparked by that title that calls for serious reflection. We are led to ask in what sense it is appropriate to attribute to Jesus, the Son of God, the title Eternal Father. Does this confuse our understanding of the Triune character of God? Not at all. The title does not mean that all of God sits in the manger or that all of God hangs on the cross, but it does mean that the child who was laid in the manger and died on the cross was fully God and fully human.

The issue of the Trinity might have been raised earlier if Isaiah had titled the child Holy Spirit instead of Wonderful Counselor, even though the meaning of that title leads us to think of the Holy Spirit (Isa 11:2; John 14:26). *There is absolutely nothing about God's being, character, and work that cannot be attributed to this child who was born for the sake of the human race.* What the prophet Isaiah affirms in the title Everlasting Father is profoundly explored in the Gospel of John. The prologue addresses the essential relationship between Jesus and the Father: "The Word became flesh and made his dwelling among us. We have seen his glory, the glory of the one and only Son, who came from the Father, full of grace and truth" (John 1:14 NIV). The Son's authority could not be greater: "The Father loves the Son and has given all things into his hand" (John 3:35). To worship the Father in spirit and in truth is to accept Jesus as the Messiah (John 4:23–26). All the activity of Jesus is consistent with and dependent on the work of the Father. As Jesus says, "My Father is working until now, and I am working" (John 5:17).

Each of the four Gospels develops the truth of the Incarnate One in a way that gives our picture of Christ greater depth and meaning. What follows is a sample of approaches to serve as a catalyst for developing Advent and Christmas sermons from the Gospels.

MATTHEW'S GENESIS (MATTHEW 1:1–17)

"... and Jacob the father of Joseph the husband of Mary, of whom Jesus was born, who is called Christ" (Matt 1:16). Making a similar point, the Apostles' Creed begins, "I believe in God the Father Almighty, Maker of heaven and earth. And in Jesus Christ, His only Son, our Lord, Who was conceived by the Holy Spirit, born from the Virgin Mary ..." Christians believe that the paternity of Jesus has no biological explanation, yet they also believe that his lineage can be known with certainty. The mystery of Jesus's birth is like the mystery of the origins of the cosmos, a reality that is beyond our figuring out, but not beyond our amazement. The virgin birth is above us in mystery, but not beyond us in truth. The historical reality exists without a naturalistic explanation.

Thirty-nine times, Matthew says "the father of," but when he comes to Jesus, he leaves that blank and says, "Joseph the

husband of Mary, of whom Jesus was born, who is called Christ."
Dale Bruner writes that he goes "to all the trouble of tracing
Jesus' Abrahamic-Davidic family line down to Joseph, only at
the last minute to deny Joseph *biological* paternity." However,
that last-minute switch did not deny Joseph legal paternity.
According to Palestinian law, the head of a family was no less
the father of an adopted son than he was of his biological children, but the obvious omission leaves room for the miraculous
conception. "By far the most exciting 'father' in this genealogy
of fathers is the unnamed Father in the climactic 'fourteenth'
generation.'"[9] Matthew has a few surprises in store for those
who think he begins his Gospel with a boring list of forty-three
names. This is not a perfunctory ancestral roll call, as if Matthew
were taking attendance, but the dramatic telling of a true story
in shorthand with its own unexpected twists and turns.

The title of Matthew's Gospel says more than we might
imagine at first glance: "The book of the genealogy of Jesus
Christ, the son of David, the son of Abraham." Matthew's new
Genesis is about Jesus the Messiah, whose life and work take
precedence over the old creation of the world and the old covenant of the law. He declares Jesus to be the personal fulfillment
of creation, salvation, and the covenant promises.

There are parallels between Genesis 1 and Matthew 1,
between the genesis of the world and the genesis of the Savior
of the world. A scientific view of creation "assumes that the
world contains its own mysteries and can be understood in
terms of itself without any transcendent referent," whereas a
biblical worldview affirms "that the ultimate meaning of creation is to be found in the heart and purpose of the Creator."[10]
"By faith we understand that the universe was created by the
word of God, so that what is seen was not made out of things

that are visible" (Heb 11:3). The primary purpose for Moses's Genesis was not to provide scientific data. Nor was Matthew's Genesis meant to present a precise historical record. Moses shows the believer that, when you add up the meaning of creation, the bottom line is an all-powerful, all-knowing, all-loving, sovereign God.

There are irregularities in Matthew's account of the genealogy of Jesus, but these alterations transform an otherwise mundane historical list of names into an implicit theology of God. He does this by highlighting the names of four women, substituting two names, and shortening the list of names to keep three sections of fourteen generations each. Matthew's purpose was not to give all the names of all the generations between Abraham and Jesus. In some cases, he compresses the generations. In other cases, he substitutes different names. Obviously, Matthew was not on an DNA fact-finding search for ancestors. His purpose was to see the sovereign hand of God throughout the course of salvation history. In the three main eras of salvation history—from Abraham to David, from David to the exile, and from the exile to Jesus—Matthew sought to reflect on the character of God: God's mercy, God's justice, and God's faithfulness.

God's Mercy

In the first section (Matt 1:2–6; note that the last line of each section is the first line of the next section), four names stand out: Tamar, Rahab, Ruth, and the wife of Uriah. Craig Keener writes,

> Genealogies need include only men (those in 1 Chronicles exemplify this pattern), so the unexpected appearance

of four women draws attention to them. Had Matthew merely meant to evoke the history of Israel in a general way, one would have expected him to have named the matriarchs of Israel: Sarah, Rebekah, Leah and Rachel. Or to evoke supernatural births as a prelude to Mary's, he could cite Sarah, Rebekah and Rachel, whose wombs God opened. Instead, he names four women whose primary common link is their apparent Gentile ancestry: Tamar of Canaan, Rahab of Jericho, Ruth the Moabite and the ex-wife of Uriah the Hittite.[11]

The second section of fourteen generations begins with David and ends with the exile (Matt 1:6–11). The upward ascent from Abraham to David in the first section becomes a downward slope from King Solomon to the Babylonian exile. The theme of the second section is judgment. "From the height of Israel's political and spiritual glory under King David, Israel first gradually but then precipitously declines until she falls into the pit of exile, losing her land, temple, kings, and thus, seemingly, almost all of God's promises."[12]

God's Justice

To bring the message home, Matthew makes four alterations. This is complicated because most of our versions have "corrected" two of Matthew's alterations even though our best Greek texts support them. Here are the four irregularities:

1. Instead of "Asa" (Matt 1:7), the best manuscripts read "Asaph," Israel's worship leader and author of fifteen psalms.

2. After Jehoram (or Joram), Matthew skips three generations (Ahaziah, Joash, and Amaziah, 842–783 BC; 2 Chr 22–25).

3. Instead of "Amon" (Matt 1:10), the best manuscripts read "Amos," Israel's eighth-century prophet.

4. Matthew skips Jehoiakim just before Jehoiachin (or Jeconiah).

If these alterations were in Matthew's original text, it appears that Matthew intentionally altered history just enough to send a message. By changing two names, he stressed the theme of judgment, and by subtracting four names, he got his fourteen generations. We might think that Matthew was too footloose and fancy free with history, but his purpose went beyond the genealogical record to the gospel of redemption.

Not unlike Moses in the first genesis account, Matthew dis-chronologizes to make his point. He switches out Asa for Asaph and Amon for Amos to emphasize judgment and justice. These two men, whose ministries roughly begin and end this era, pronounced judgment against Israel's disobedience. Matthew includes four women in the first section to emphasize God's mercy; he includes these two men to emphasize God's justice. By interjecting these two names—Asaph the psalmist and Amos the prophet—Matthew is conveying his message in code. His Jewish readers knew the list of Israel's kings the way schoolchildren know the list of American presidents. He was not trying to trick them; he was trying to get their attention. As Bruner writes, "Asaph, after only David, is the most important psalmist and is the author of Psalms 50 and 73–83. Amos is the well-known eighth century prophet ... the prophet of social justice par excellence. ... So Asaph and Amos spell, respectively, psalmic 'spiritual renewal' and prophetic 'social justice.' "[13]

God's Faithfulness

The downward movement from David to exile is reversed in the third section (Matt 1:11–16). Everything is pointing up to Jesus Christ, and the theme is God's faithfulness. Bruner writes, "God had promised Abraham a Seed for Everyone, and Israel waited; God had promised David a Son Forever (2 Sam 7:12; 1 Chron 17:11) and Israel hoped. And on route God brought Israel *up* in mercy, *down* in judgment, and finally [forward] *in* by faith—by God's good faith in conceiving the Seed of Abraham and the Son of David in the womb of Mary."[14]

Once again Matthew compresses the generations. He refers to only nine names covering a five-hundred-year period from Zerubbabel to Joseph, whereas Luke refers to eighteen names to cover this period in his genealogy. Most of these names cannot be found elsewhere in the biblical record. But there is something more surprising than Matthew's compressed chronology and abbreviated list of names, which knits together the tapestry of the whole genealogy. Matthew ends his genealogy by naming a fifth woman, Mary, and making a fifth alteration. Instead of saying "Joseph the father of Jesus," he deliberately says, "Joseph, the husband of Mary, and Mary was the mother of Jesus who is called the Messiah" (Matt 1:16 NIV).

The most striking feature of the last section is the last line. It lacks any mention of Jesus's father and a fourteenth generation! The unnamed father has been there from the beginning. He is none other than God the Father Almighty—as Bruner writes,

> Almighty in mercy (by including outsiders and forgiving sinners), almighty in judgment (on particularly the incorrigible) and, with special force, almighty in

good faith (in keeping faith with promises seemingly unkept—bringing a Seed of Abraham for all people and a Son of David for all time). And this Almighty Father is indeed "Maker of heaven and earth," not only at the beginning of history in Creation but also and especially at the heart of the history of redemption—in the "New Genesis wrought by Jesus Christ, son of David, son of Abraham."[15]

Who is included in the unnamed fourteenth generation is especially significant. In a genealogy of three times fourteen ($3\times[7\times2]$), Matthew uses numbers to indicate the completeness of salvation history. Like the seven days of creation, the number seven symbolizes the essence, the completeness, the comprehending reality of what is signified. Matthew stresses the sovereign rule of the kingdom of God. Bruner asks, "Is it possible that the fourteenth generation (in the third section) is the unnamed but major 'generation' in the whole series—the divine 'generation' of Jesus in the womb of Mary?"[16]

If so, this means all those who follow the Lord Jesus Christ are included in this family tree. We are that fourteenth generation. To begin our story, conscious of the twofold genesis, implies a hidden spiritual discipline. Many of us are in the habit of telling our story with a secular slant. Some talk as if we were masters of the universe, in control of our destiny, while others lament our vulnerability as victims of despair. In either case, the secular nature of our self-understanding comes out in our storytelling. Practically speaking, we tend to talk about our lives as if there were no God of creation, no God of redemption. Whatever the pride or pathos of our past may be, faith in Christ reorients our personal story and gives us a new beginning.

We begin the way the Bible begins, by intentionally orienting our story to the will and work of God. The apostles were true to this reorientation when they emphasized predestination and election. To be chosen "in him before the foundation of the world, that we should be holy and blameless before him" (Eph 1:4) is another way of emphasizing the twofold genesis, "In the beginning God ..." and "The book of the genealogy of Jesus Christ, the son of David, the son of Abraham." To say that the Lamb of God, Jesus Christ our Savior, was slain from before the foundation of the world emphasizes both "In the beginning, God ..." and "Immanuel, God with us" (Rev 13:8; Matt 1:23).

A CHRISTMAS STORY (MATTHEW 2:12–18)

We would like to avoid the tragedy of King Herod's Bethlehem massacre, but it cannot be ignored. Right from the beginning, the coming of Jesus gave rise to painful historical consequences. "Enemy-occupied territory—that is what this world is," writes C. S. Lewis. "Christianity is the story of how the rightful king has landed, you might say in disguise, and is calling us all to take part in a great campaign of sabotage."[17] Before Jesus spoke a word, performed a miracle, or challenged the Jerusalem establishment, he was pursued with vengeance by a violent, paranoid, and maniacal political ruler. Innocent lives were put at risk. The magi escaped. Having been warned in a dream not to go back to Herod, they returned to their country by another route. Joseph was warned in a dream by the angel of the Lord to flee from Bethlehem immediately. "Get up. Take the child and his mother and escape to Egypt. Stay there until I tell you, for Herod is going to search for the child to kill him" (Matt 1:13 NIV).

Herod sent soldiers to Bethlehem with orders to kill all the boys in Bethlehem and its vicinity who were two years old and under (Matt 2:16). If the population of the small town were about two thousand inhabitants, with three to four dozen children two years old and under, that would mean that twenty to twenty-five infant and toddler boys were killed. Only one baby boy was spared. The first Christian martyrs were name-less Jewish boys living in Bethlehem. None of them realized what they were dying for, but by the grace of God, we can say that before Jesus died for them, they died for Jesus. Joseph gave up his dignity, Mary gave up her womb, but the infant boys of Bethlehem gave up their lives.

When Matthew describes what Herod did in Bethlehem, he recalls the prophecy of Jeremiah: "A voice was heard in Ramah, weeping and loud lamentation, Rachel weeping for her children; she refused to be comforted, because they are no more" (Matt 2:18, from Jer 31:15). What Matthew does not say speaks as loud as what he does say. Jeremiah's reference to Rachel's weeping and the sorrow of Ramah comes out of the same chapter that promises the new covenant. It is as if the mourning in Ramah and the grieving of Rachel gather up all the sorrow and grief of the past. The wailing cry of Bethlehem's mothers echoes through the ages, but the One whose life was spared will die and rise again in order to redeem all those who are lost, including those twenty-five or so young boys.

Matthew's account of King Herod and the magi dispels whatever sentimentality or nostalgia we may associate with Christmas. All the surprising twists and tragic turns of Jesus's life only go into fulfilling the sovereign will of God. Even Egypt fits into the will of God (Hos 11:1). This should help all those who follow Christ to accept the chaotic twists and turns of their lives. Sentimentality cannot stand up under the pressure of human depravity, but trusting in the sovereign will of God can. The God of Christmas is not a sentimentalist, and the sending of his Son was the costliest sacrifice God could have ever given.

Bruner writes, "Those who begin by hating the Child end by hurting children. Hating revelation leads to hurting people."[18] Parents who take after Herod make it difficult for their children to believe in Christ. Adult self-rule, especially when disguised by religion, makes it nearly impossible for sons and daughters to escape the slaughter of innocents. Parents who take after the magi bring their children along on this arduous faith journey. They teach their children to take God at his word. They show them how to turn faith to action and to give gifts worthy of Christ the King.

JESUS UNEMBELLISHED (MARK 1:9–13; 10:45)

The Gospel of Mark is unique in its nothing-but-Jesus beginning. Mark dispenses altogether with Christmas carols and angel choirs. He eliminates visitations and revelations. He gives nothing to his Greek audience to embellish—nothing to distract. John gives us the cosmic Christ and the Word made flesh. Matthew introduces Joseph and the magi. Luke paints the nativity with Elizabeth and Zechariah, Mary and Joseph, angels and shepherds, and Anna and Simeon. But Mark skips it all and jumps right to Jesus's public ministry.

John the Baptist is the voice of one calling in the wilderness. He has the honor of delivering Mark's Christmas greeting, "Prepare the way of the Lord, make straight paths for him." It would be as if we added one more figure in the usual nativity scene—John the Baptist, a wilderness loner, clothed in camel hair, living off locusts and wild honey. Christmas comes late in Mark's Gospel. Mark, the Evangelist and close colleague of the apostle Peter, waits until the baptism of Jesus to introduce the Savior. He needs only one line to sum up the Christmas message: "And a voice came from heaven: 'You are my Son, whom I love; with you I am well pleased'" (Mark 1:11 NIV). For those who are celebrating Christmas when it does not feel like Christmas, Mark does a nice job. He gets to the point quicker than anyone else. By leaving out the familiar, Mark focuses our attention on why Jesus came. Jesus sums it up when he says,

"For even the Son of Man came not to be served but to serve, and to give his life as a ransom for many" (Mark 10:45).

Of the four Gospels, Mark's gospel is the most consistent with Jesus's preferred title of Son of Man. Jesus interpreted the meaning of his sonship through his familiar self-designation as the Son of Man. He chose this title apparently because it was least likely to be misunderstood and afforded the best opportunity to reshape the popular concept of the Messiah. Jesus combined as never before two significant Old Testament themes. Salvation on the universal and eternal scale envisioned by Daniel and others was to be accomplished through suffering, humiliation, and death. According to Jesus, salvation was to come not through political triumph but through God's gracious acceptance of the redemptive sacrifice provided by a "man of sorrows" who was "led like a lamb to the slaughter."

Some of our most memorable Christmases are the ones where everything but Christ is stripped away, and we are left with a Gospel of Mark Christmas. When the usual pattern of celebration, tradition, and sentiment is broken, there is hope for God to do a new and deeper work in us. There is a kind of service that Jesus does not want. "For the Son of Man did not come to be served." This rules out all forms of service that are for our glory and at Christ's expense. For it is possible to serve ourselves under the pretense of serving Christ. David Augsburger writes, "Service whose goal is to elevate the servant is no service at all."[19]

We come closest to celebrating the true meaning of Christmas when, in the providence of God, we experience hardship and loss at Christmas—or when we give ourselves to others who are experiencing hardship and loss. It may be the loss of a loved one, or a life-threatening illness, or a family crisis, but whatever it is, it forces us to seek a truer and more lasting comfort than the familiar rituals. We turn to Christ for comfort.

Holiday cheer may mock either our grief or the grief of the one we are called to serve. Happy holidays may intensify our suffering or provoke our compassion to serve others. The festive sights and sounds of the season are no match for the stark realities of those who suffer. All the color is drained out of our holiday picture, and we seem to be left in the dark. But it is then, when our lives are swept clean of all diversions and distractions, that our devotion to Christ grows. Everything else is in the shadows, but the light of Christ shines in our lives. We become impressed with one overwhelming, awesome truth: Jesus is our Savior.

One year, pastor J. Sidlow Baxter sampled what various preachers had to say about Christmas. "To one, Christmas was a symbol of intangible aspirations. To another, it was an idealistic enshrinement of motherhood and family life. To another it was 'the most significant domestic festival in the Church's calendar.' But when I turned back again to our Lord's own explanation," Baxter said, "this is what I found: 'The Son of Man came not to be served, but to serve, and to give his life a ransom for many' (Matt 20:28). If *anyone* knows, 'the reason why,'" Baxter emphasized, "*He* does. His is the one explanation of Christmas which really matters."

Ironically, the more we add to Jesus's own explanation, the more inadequate our understanding will be. Baxter says it well,

> In view of our Lord's words, it is intolerably inadequate to offer some beautifully worded yet merely aesthetic explanation of Christmas. Our Lord's incarnation was not merely idealistic; it was redemptive. ... Bethlehem and Golgotha, the Manger and the Cross, the birth and the death, must always be seen together, if the real Christmas is to survive with all its profound inspirations;

for "the Son of Man came not to be served, but to serve,
and to give his life a ransom for many."[20]

This may be a Gospel of Mark Christmas for you, either because
of your experience of loss or because the Lord has called you
into his service for the sake of others. Either way, we come
closest to celebrating the true meaning of Christmas when we
agree with the Son of Man, who came not to be served but to
serve and give his life a ransom for many.

The incarnation is the grand miracle of the Christian faith,
merging creation and redemption. God-in-person is embodied in
flesh and blood. "The Word became flesh and made his dwelling
among us. We have seen his glory, the glory of the one and only
Son, who came from the Father, full of grace and truth" (John
1:14 NIV). The early Christians proclaimed in creedal form, "We
all unanimously teach that we should confess that our Lord Jesus
Christ is one and the same Son, truly God and truly man, one
with the Father in his deity and one with us in our humanity,
like us in all things except sin" (Chalcedonian Definition 451).
Mary wrapped the Christ child in strips of cloth and laid him
in a manger. God wrapped his birth in prophecy and promise.

A GREAT AND WONDROUS SIGN!
(REVELATION 12:1–17)

The apostle John's Christmas message hurls us into history
and flings us into eternity. Past, present, and future are packed
together in a single scene. His nativity is ablaze with light. A
pregnant woman clothed in the sun, with the moon under her
feet and a crown of stars on her head, is in labor. She cries in
pain. An enormous and powerful red dragon threatens her. Like
the shepherds and the magi, the dragon stands before the child,
not to adore but to annihilate. This is not a Norman Rockwell

painting, and Rembrandt never painted St. John's nativity. In the Spirit, John describes Christmas like we have never seen it before. Salvation history is compressed into a vision that includes the fall of Satan, the incarnation, the ascension, and the church.

The woman in travail is the true Israel "in her pre-messianic agony of expectation."[21] She shines radiantly, stands powerfully, and rules mightily. She is the people of God, spanning Old and New Testaments, the bride of Christ. The Bethlehem birth of the Christ child is God's D-Day invasion. Luke's manger scene and John's vision of the woman clothed with the sun cover the range that invokes worship and witness. In John's vision, hell itself threatens heaven. The devil shows up with his strategies of annihilation (Matt 16:18; Luke 10:18). John insists on the true meaning of Christmas, undeterred by either trivialization or tribulation. Heaven's Christmas carol is a victory song (Rev 12:10–12).

FROM THE CRADLE TO THE CROSS

The trajectory of salvation history leads downward to the manger. Most Christians are familiar with Israel's early history. God called Abraham out of nowhere to make of him a great nation. Under the patriarchs, Isaac, Jacob, and Joseph, the family grew. Then, famine led the Israelites into four hundred years of Egyptian bondage. We remember the first exodus, when the Israelites escaped from Egypt, crossed the Red Sea, and were led through the wilderness by Moses and Joshua into the promised land. The stories of Deborah, Gideon, and Ruth lead to kings Saul and David. Here, Israel is at its height. David's son Solomon begins the descent.

We begin to lose interest when the kingdom is divided between Jeroboam's Israel in the north and Rehoboam's Judah in the south. Against a litany of bad kings, Elijah and Elisha keep Israel's history alive. From there the story line belongs to the prophets. It is hard to keep sixteen prophets straight.

Their ministry, from Joel to Malachi, spanned four hundred long years. Joel, Jonah, Amos, Hosea, Isaiah, Micah, Nahum, Zephaniah, and Jeremiah tried to turn the hearts of the people to God. Embedded in their message is the story of the coming Messiah, but few grasped the promised hope, and few honored the faithfulness of God with obedience and devotion. God judged his people and sent them into exile. The Babylonian captivity ran for seventy years. Habakkuk, Daniel, Ezekiel, Obadiah, Haggai, Zechariah, and Malachi cover this period. This is where Nehemiah and Ezra come in as well.

The first exodus was powerful. God's ten plagues, the Passover meal, and the solidarity of the people of Israel leaving Egypt in mass, crossing the Red Sea on dry ground, feeding on manna in the wilderness, and receiving the law on Mount Sinai all add up to a spectacular defining moment. But the second exodus from Babylon was nothing by comparison. Israel trekked back to their homeland as refugees. We remember the first exodus, but few of us know much about the second exodus. Nehemiah and Ezra describe a beleaguered people, barely hanging on. When the temple was rebuilt, those who remembered the glory days under Solomon and the first temple cried because they were disappointed. Malachi's cry for faithfulness is the last word in this downward trajectory, followed by four hundred years of silence. The people of God, through whom God promised to bless all the nations, were taken down to rock bottom. The descent of the Messiah was proceeded by the descent of the people of God.

Martin Luther likened the Old Testament to Christ's swaddling clothes and the manger in which Christ was laid. In his preface to the Old Testament, he writes:

There are some who have little regard for the Old Testament. They think of it as a book that was given to the Jewish people only and is now out of date, containing only stories of past times. ... But it says in John 5, "Search the Scriptures, for it is they that bear witness to me." ... The Scriptures of the Old Testament are not to be despised but diligently read. ... Therefore dismiss your own opinions and feelings and think of the Scriptures as the loftiest and noblest of holy things, as the richest of mines which can never be sufficiently explored, in order that you may find that divine wisdom which God here lays before you in such simple guise as to quench all pride. Here you will find the swaddling cloths and the manger in which Christ lies. ... Simple and lowly are these swaddling cloths, but dear is the treasure, Christ, who lies in them.[22]

All the work that went into Israel's postexilic period was God's way of building a cradle for his ultimate revelation. God restored the Jewish people, the Jerusalem temple, the Mosaic law, the Passover, the sacrificial system, the priesthood, and the walls of Jerusalem in order to cradle the Incarnate One. Even though everything seemed to be on a smaller, humbler scale than the first exodus, anticipation grew. There was little room for pride of country and race among a people who longed for God's mercy and justice. The promised land may be less promising than in the days of Moses, but the Promised One is coming, and God is at work.

When Luke quotes the angelic announcement, "And this will be a sign for you; you will find a baby wrapped in swaddling cloths and lying in a manger," he introduces a powerful metaphor for God's self-imposed, sacrificial powerlessness (Luke 2:12). In this divinely appointed object lesson, the manger becomes a profound illustration of the humility of God. It is a radical picture of God's self-emptying. God himself, the Incarnate One, condescends to join our helpless state in order to bring redemption and restore us to right relationship with himself. Like the cross, the manger illustrates the extent of Christ's love. If Christ and his word shape the meaning behind the metaphor, then God's visual aids will retain their effectiveness in shaping discipleship. We begin with the cradle and end with the cross. The manger and the empty tomb are on God's revelational continuum. The hymns and carols we sing at Christmas proclaim an important truth. They do not leave us at the manger; they lead us to the cross.

The story we tell at Christmas is the beginning of the story of the cross: "His name will be called Jesus, because he will save his people from their sins." We cannot look at the babe in the manger without seeing the shadow of the cross. The angels announced, "Fear not, for behold, I bring you good news of a great joy that will be for all the people. For unto you is born this day in the city of David a Savior, who is Christ the Lord" (Luke 2:10–11). Story, song, and symbol move us from the cradle to the cross; from Christmas to Easter; from celebrating the Christ-child to worshiping the crucified and risen Lord Jesus, the coming King of kings and Lord of lords. "The Gift we celebrate at Christmas was not wrapped, it was crucified. It was not under the tree, it was nailed to the tree; and it was not opened on Christmas day, it was opened on Easter morning."[23]

Every year pastors are privileged to explore how wide and long and high and deep is the love of Christ. A lifetime of Advent sermons and Christmas meditations is not sufficient to exhaust the scope of salvation history and the depth of Christ's incarnational love. It is a labor of love and worship.

*I want to know Christ—yes, to know the power of
his resurrection and participation in his sufferings,
becoming like him in his death, and so, somehow,
attaining to the resurrection from the dead.*

Philippians 3:10–11 NIV

*Near the cross! O Lamb of God,
bring its scenes before me.*

Fanny Crosby, "Near the Cross"

8

Preaching Lenten Sermons

Lent is forty days, plus seven Sundays, leading up to Easter. Through the centuries the church has set aside this time for penitential preparation to remember Christ's passion for us and to grow in Christ. Our focus is on Jesus's path to the cross and our cross bearing. Whether or not your church tradition practices Lent, all Christians will want to explore the meaning of Christ's atoning sacrifice and what it means to take up our cross and follow Jesus.

Salvation history moves to the cross of Christ out of redemptive necessity. The Lord of history has designed it that way. From Genesis to Revelation, the meaning of the cross and the mystery of the atonement unfold under the sovereign direction of God. We are prepared for the cross through images, events, allusions, symbols, parables, prophecies, and poetry. Every form, phase, type, and strata of the Bible points to the cross. From the garden of Eden to the return of the exiles from Babylon, and from the birth of Christ to the garden of Gethsemane, we are moving toward the cross.

To most historians, the importance of Jesus's cross is by no means obvious. Divine necessity is hidden in the course of human affairs. Current events, political leaders, and natural catastrophes grab the headlines. Yet, those with eyes to see and ears to hear testify to the inevitability of the cross. God's word declares its meaning in ways that convict and comfort.

Salvation is woven into the very fabric of history. The history of God's revelation points to the cross, and the nature of God's creation points to the resurrection. We are prepared for the resurrection of Jesus through the big bang, the language of DNA, the human quest for knowledge, the periodic table, mathematical patterns and formulas, the human capacity for beauty, the anthropic principle of the universe, the incredible complexity of the living cell, and the meaning of the human drama. As history moves to the cross, creation moves to the resurrection. Salvation is woven into the very fabric of nature. The cross and the resurrection of Christ cannot be separated from each other. They are revealed by God in history, but they are not of history. They are space-time historical events, embraced by faith.

Lent provides an opportunity for the church to pay attention to some difficult biblical texts. Our church reorganized our small groups for Lent. For seven weeks, instead of meeting in our regular small groups, we mixed it up and met geographically. This brought us together in new ways and generated greater diversity in our groups. The focus of these midweek groups was to pray over and discuss the biblical text that was to be preached the coming Sunday. Group leaders met on Sunday during the Sunday school hour to prepare for the coming week's passage. This meant that about a quarter of our Sunday morning worshipers spent several hours studying the biblical passage before it was preached. This heightened our sense of participation in the biblical text and our anticipation of the preached word. We also prepared a study guide for the seven weeks that included lessons for Maundy Thursday, Good Friday, and Easter Sunday.

Each year we studied a challenging text, such as what we titled "Jeremiah's Gethsemane Life" or "The Book of Revelation's Followers of the Lamb" or "The Gospel according to Job." We explored the supremacy of Christ in Hebrews and a passion for Christ in Matthew's Gospel. For seven weeks, we worked hard on the biblical text both in a midweek Bible study and Sunday morning. This Lenten exercise carried over into a forty-day devotional series on Jesus's upper-room discourse: "The God Who Kneels" (John 13), "The God Who Comforts" (John 14–15), and "The God Who Prays" (John 16–17).

One year we focused our Lenten preaching series on the seven last sayings of Christ. It was a series seven years in the making, because for every Good Friday seven years running, I joined six African American pastors at Bethel African Methodist Episcopal Church in San Diego for a three-hour worship service in which we preached the seven last sayings of Christ.

THE SEVEN LAST
SAYINGS OF CHRIST

The first thing that everyone sees when they enter the sanctuary of Cherry Creek Presbyterian Church in Denver is a twelve-foot, free-standing wooden cross off to the side of the pulpit. I have always found it to be a powerful reminder of God's grace and our Lord's call to a life of discipleship. Once an engaged couple new to the church surprised us by requesting that the cross be removed for their wedding service. They complained that the cross was "so religious" and that it was bound to show up in some of their wedding pictures. We were happy to inform them that the cross in the sanctuary could not be removed; it was permanent. It was set in concrete.

The fullness of Christ's sevenfold message from the cross encompasses doctrinal truth and devotional passion. The biblical doctrines of forgiveness, salvation, incarnation, atonement, and resurrection are profoundly presented by Jesus himself on the cross. On the cross theology and ethics, truth and practice, meaning and ministry converge. These seven last prayers and sayings from the cross underscore the identity of the crucified and risen Messiah.

1. "Father, forgive them, for they know not what they do" (Luke 23:34)

2. "Truly, I say to you, today you will be with me in paradise" (Luke 23:43)

3. "Woman, behold your son!" (John 19:26)

4. "My God, my God, why have you forsaken me?" (Mark 15:34)

5. "I thirst" (John 19:28)

6. "It is finished" (John 19:30)

7. "Father, into your hands I commit my spirit" (Luke 23:46)

1. "FATHER, FORGIVE THEM, FOR THEY KNOW NOT WHAT THEY DO" (LUKE 23:26–34)

The prophet Isaiah was impressed by what the suffering servant did *not* say: "He was oppressed, and he was afflicted, yet he opened not his mouth; like a lamb that is led to the slaughter, and like sheep that before its shearers is silent, so he opened not his mouth" (Isa 53:7).

The silence of Jesus on the cross is extraordinary. We do well to consider what he did not say. He offered no criticism, gave no excuses, provided no defense, and uttered no blame. He was "despised and rejected" (Isa 53:3), but he did not respond to his captors and torturers. He "has borne our griefs and carried our sorrows" (Isa 53:4) without a word of indignation or self-pity. He was "stricken, smitten by God, and afflicted" (Isa 53:4), yet he remained silent. Everything God's word says about how we should respond to our persecutors is illustrated for us in Jesus.

Consider what Jesus went through: Luke tells us that Jesus was in anguish and the disciples were "exhausted from sorrow" (Luke 22:45 NIV). He was abandoned by the disciples emotionally before they left him physically. He was left to carry out the will of the Father alone. The disciples were confused, ignorant, ready to flee. He was arrested late Thursday night and kept up all night by guards who blindfolded him. They beat him and demanded, "Prophesy! Who hit you?" (Luke 22:64 NIV).

At daybreak on Friday, he went before the Jewish Sanhedrin. They reaffirmed their predetermined verdict based on false accusers and sent Jesus to Pilate, whose authorization was needed to pass the death penalty. "We found this man misleading our nation and forbidding us to give tribute to Caesar, and saying that he himself is Christ, a king" (Luke 23:2). Pilate examined Jesus and answered the chief priests and the crowds, saying, "I find no guilt in this man" (Luke 23:4). Then Pilate sent Jesus to Herod, who interrogated him in the presence of the chief priests, who persisted in shouting accusations against him. Herod ridiculed and mocked Jesus. He had him dressed in an elegant robe and sent him back to Pilate.

Pilate played out his own little drama, washing his hands before the people, declaring that innocent blood would not be on his hands. Meanwhile, a hostile mob raged against Jesus. They shouted, "Crucify him! Crucify him!" The ordeal of the trial and the public indictment was followed by an excruciating walk to Golgotha bearing the cross. Jesus was stripped, mocked, and nailed. He hung on the cross for six hours and uttered seven short sentences. Each one was deeply personal and genuinely indicative of his God-centered, sacrificial life.

Reflection on the suffering and silence of Jesus on the cross naturally focuses our attention on the speech of Jesus from the cross. What form did his speech take, and for what purpose did he speak? Not surprisingly, Jesus prayed. Of these seven last sentences, three are prayers:

"Father, forgive them."

"My God, my God, why have you forsaken me?"

"Father, into your hands I commit my Spirit."

Jesus began and ended the experience of the cross in prayer, and in the middle, he cried out to God. The second and sixth words from the cross contemplate the eternal perspective of the immediate present and climactic completion of the Father's will. Dying is swallowed up in victory. At the point of his greatest earthly pain, Jesus contemplates heaven and the accomplishment of the Father's purposes.

"Today you will be with me in paradise."

"It is finished."

The third and fifth words from the cross are immediate and practical, reflecting the real-world consciousness of our Savior.

"Woman, behold your son."

"I thirst."

We are not surprised at either Jesus's readiness to pray or his focus on forgiveness even in these extraordinary and excruciating circumstances. But we may be surprised that Jesus expects us to be like him. Prayer and forgiveness are meant to go hand in hand not only in Jesus's life but in our lives. Prayer was always the first act of Jesus's life and ministry, and forgiveness followed naturally. "You shall call his name Jesus, for he will save his people from their sins" (Matt 1:21). "I have not come to call the righteous but sinners to repentance" (Luke 5:32).

The first word of the cross shows God's readiness to forgive. Remember the Lord's word in Isaiah: "For my thoughts are not your thoughts, neither are your ways my ways, declares the LORD. For as the heavens are higher than the earth, so are my ways higher than your ways and my thoughts than your thoughts" (Isa 55:8–9). When we hear this description of the Lord, we are inspired to think of God's mystery and majesty, but in the context of Isaiah, we are drawn to think of God's mercy! The prophet admonishes, "Seek the LORD while he may be found; call upon him while he is near; let the wicked forsake his way, and the unrighteous man his thoughts; let him return to the LORD, that he may have compassion on him, and to our God, for he will abundantly pardon" (Isa 55:6–7).

If we are serious about fellowship with God, we are serious about forgiveness. To seek the forgiveness of those who have wronged us is fundamental to our relationship with the Lord. The petition in the Lord's Prayer that Jesus singles out for special commentary is, "Forgive us our debts, as we also have forgiven our debtors" (Matt 6:12), or "Forgive us our sins, for we also forgive everyone who sins against us. And lead us not into temptation" (Luke 11:4 NIV). Jesus says, "For if you forgive others their trespasses, your heavenly Father will also forgive you, but if you do not forgive others their trespasses, neither will your Father forgive your trespasses" (Matt 6:14–15). What Jesus taught, he practiced: "Love your enemies and pray for those who persecute you" (Matt 5:44).

Our communion with God depends on our willingness to forgive and our anticipation of God's work in a person's life leading to repentance and forgiveness. To forgive those who have wronged us is a sign that we ourselves have been forgiven. The clarity of our responsibility in the light of the cross is beyond debate. With these words Jesus showed not only his readiness to forgive, but to what extent he would go to provide for our forgiveness. The will and purpose of the Son is one with the will and purpose of the Father. "For even the Son of Man came not to be served but to serve, and to give his life as a ransom for many" (Mark 10:45). The forgiveness offered by the Father is based on the obedience of the Son.

Who, then, did Jesus pray for, and what were they ignorant of? Did Jesus pray for the soldiers who nailed his hands and feet and thrust the crown of thorns on his head? Yes, Jesus prayed for them. Did Jesus pray for Pilate, the Roman governor, who washed his hands in front of the crowd and declared, "I am innocent of this man's blood. It is your responsibility" (Matt 27:24 NIV). Yes, Jesus earnestly sought the Father on behalf of Pilate. Did Jesus pray for the crowds who shouted, "Crucify him! Crucify him!" Most certainly. What about the Jewish ruling body, the Sanhedrin, who sought to condemn Jesus on false chargers? Did Jesus pray for them and the chief high priest, who charged Jesus with blasphemy? Yes, Jesus persevered in praying for the people of Israel, including their evil leaders. Did Jesus pray for the disciples who disowned him and fled out of fear? Yes, Jesus interceded on behalf of his disciples.

Did the soldiers know they were crucifying the King of kings and Lord of lords? Did Pilate know that he would one day stand before this very same Jesus, who would decide his eternal fate? Did the crowds know that they were jeering at the Lord of glory? Did the Jews know they were mocking and spitting in the face of their Messiah? Did the disciples know that they were disowning the one who would be their risen Lord?

Forgiveness is not imposed; it is received. It is received through repentance and the acceptance of the mercy of God. It is conceivable that many of those who shouted "Crucify him! Crucify him!" were in the crowd on Pentecost when Peter declared: "Now, brothers, I know that you acted in ignorance, as did also your rulers. But what God foretold by the mouth of all the prophets, that his Christ would suffer, he thus fulfilled. Repent therefore, and turn back, that your sins may be blotted out, that times of refreshing may come from the presence of the Lord" (Acts 3:17–20).

But who is missing from this picture? We are missing from this picture. It is our sins that nailed Jesus to the cross. I have never met anyone who mourned more painfully and in greater agony than David Conner. The lines on his face seemed frozen and contorted in a cry of pain. His eyes, swollen and red, filled with a seemingly endless supply of tears. When he spoke, the trembling of his lips seemed to spread throughout his body. He shivered as if he were always cold. I believe David grieved as deeply as anyone could grieve. And when I visited him in prison, even his faint smile seemed to hurt. David was in prison because he killed a mother and child accidentally on a two-lane road in Indiana. It was a Saturday afternoon, and David had been drinking. He was impatient and provoked when he was cut off by a motorcyclist who had passed him on a curve. He sped up to pass and lost control of his car on the next curve. He hit the oncoming car head-on. The mother and child died instantly.

It was as if in the twinkling of an eye David entered hell itself. Every evil thing he had ever done was now dumped in his despairing soul. How could a human being do what he had done? He went from being an ordinary husband, OK father, average worker, to the very personification of evil. Overnight David became an object of hate in our small town. The victim's family could not have condemned David more if he had been solely responsible for the Nazi Holocaust of the Jews or singularly culpable in the crucifixion of Jesus. And who could blame the grieving family? Two white crosses marked the spot on the highway where the accident occurred. Yet throughout the ordeal David reminded me of myself. When I visited him in prison, his pain reminded me of my own sin and moral culpability. He was not alone in his need. There was a glaring obviousness about his evil, but it did not obscure my own.

Martin Luther used a graphic picture to depict our responsibility in the death of Christ. He said we carry around the nails of Christ's cross in our pocket. We cringe at the very thought of the crucifixion; we hardly feel responsible for the spikes driven through the hands and feet of Jesus. But that is what our sins did. He "was pierced for our transgressions; he was crushed for our iniquities; upon him was the chastisement that brought us peace, and with his wounds we are healed. ... The LORD has laid on him the iniquity of us all" (Isa 53:5–6).

David Connor honestly mourned for what he had done. His soulful conviction was very different from feeling pity for what he had become. He tried to understand his actions, but he did not excuse them. He was truly filled with remorse and repentance. Did Jesus have David in mind when he said, "Father, forgive them, for they know not what they do"? Yes, indeed, I believe he did. Whether there is an empty six-pack in the trunk or some leftover crucifixion spikes in our pockets, we all need to repent and turn to Christ for forgiveness. Only then can we begin to experience the comfort we need.

2. "TRULY, I SAY TO YOU, TODAY YOU WILL BE WITH ME IN PARADISE" (LUKE 23:43)

Despite all the confusion and ambiguity that surround life today, the gospel picture is clear and simple. Amid an array of options, choices, and identities, the gospel slices life in two. There is no neutral ground. Two men were crucified, one on either side of Jesus. Their responses to Jesus represent the only two options available: rejection or acceptance, disdain or devotion, unbelief or belief. Jesus was either a person to be mocked or the merciful Savior. The options before them were momentous. Their opportunity was truly unique. Their decisions were irreversible, and the stakes could not have been higher.

Most people do not feel the pressure to take sides about Jesus the way these two criminals did. That is a shame. They were forced to decide. Indifference or apathy in the face of ridicule was hardly an option. The situation imposed on the two criminals did not allow for any other options but these two: belief or unbelief. When C. S. Lewis wrote *Mere Christianity*, he wanted to bring the reader to a hard choice, to an either/or choice. He appealed to reason to force a decision. He writes,

> I am trying to prevent anyone saying the really foolish thing that people often say about Him: "I'm ready to accept Jesus as a great moral teacher, but I don't accept His claim to be God." That is the one thing we must not say. A man who was merely a man and said the sort of things Jesus said would not be a great moral teacher. He would either be a lunatic—on a level with the man who says he is a poached egg—or else he would be the Devil of Hell. You must make your choice. Either this man was, and is, the Son of God: or else a madman or something worse. You can shut Him up for a fool, you

> can spit at Him and kill Him as a demon; or you can fall
> at His feet and call Him Lord and God. But let us not
> come with any patronizing nonsense about His being
> a great human teacher. He has not left that open to us.
> He did not intend to.[1]

The rich young ruler wanted to keep his options open, but Jesus forced him to make a decision: "One thing you still lack. Sell all that you have and distribute to the poor, and you will have treasure in heaven; and come, follow me" (Luke 18:22).

Jesus pushed his disciples to the crisis of decision as well. Following the feeding of the more-than-five-thousand, Jesus said, "Whoever feeds on my flesh and drinks my blood has eternal life, and I will raise him up on the last day" (John 6:54). This caused many to turn away from following Jesus. "You do not want to leave too, do you?" Jesus asked (John 6:67 NIV). Peter answered, "Lord, to whom shall we go? You have the words of eternal life. We have come to believe and know that you are the Holy One of God" (John 6:68–69 NIV).

The word of Jesus, the force of circumstances, the power of reasoning, and the conviction of the heart drive people to decide one way or the other for Jesus. We may be lying on a hospital bed or in the throes of depression, but we have to decide one way or the other. We are either for Jesus or against Jesus. We are like either the criminal who rejected Jesus or the criminal who believed in Jesus. The first criminal to speak joined the chorus of mockers (see Ps 22:12–18). The humiliations suffered by Jesus were many. He was brutally treated, falsely accused, abandoned by friends, taunted by enemies, exposed in the sight of the people, and nailed to the cross. He hung between two criminals, who were most likely insurrectionists—enemies of the state. Isaiah's prophecy was accurate:

"He was despised and rejected by men, a man of sorrows and acquainted with grief; and as one from whom men hide their faces he was despised, and we esteemed him not. ... [He] was numbered with the transgressors; yet he bore the sin of many, and makes intercession for the transgressors" (Isa 53:3, 12).

The issue surrounding the cross was not the death of an innocent man, but the death of one who claimed to be the Messiah. With their taunts and jeers, the chorus of mockers made that clear. The rulers sneered, "He saved others; let him save himself, if he is the Christ of God, the Chosen One" (Luke 23:35). The soldiers mocked, "If you are the king of the Jews, save yourself" (23:37). The third member of this trio of mockery was a criminal. Luke tells us, "One of the criminals who hung there hurled insults at him, 'Aren't you the Christ? Save yourself and us!'" (23:39 NIV).

This chorus of scorn sang from the same score. They played the same tune. Just as Satan had tempted Jesus at the outset of his ministry, saying, "If you are the Son of God, tell these stones to become bread" (Matt 4:3 NIV), all three groups, rulers, soldiers, and a terrorist, taunted him with his true titles: the Christ, the Chosen One, and the King of the Jews. Encircling the cross, each of these mockers sneered at Jesus and ridiculed him, shouting, "Save yourself." In their shameful anger and outrage, the mockers underscored the meaning of the cross. They unwittingly publicized the identity of the Crucified One and echoed the purpose of the cross, salvation.

Who are these proud mockers who jeer and taunt the Prince of Peace and the Lord of glory? The humiliations and wrongs inflicted on Jesus climax with the word of a terrorist. Who could have legitimately spoken against Jesus? The religious leaders? Herod? Pilate? By accusing and condemning an innocent man, they abused the power of their authority. The officers of the system, religious and political, betrayed the principles of justice and order and used the power of the system against an innocent man. Even in their mockery, they admitted his innocence: "He saved others; let him save himself if he is the Christ of God, the Chosen One."

But the most ironic accuser of all and the very last person in the world to have the floor in condemning Jesus was an insurrectionist, about to be executed for being an enemy of the state. A terrorist gave the world's final curses and accusations against Jesus as he hung dying on the cross. The case of *Sinful Humanity v. Jesus* comes down to this: a man on a cross hurling curses against Christ. The case against Jesus comes to this: a convict cursing Jesus, a killer sneering at the Savior. This is mockery at its worst, but it is what all mockery against Christ eventually comes down to.

It is important to ask, Who, then, speaks for you? Is your voice heard at the foot of the cross? Does the criminal hurling insults against Jesus represent you? Herod used Jesus to boost his ego. Pilate played Jesus like a pawn in a political chess game. The Sanhedrin made Jesus out to be their archenemy. Yet, in the end, they are all like the criminal in their rejection of Jesus. These two men on either side of Jesus are strikingly representative of the human response for and against Jesus.

If you reject Jesus, you may be offended that I would link your unbelief to the cursing terrorist on the cross. You are not rude in your unbelief. You are not mean. You are in fact very reasonable and polite in your unbelief. So, I don't mean to offend you, but I do mean to warn you. You are at the foot of the cross faced with a formidable life-and-death decision. If you have come to believe that Jesus is the Christ, your Savior from sin and death, and the giver of everlasting life, you are closer to the believing criminal on the cross than you might realize. His conversion to Christ, like our own, is entirely and absolutely based on mercy, not merit. In Christ, we are all more like death-row inmates than we realize. People mock jailhouse conversions, but we should not. They remind me too much of my own.

Why did one rebel against the state believe in Jesus and the other did not? Was the hate surrounding the cross so palpable and the love of Jesus so real that Jesus made a believer out of him? Do not forget that the rebel heard the first word of the cross, "Father, forgive them, for they know not what they do." He must have been moved by the word of forgiveness. He rebuked the cursing criminal, "Do you not fear God, since you are under the same sentence of condemnation? And we indeed justly, for we are receiving the due reward of our deeds; but this man has done nothing wrong" (Luke 23:40–41). The rebel who believed became convicted of his own guilt and convinced of Jesus's righteousness. The first word from the cross expressed the power of the gospel: God's readiness to forgive and the power of God's love and grace. The rebel heard the gospel and believed.

Jesus preached the gospel from the beginning of his earthly ministry to the end. He began in Nazareth, preaching good news to the poor, proclaiming freedom for the prisoners, and announcing the year of the Lord's favor. He concluded his first sermon by saying, "Today this Scripture has been fulfilled in your hearing" (Luke 4:21). He ended his last sermon by saying, "Today you will be with me in paradise." It is never too late to come to Christ. The preacher in Hebrews confirms, "Today, if you hear his voice, do not harden your hearts as in the rebellion" (Heb 3:7–8, 15). At the foot of the cross, there is no neutral ground. We are either taunting or trusting. We say with the apostle, "Behold, now is the favorable time; behold, now is the day of salvation" (2 Cor 6:2).

The second saying from the cross is a beautiful exchange between Jesus and his newest disciple. The dialogue between sinner and Savior is matched thought by thought. It is immediate, direct, and personal. He calls out, "Jesus," and the Savior responds, "I tell you the truth."

"Remember me," says the new believer, and Jesus responds, "You will be with me in paradise." The plea for help was answered with the promise of fellowship. The disciples' expectation, "When you come into your kingdom," is exceeded dramatically by Jesus's assurance, "Today you will be with me in paradise." Amen.

3. "WOMAN, BEHOLD YOUR SON!" (JOHN 19:16–27)

"So the soldiers took charge of Jesus" (John 19:16 NIV). Can anyone really take charge of Jesus? He was convicted by the Jews, sentenced by Pilate, and crucified by the soldiers, but can anyone take charge of Jesus? The words from the cross are a declaration of independence. They are filled with authority, passion, and conviction. Yes, in one sense, the soldiers took charge of Jesus, but in a deeper, more profound sense, Jesus demonstrated his freedom. The power of Jesus comes through even at the point of his powerlessness. On the cross, his words remind us of forgiveness, salvation, and compassion. Jesus was free to preach the gospel from the cross.

The second and third sayings of Jesus from the cross demonstrate the all-encompassing power of the gospel. After Jesus said to his newest disciple, "Today you will be with me in paradise," he said to Mary, "Woman, behold, your son!" and then, turning to John, he said, "Behold, your mother!" "This is one of the greatest wonders of his person," writes Arthur Pink, "the blending of the most perfect human affection with his divine glory."[2]

On the cross the Incarnate One offered a final testimony. He not only offered himself, the atoning sacrifice for the sins of the world, but he cared for his mother. He showed us how to unite the Great Commission to go into all the world to preach the gospel with the Great Commandment to love our neighbor as ourselves. He demonstrated the inseparable nature of evangelism and ethics. Eternal glory and temporal concerns share the same stage of life. The physical and the spiritual dimensions of our humanity are united.

Until now we have seen only cruelty at the cross. We have witnessed raw evil. But there at the foot of the cross, we find Mary, Jesus's mother, with her sister, together with Mary the wife of Clopas and Mary of Magdala. The women are joined by John, who is described not by name but by affection as "the disciple whom Jesus loved." The rest of the disciples fled the scene, but John returned. Our "brother and companion in the suffering and kingdom and patient endurance that are ours in Jesus" made it to the foot of the cross (Rev 1:9 NIV).

Mary was confronted with a dual role, a mother's love and a disciple's faithfulness. Mary's response to the angel's announcement at the very beginning held true her whole life through: "Behold, I am the servant of the Lord; let it be to me according to your word" (Luke 1:38). Situations throughout Jesus's life reveal both Mary's confusion and her character—the Jerusalem Passover journey when Jesus was twelve and his parents spent several anxious days searching for their son, the wedding reception in Cana of Galilee when Jesus turned water to wine, the awkward intervention when Mary and Jesus's siblings came to take Jesus back home and Jesus curtly reacted, "Who is my mother, and who are my brothers?" Looking around at his disciples, Jesus said, "Here are my mother and my brothers! For whoever does the will of my Father in heaven is my brother and sister and mother" (Matt 12:49–50).

We recall Simeon's sober words to Mary when Jesus was dedicated in the temple: "Behold, this child is appointed for the fall and rising of many in Israel, and for a sign that is opposed (and a sword will pierce through your own soul also), so that thoughts from many hearts may be revealed" (Luke 2:34). The spiritual formation of Mary was painful, from the time she and Joseph were forced to flee from Herod's soldiers with their newborn son to the moment she stood near the cross, watching Jesus die. But at each stage she grew and saw her Lord more clearly.

The way in which Jesus showed his concern and compassion for Mary is a model of filial love and support. Jesus addressed her first, before turning to John. He respected her dignity, and he did so in a timely fashion. He was considerate. Jesus cared for more than her physical needs. He showed how to care for others with love and compassion. Augustine recognized Jesus's example of moral responsibility: "The very Master of the saints set the example" for us how we should be willing to love those whom the Lord has entrusted into our care.[3]

On the cross Jesus proved that love embraces family responsibility. He not only fulfilled the fifth commandment, but he surpassed it. Now "the tie that binds our hearts in Christian love" goes beyond our biological family to the body of Christ. Jesus's concern for Mary fits with his promise, "Truly, I say to you, there is no one who has left house or brothers or sisters or mother or father or children or lands, for my sake and the gospel, who will not receive a hundredfold now in this time, houses and brothers and sisters and mothers and children and lands, with persecutions, and in the age to come eternal life" (Mark 10:29–31). Jesus goes beyond honoring his mother when he defines a new relationship for Mary: "Woman, behold, your son!"

In his final moments on the cross, Jesus gave his mother into the care of a beloved disciple. He turned to John and said simply, "Here is your mother." In that moment, we are reminded that the gospel embraces the fullness of life (Jas 1:27). Does anyone expect to draw near the cross and leave without a responsibility? Nailed to the cross, Jesus was silent of all pain and bitterness, but when it came to the gospel, he was not silent. At the cross Jesus declared forgiveness for his enemies, salvation for the repentant, and affection for the needy.

4. "MY GOD, MY GOD, WHY HAVE YOU FORSAKEN ME?" (MARK 15:33–39)

The brevity and intensity of Mark's description heightens the drama of the cross. He leads us into the passion of Christ's cross, into its darkness and trauma. Of all the words of the cross, this is the hardest one to hear. Charles Spurgeon describes the fourth word as "measureless, unfathomable, inconceivable. The anguish of the Savior on your behalf and mine is no more to be measured and weighed than the sin which needed it, or the love which endureth it."[4]

Jesus cried out to God in a loud voice, "My God, my God, why have you forsaken me?" This word from the cross has no prior reference in Jesus's public ministry. Until Gethsemane, there was no hint of pain or tension between the Father and the Son. Jesus's ministry had been marked by an absolute oneness with the Father. The very essence of Jesus's ministry was his fellowship with the Father. Everything he did reflected this immediate and intimate relationship (Matt 11:27; Luke 9:35; John 14:6). Even in Gethsemane, Jesus experienced fellowship with the Father. He prayed repeatedly, "My Father, if it be possible, let this cup pass from me; nevertheless, not as I will, but as you will" (Matt 26:39). He was completely in sync with the Father's will as he said to Peter, "Do you think I cannot appeal to my Father, and he will at once send me more than twelve legions of angels? But how then should the Scriptures be fulfilled, that it must be so?" (Matt 26:53–54).

Jesus knew from the outset that he was headed to the cross, and he knew why, "For even the Son of Man came not to be served but to serve, and to give his life as a ransom for many" (Mark 10:45). The one in whom fellowship with the Father was his right by virtue of his being, and the one in whom fellowship with the Father was his right by virtue of his faithfulness and obedience, was completely forsaken and totally abandoned by the Father *because of us*. Instead of being honored, he was condemned; instead of being praised, he was accused (Isa 53:4–6, 10).

There have been many throughout salvation history who have cried out to God, asking the heart-rending, soul-searching question, "Why?" Sometimes the line between devotion and defiance seems thin. When Moses asked "Why?" he sounded like an adolescent son angry at his father: "O Lord, why have you done evil to this people? Why did you ever send me?" (Exod 5:22; see Josh 7:7; Judg 6:13). Those who have not walked with God through intense struggles may find Job's "Why?" troubling. His lament's radical honesty is unnerving. "If I sin, what do I do to you, you watcher of mankind? Why have you made me your mark? Why have I become a burden to you?" (Job 7:20). Or "Why do you hide your face and count me as your enemy?" (Job 13:24).

The Psalms make the "Why?" of lament and confusion a catalyst for true worship. True worship neither hides nor parades the "Why?" of honest lamentation. The prophet Jeremiah asked

"Why?" not for himself alone, but on behalf of the people of God (Jer 20:18). At times Jeremiah felt like God was a stranger: "Why should you be like a stranger in the land, like a traveler who turns aside to tarry for a night?" (Jer 14:8). He lamented, "Why do you always forget us? Why do you forsake us for so long?" (Lam 5:20 NIV).

The redeeming quality found in all of these heart-rending pleas is devotion directed to God. From Moses to Jeremiah, they cry out to God, "My God! My God!" They are not accusing God behind his back; they are crying out to God in his presence. The power of the lament can be measured by the intensity of the relationship to God. But of all the lamentations, all the cries of anguish from God's people, there is none more poignant, more impassioned, than Jesus's cry from the cross, "My God, my God, why have you forsaken me?" This one cry embraces and comprehends all the lamentations of all God's people throughout all of time. All other cries of anguish, all other Gethsemanes, both before and after the cross, look to this moment for resolution. It is as if Jesus literally gathered up all the lamentations of God's people and shouted them from the cross in a loud voice.

Abraham's unspoken anguish on Mount Moriah when he was asked to sacrifice his son Isaac is echoed in the cry of Jesus. Job's passion, the cry of a righteous man afflicted beyond measure for the cause of God, can be heard in the cry of Jesus from the cross. David's utter feeling of desperation and disorientation became the very words of Jesus on the cross.

The difference between their feelings of anguish and abandonment and Jesus's experience of godforsakenness was that they all *felt* like God had rejected them, but in reality, God had never been closer. God may have seemed to withdraw his protective presence, the evidence of his providential care, the demonstration of his redeeming love, but this was only for a time. What felt like utter abandonment was in reality God's special attention. In what seemed to be God's absence, Abraham, Job, and David proved their faithfulness to God, in the absence of any worldly reason for their commitment. At the right time, God made himself known in a deeper and more profound way than they could have imagined. As Job said in the end, "I know that you can do all things, and that no purpose of yours can be thwarted. ... I had heard of you by the hearing of the ear, but now my eyes see you" (Job 42:2, 5).

Elijah was delivered from death and taken to heaven in a whirlwind. When Stephen, one of the church's early martyrs, was dying, he beheld the glory of God and Jesus. "Behold, I see the heavens opened, and the Son of Man standing at the right hand of God" (Acts 7:56). This was not the case for Jesus. He saw no vision of heaven from the cross (see 1 Pet 3:19). Utterly abandoned by God, he suffered like the worst sinner who ever lived. He suffered the same as if he had gone to the grave damning God with his last breath.

No one ever said, "My God, my God, why have you forsaken me?" the way Jesus said it. No one ever experienced the fellowship of the Father the way Jesus did, and no one experienced the judgment for depravity the way Jesus did. Jesus's agony of soul was ultimately and most intensely spiritual. Spurgeon explains, "Grief of mind is harder to bear than pain of body. ... Spiritual sorrows are the worst of mental miseries. ... We can bear a bleeding body, and even a wounded spirit, but a soul conscious of desertion by God is beyond conception unendurable."[5] The crisis of Gethsemane and the pain of the cross were Jesus's experience of being forsaken by God. He deliberately identified with our sin and our alienation from God. In Gethsemane he anticipated the wrath of God, and on the cross he took it on himself. "For our sake he made him to be sin who knew no sin, so that in him we might become the righteousness of God" (2 Cor 5:21). "He was delivered over to death for our sins and was raised to life for our justification" (Rom 4:25 NIV). "He himself bore our sins in his body on the tree, that we might die to sin and live to righteousness. By his wounds you have been healed"(1 Pet 2:24). The intensity of his struggle came not from a fear of death, but from his separation from the Father. Spurgeon writes,

> This marks the lowest depth of the Savior's grief. The desertion was real. ... It was no delirium of mind, caused by weakness of body, the depression of his spirit, or the near approach of death. His mind was clear to the last. He bore up under pain, loss of blood, scorn, thirst, and desolation. ... All the tortures on His body He endured in silence; but when it came to being forsaken by God, then His great heart burst out. ... It was a real absence he mourned.[6]

This was a *singular* and absolutely unique desertion. Never before had the Father abandoned the Son. This godforsakenness could only be described as *terrible*. For one who knew the intimacy of the Father's fellowship (Matt 11:27), this must have been agonizing. We cannot say "that Jesus felt abandoned but was not truly abandoned," especially when we believe that Jesus lived in the most intimate fellowship possible with the Father. It seems impossible for Jesus not to have known that he was utterly abandoned because of our sin.[7] The Father's abandonment of the Son in that hour was absolutely real.

Jesus's cry from the cross was met with confusion and confession. The cynical bystanders misconstrued it as a plea for help from Elijah, giving them another excuse to taunt and ridicule Jesus. They filled a sponge with wine vinegar and poked it in his face, saying, "Let's see if Elijah comes to take him down." But the Roman centurion, "who stood there in front of Jesus" and "saw how he died," was deeply moved by the experience (Mark 15:39 NIV). He "praised God, saying, 'Certainly this man was innocent!'" (Luke 23:47). Mark describes the centurion's testimony more dramatically: "Truly this man was the Son of God!" (Mark 15:39). No other human being in the Gospel of Mark uses this title for Jesus. The title is used by God at Jesus's baptism (Mark 1:11), at the transfiguration (9:7), and "by demons on several occasions (Mark 3:11; 5:7; 1:24, 34), but never by a human character (the demoniacs are pictured as being used by the demons as mouthpieces)."[8]

The startling truth is that at that very moment when Jesus hung dying on the cross, when our Savior not only felt godforsaken but was in fact godforsaken because of our sin, the Roman centurion, who was in charge of the crucifixion, confessed the true identity of the one who hung dying. Spurgeon concludes, "You shall measure the height of His love, if it be ever measured, by the depth of His grief, if that can ever be known."[9]

5. "I THIRST" (JOHN 19:28–30)

The fifth saying from the cross is a final exclamation of the Incarnate One. Literally one word in the original, it underscores the humanity of Jesus. Moments before he died, Jesus offered a final testimony to the reality of his humanity. It is an exclamation mark to the incarnation, a commentary on the human dilemma, and a powerful lesson in true spirituality.

John informs his readers, "Later, knowing that everything had now been finished, and so that the Scripture would be fulfilled, Jesus said, 'I am thirsty'" (John 19:28 NIV; see 13:1). In time, the disciples became aware of the many divinely orchestrated details surrounding the cross. They discovered in the Old Testament numerous pointers that confirmed the circumstances experienced in the trial and crucifixion. Jesus's death was not following a script, but there was a convergence of circumstances beyond human control that pointed the apostles to the sovereign, redemptive plan of God at work. They were impressed by the prophetic preview of Jesus's passion, particularly in the Psalms. They read the Psalms in a new light, finding in Israel's prayerbook details that confirmed that the cross was not an accident of history but God's well-laid-out plan. Every detail was significant, every act purposeful, and every utterance meaningful.

Thirst is a potent metaphor in the Bible. The physical experience of thirst is analogous to our spiritual need for God (Pss 42:1–2; 63:1). This fifth saying from the cross is not metaphoric but literal. It describes Jesus's desperate physical condition. Thirst is often the last physical symptom mentioned by the dying. The heart may be failing, the brain may be shutting down, but it is the experience of thirst that is felt. After surgery, the first thing a patient often experiences is an acute sensation of thirst, and the most immediate relief comes by moistening the patient's lips with a lemon swab.

Jesus was on the verge of death when he gasped, "I thirst." Jesus's physical trauma began in Gethsemane, where Luke reports that Jesus's "sweat was like drops of blood" (Luke 22:44 NIV). This bloody sweat "may occur in highly emotional states or in persons with bleeding disorders."[10] He was tried before the Sanhedrin, blindfolded, and beaten. He was struck with fists and forced to walk two-and-half miles (Mark 14:65). He was flogged with a short whip with leather thongs embedded with small iron balls or sharp pieces of sheep bones. The lacerations were severe enough to cause blood loss and were intended to weaken the victim to prevent resistance. In his weakened condition, Jesus was unable to carry his cross a third of a mile to Golgotha. The five-to-seven-inch tapered spikes were driven through his wrists between the carpals and radius, rather than the palms. His feet were fastened to the cross with one spike through the top of each foot. The nerve damage alone caused excruciating bolts of pain in both arms and legs. On the cross his body weight pulled down on his muscles, making breathing, especially exhaling, nearly impossible. Searing pain, intense muscle cramps, dehydration, hypovolemic shock, exhaustion asphyxia, stress-induced arrhythmias, and congestive heart failure were excruciating (the Latin word *excuciatus* means literally "out of the cross"). "Death by crucifixion was, in every sense of the word, excruciating."[11]

All that Jesus endured physically on the cross is summed up in an utterance, "I thirst." He identified with the desperate, fallen human condition. "And being found in human form, he humbled himself by becoming obedient to the point of death, even death on a cross" (Phil 2:8). Jesus waited to the very end to comment about his physical condition. The order of Jesus's sayings from the cross may be significant. He spoke words of forgiveness, salvation, affection, and spiritual anguish before he mentioned his physical condition. The physical rigors and discipline of Jesus's ministry assured his physical stamina. The portrayals of a weak and wimpy cinematic Jesus are out of character compared to the biblical Jesus. Strength of soul mattered most to Jesus, but his body was in good physical condition. Jesus prioritized the spiritual over the physical when he said, "Do not be anxious about your life, what you will eat or what you will drink, nor about your body, what you will put on. Is not life more than food, and the body more than clothing?" (Matt 6:25). But the priority of the spiritual over the physical does not depreciate the physical. The purpose of the incarnation and the cross was to redeem the entire person, body, mind, and soul.

Early Christian heretics depreciated human physicality. They alternated between depriving the flesh and indulging the flesh. They mistakenly assumed that the body could be divorced from the soul. The beauty and power of Christ's redemption is that it restores the physical side of life to its true spiritual, God-centered significance. Jesus assumed every aspect of our humanity in order to redeem all of our humanity. Gregory of Nazianzus argued that, if Christ was not completely man, then our salvation is incomplete: "What he did not assume, he did not heal [or redeem]."[12] Jesus endured our weaknesses in order to empower our sanctification. As Hebrews says, "For we do not have a high priest who is unable to sympathize with our weaknesses, but one who in every respect has been tempted as we are, yet without sin" (Heb 4:15).

Jesus's "I thirst" offers insight into the meaning of the cross by emphasizing the physical condition of human suffering, the fullness of God's redemptive plan, and the importance of the disciplined mind. We are reminded that following Jesus can be physically demanding. "I thirst" underscores the physical cost of following Jesus. His fifth saying from the cross uses thirst as a potent metaphor for life. There is only one way to satisfy the thirst for life. Jesus said to the woman at the well, "If you knew the gift of God and who it is that is saying to you, 'Give me a drink,' you would have asked him, and he would have given you living water" (John 4:10). The risen Lord Jesus is the only one who can satisfy our thirst for life.

6. "IT IS FINISHED" (JOHN 19:28–37)

Jesus's identification with us in our suffering is significant, but his sacrifice for our sin remains the primary purpose of the cross. We all have sinned and fallen short of the glory of God, and we are justified "by his grace as a gift, through the redemption that is in Christ Jesus" (Rom 3:24). This is true because God presented Jesus "as a propitiation by his blood, to be received by faith" (Rom 3:25). And again, "God shows his love for us in that while were still sinners, Christ died for us" (Rom 5:8).

The Savior said, "It is finished," because he is the sacrifice that makes our salvation possible. The significance of the sixth saying of the Savior has everything to do with the identity and the purpose of the one who uttered these words. The power behind Jesus's cry "It is finished" lies in who said it and why. Jesus laid out the overarching purpose for his incarnation from the beginning: "For even the Son of Man came not to be served but to serve, and to give his life as a ransom for many" (Mark 10:45). Following Peter's confession, "You are the Christ, the Son of the living God," Jesus "began to explain to his disciples that he must go to Jerusalem and suffer many things" and "that he must be killed and on the third day be raised to life" (Matt 16:16, 21 NIV). The meaning of the atonement takes us well beyond Jesus's identification with us in our suffering. Jesus is more than a fellow sufferer or a hero or a martyr. He is the Savior. "If Christianity was something we were making up," writes C. S. Lewis, "of course we could make it easier. But it is not. We cannot compete, in simplicity, with people who are inventing religions. How could we? We are dealing with Fact. Of course, anyone can be simple if he has no facts to bother about."[13]

The Father's will and the purpose of Jesus's life could only be fulfilled through his atoning sacrifice on the cross. This is the reason Luke records, "When the days drew near for him to be taken up, he set his face to go to Jerusalem" (Luke 9:51).

This is why Jesus instituted the Lord's table: "This cup that is poured out for you is the new covenant in my blood" (Luke 22:20). This is why he prayed in Gethsemane, "Father, if you are willing, remove this cup from me. Nevertheless, not my will, but yours be done" (Luke 22:42). The meaning of the cross loomed large in Jesus's mind, not as a painful end to a challenging ministry, but as the sacrificial atonement for the sins of the world. "For God so loved the world, that he gave his one and only Son, that whoever believes in him should not perish but have eternal life" (John 3:16).

The author of Hebrews declares the meaning explicitly:

> Long ago, at many times and in many ways, God spoke to our fathers by the prophets, but in these last days he has spoken to us by his Son, whom he appointed the heir of all things, through whom also he created the world. He is the radiance of the glory of God and the exact imprint of his nature, and he upholds the universe by the word of his power. After making purification for sins, he sat down at the right hand of the Majesty on high. (Heb 1:1–3)

"It is finished" is a statement that gains significance because of who said it and why. It is a victory cry uttered by the one who fulfilled the Father's will completely (see John 17:4). The sixth cross saying can be translated, "It is accomplished!" This is Jesus's last saying from the cross in John's Gospel, and the apostle "interprets his suffering and dying as the crowning conclusion and high point of the work that he has performed in obedience—the obedience of the Son finds here its most radical expression and enables the believing eye to see the glorifying of the Son through the Father."[14] Oswald Chambers exclaims, "The greatest note of triumph ever sounded in the ears of a startled

universe was that sounded on the Cross of Christ—'It is finished.' That is the final word in the redemption of humankind."[15]

"It is finished" marks the climax of salvation history. Here is
"the Lamb that was slain from the creation of the world" (Rev
13:8 NIV). It was anticipated in Abel's sacrifice and Abraham
on Mount Moriah. It was foreshadowed in Israel's Passover
lamb and in exodus from bondage. It was envisioned in the
tabernacle's sacrificial system and the Day of Atonement. It
lies behind Job's ash-heap theology and Isaiah's suffering servant. These were all shadows of anticipation pointing toward
Christ's atoning sacrifice. "But he has appeared once for all at
the culmination of the ages to do away with sin by the sacrifice
of himself" (Heb 9:26 NIV).

Christ's death on the cross is the conclusion that salvation
history had long anticipated. C. S. Lewis offers a helpful analogy
to illustrate this redemptive climax:

> Let us suppose we possess parts of a novel or a sym-
> phony. Someone now brings us a newly discovered piece
> of manuscript and says, "This is the missing part of the
> work. This is the chapter on which the whole plot of
> the novel really turned. This is the main theme of the
> symphony." Our business would be to see whether the
> new passage, if admitted to the central place which the
> discoverer claimed for it, did actually illuminate all the
> parts we had already seen and "pull them together." Nor
> should we be likely to go very far wrong. The new pas-
> sage, if spurious, however attractive it looked at the first
> glance, would become harder and harder to reconcile
> with the rest of the work and the longer we considered
> the matter. But if it were genuine, then at every fresh
> hearing of the music or every fresh reading of the book,

we should find it settling down, making itself more at home, and eliciting significance from all sorts of details in the whole work which we had hitherto neglected. Even though the new central chapter or main theme contained great difficulties in itself, we should still think it genuine provided that it continually removed difficulties elsewhere.[16]

All the types, prophecies, and promises found in the Bible find their conclusion and fulfillment in the cross of Christ. The apostle declares, "In him we have redemption through his blood, the forgiveness of our trespasses, according to the riches of God's grace, which he lavished upon us, in all wisdom and insight" (Eph 1:7–8). The finished work of Christ on the cross is the most important reality of history. Lewis says it well:

We believe that the death of Christ is just that point in history at which something absolutely unimaginable from outside shows through into our own world. And if we cannot picture even the atoms of which our own world is built, of course we are not going to be able to picture this. ... A person can eat his dinner without understanding exactly how food nourishes him. A person can accept what Christ has done without knowing how it works: indeed, he certainly would not know how it works until he accepted it.[17]

Charles Spurgeon declares that it is important to tell the world, "It is finished!" Go tell all "those who are torturing themselves, thinking that through obedience and mortification" they can somehow earn their salvation. People all over the earth are thinking that they can make themselves more acceptable to God by punishing themselves and doing penance. "Cease, false worshiper, Cease!" cries Spurgeon. "God neither asks nor accepts any other sacrifice than that which Christ offered once for all upon the cross."[18] Spurgeon insists that we should also go to the churchgoer who feels that by attending church services and doing good deeds he is making himself more acceptable to God. Does he not know that "all our righteous deeds are like a polluted garment" (Isa 64:6)? "Why will you pin your rags to the fine linen of Christ's righteousness? Why improve on what is finished! ... Go to the poor, despairing wretch, who has given himself up, not for death merely, but for damnation— he who says, 'I cannot escape from sin, and I cannot be saved from its punishment.' Say to him, 'Sinner, the way of salvation is finished once for all.' "

Spurgeon continues, "Go, as well, to the poor souls, who love the Savior, but don't have the assurance of their salvation. Why, we have hundreds and thousands that really are converted, who do not know that 'it is finished.' They never know that they are safe. ... They think they have faith today, but perhaps they may become unbelieving tomorrow. They do not know that 'it is finished.'" "Child of God," Spurgeon pleads, "will you have Christ's finished righteousness right now, and will you rejoice in it more than you ever have done before?"[19]

7. "FATHER, INTO YOUR HANDS I COMMIT MY SPIRIT" (LUKE 23:44–24:8)

The meaning of the cross is not in the eye of the beholder, but in the voice of Jesus, who spoke from the cross. Augustine suggests that Jesus turned the cross into a pulpit from which he preached the gospel. The meaning of the cross is specific and definable. The Holy Spirit reveals the truth of the cross of Christ. It means the free gift of forgiveness, the catalyst for our repentance, the provision for our redemption, and the sacrifice necessary for our salvation.

The significance of what transpired on the cross rests in the identity of Jesus. Was he a traveling preacher from Galilee, a nonconformist rabbi, a spiritual revolutionary who was ahead of his time, or is he the Christ, the Son of the Living God? Is he the Incarnate One, the Word made flesh, the Alpha and Omega, the Great Shepherd of the sheep, the Savior of the world? By God's grace, we have come to take him at his word. Jesus says, "I am the way, the truth, and the life" (John 14:6). We agree with the disciples who declared, "Lord, to whom shall we go? You have the words of eternal life, and we have believed, and have come to know, that you are the Holy One of God" (John 6:68–69).

Each of Jesus's sayings from the cross focuses on the scope of God's great salvation. "Father, forgive them, for they know not what they do" emphasizes the mercy of God, not only to those who were there, but to us who are here. "Surely he took up our pain and bore our suffering, yet we considered him punished by God, stricken by him, and afflicted. But he was pierced for our transgressions, he was crushed for our iniquities; the punishment that brought us peace was on him, and by his wounds we are healed" (Isa 53:4–5 NIV).

The words of Jesus to the repentant thief who feared God, "Truly, I say to you, today you will be with me in paradise," captures the quickness of the gospel of grace to rescue the perishing, care for the dying. No one, absolutely no one, is outside the scope of God's redemptive provision in Jesus Christ. Make no mistake, this good news is for you, "for there is no other name under heaven given among men by which we must be saved" (Acts 4:12).

The holistic character of the gospel is evident in Jesus's third saying from the cross, "Woman, behold your son." The work of salvation does not deny the physical, relational, and emotional self. From the cross, Jesus not only saved our souls, but he inspired our service. We are commissioned to preach the gospel, and we are commanded to love our neighbor as ourselves.

The fourth saying of Jesus from the cross encompasses what Jesus experienced for us spiritually in his godforsakenness, "My God, my God, why have you forsaken me?" What the prophet said is still true: we consider "him stricken, smitten by God, and afflicted. ... All we like sheep have gone astray; we have turned—every one—to his own way; and the LORD has laid on him the iniquity of us all" (Isa 53:4, 6).

The fifth saying reveals the full extent of his physical suffering, summarily expressed in his dying comment, "I thirst." There is no part of the human trauma that Jesus did not experience. He assumed it all and redeemed it all.

The sixth saying gathers up the full sweep of salvation history from the Passover lamb to the passion and pronounces, "It is finished." "The Lamb who was slain from the creation of the world" (Rev 13:8 NIV) has "appeared once for all at the end of the ages to put away sin by the sacrifice of himself" (Heb 9:26). "For the wages of sin is death, but the free gift of God is eternal life in Christ Jesus our Lord" (Rom 6:23).

The power of the resurrection establishes each one of these sayings from the cross. If Jesus Christ was not raised from the dead, there is no forgiveness, no offer of salvation, no comfort in the midst of sorrow, no resolution of spiritual anguish, no provision for pain, and no redemption for the soul. Apart from the resurrection, we have a Buddhist lesson in suffering, an Islamic example of martyrdom, a Jewish act of nonconformist zeal, and a humanist illustration of fate. As the apostle Paul bluntly says,

"And if Christ has not been raised, then our preaching is in vain and your faith is in vain" (1 Cor 15:14).

Jesus died on Friday, but by Sunday he was explaining the meaning of his sacrificial death to two of his followers heading home from Jerusalem to Emmaus. Before leaving Jerusalem, they heard reports that the tomb was empty. "Some women of our company amazed us," they said. "They came back saying that they had even seen a vision of angels, who said that he was alive" (Luke 24:22–23). That they left Jerusalem and were returning to Emmaus may indicate what they thought of the women's report. They were discouraged and confused, unaware that they were in the presence of their risen Lord, but Jesus expected to find believing believers, not downcast, unbelieving believers. Jesus offered them no sympathy for their confusion, no solace for their grieving spirits. He declared, "O foolish ones, and slow of heart to believe all that the prophets have spoken! Was it not necessary that the Christ should suffer these things and enter into his glory?" (Luke 24:25–26). Along the way, Jesus recounted the facts, discussed the truths, and explained the Scriptures. Eventually, they recognized him. When he took bread, gave thanks, broke it, and began to give it to them, they knew it was him. Yet it wasn't the appearance of Jesus alone that impressed them as much as their conversation with Jesus. "They said to each other, 'Did not our hearts burn within us while he talked to us on the road, while he opened to us the Scriptures?' " (Luke 24:32).

In the end, either Jesus on the cross is a picture of human fate without hope, or he is the atoning sacrifice that we accept by faith, and Jesus himself helps us decide. We cannot be persuaded or convinced of the meaning of Jesus's death and resurrection apart from God at work. What Jesus did for those two disciples, he wants to do for us. Through the Holy Spirit, he seeks to bring us to faith and trust in him. As the apostle Paul says, "My message and my preaching were not with wise and persuasive words, but with a demonstration of the Spirit's power, so that your faith might not rest on human wisdom, but on God's power." Paul adds, "What we have received is not the spirit of the world, but the Spirit who is from God, so that we may understand what God has freely given us" (1 Cor 2:4–5, 12 NIV).

The final word from the cross unites the meaning of Jesus's death and the reality of his resurrection. They are bound together, meaning and truth, inseparable. Instead of a final word of anguish, Jesus uttered a declaration of hope: "Father, into your hands I commit my spirit." Instead of giving up, Jesus offered himself up; instead of surrendering to fate, he committed himself to God in faith. The final word is not a word of resignation, but of resurrection; not a sigh of relief, but a prayer of confidence.

This final word belongs to Jesus. Only he can speak to the Father as he did, because only Jesus can say, "I and the Father are one" (John 10:30). Only he can declare, "I am the way, the truth, and the life. No one comes to the Father except through me" (John 14:6). He who suffered at the hands of evil men (Luke 9:44; 18:32; 20:19; 22:53; 24:7) gives himself into the hands of the Father. Only he who offered his life as an atoning sacrifice can entrust himself in this way to the Father. Only Jesus can claim, "The Father knows me and I know the Father— and I lay down my life for the sheep" (John 10:15 NIV). Only Jesus can say, "For this reason the Father loves me, because I lay down my life that I may take it up again. No one takes it from me, but I lay it down of my own accord. I have authority to lay it down, and I have authority to take it up again. This charge I have received from my Father" (John 10:17–18).

Jesus's seventh and final word from the cross echoes David's prayer: "Into your hand I commit my spirit; you have redeemed me, O LORD, faithful God" (Ps 31:5). David placed his faith in God to deliver and protect.[20] David prayed for deliverance from death. Jesus prayed for deliverance through death. His resurrection makes it possible for us to pray, "Father, into your hands we commit our spirits." Stephen, the first Christian martyr, prayed, "Lord Jesus, receive my spirit" (Acts 7:59). Pastors have a unique privilege to share the meaning of the cross and the power of Christ's atoning sacrifice within the household of faith. I believe this can and must be done through the Spirit with emotional and intellectual power so that hearts are moved, minds informed, spirits lifted, and lives transformed. The power of the cross can crush the hard heart and comfort the wounded soul.

Unless I see in his hands the mark of the nails, and
place my finger into the mark of the nails, and
place my hand into his side, I will never believe.

John 20:25

Let us not mock God with metaphor, analogy,
sidestepping transcendence; making of
the event a parable, a sign painted in
the faded credulity of earlier ages.

John Updike, *Telephone Poles and Other Poems*

9

Easter Sermons

Easter is a big deal. Every Sunday is resurrection Sunday, but once a year we celebrate Christ's resurrection in a special way, on Easter. Pastors work hard on their Easter message. Everyone packs into the sanctuary expecting something special. I want to resist the pressure to try to embellish and impress and *knock people's socks off.* I want to stay within the text, within my gifts, and keep the focus where it belongs—on the risen Lord. The church I served in Bloomington, Indiana, celebrated Easter by making it into a major evangelistic outreach effort. We rented a large auditorium at the university so we could accommodate our regular Sunday-morning worshipers plus hundreds from the community. We advertised the event, recruited volunteers for parking and ushering, and worked hard to make the music special. We prayed about every aspect of the Easter service. I spent hours working on the Easter sermon. But looking back, I have some regrets. I tried too hard to get people's attention. Instead of focusing on our worship, I tried to orchestrate an event.

My text was Acts 17, Paul's evangelistic message at the Areopagus, when the apostle challenged Athenian religiosity and idolatry. He used their shrine to "an unknown god" as a bridge to launch a powerful witness to the gospel. Paul challenged Athenian idolatry, so I challenged American idolatry. On the auditorium stage we erected a free-standing cross surrounded by various symbols of our cultural idols. As I recall, we had a lot of paraphernalia on the platform—a boat, a surfboard, a bike, a basketball hoop, and a bunch of stuff. Indiana University was at the height of basketball season, and when I walked on stage, I was bouncing a basketball. I wore a white lab coat to symbolize, as I explained in the sermon, that truth was not limited to the empirical scientists. The truest of all truth was revealed in God's word.

I do not regret the sermon I preached that day, but I regret the artificial distractions that I built into the service on that special day. I substituted a shallow spectacle for respectful reflection. I was on the verge of performing instead of preaching, treating people as an audience rather than true worshipers and genuine seekers. Looking back, my positive memory is of the older saints who were patient and supportive even though I had engineered an awkward day. They cut a young pastor some slack that day, and I am grateful.

Tim Keller says the difference between a good sermon and a great sermon is the Holy Spirit. Preachers are responsible for the difference between a bad sermon and a good sermon. We have our work cut out for us: "Understanding the biblical text, distilling a clear outline and theme, developing a persuasive argument, enriching it with poignant illustrations, metaphors, and practical examples, incisively analyzing heart motives and cultural assumptions, making specific application to real life—all of this takes extensive labor." All of this is the preacher's responsibility, and it involves hard work, practice, prayer, and plenty of spiritual discipline. But "the difference between good preaching and great preaching lies mainly in the work of the Holy Spirit in the heart of the listener as well as the preacher."[1]

Lent is forty days plus seven Sundays. The reason Sundays are excluded from the cross-centered Lenten focus is that every Sunday is resurrection Sunday. This is why it has always been important to me to preach the Sunday after Easter. If a person who is seeking Christ comes on Easter Sunday and is moved by the gospel message, I do not want them to return the next Sunday and wonder what happened to all the energy, passion, and joy. I do not want them to feel that the church decided to take the Sunday after Easter off. I want every Sunday to feel as important as Easter Sunday.

Easter is the climax of the church's journey to the cross. Costly discipleship is rooted in the crucified and risen Messiah. Seven Lenten sermons frame a liturgy of the cross, and sermons on Palm Sunday, Maundy Thursday, and Good Friday bring the people of God to the foot of the cross. On Easter Sunday morning we gather to celebrate the empty tomb, the risen Lord, and the coming King.

THE FIRST EASTER

The first Easter Sunday morning began sad and sober. All the disciples awoke filled with grief and uncertainty. The two Marys "went to see the tomb" (Matt 28:1). It was still dark as they walked to the tomb carrying spices to embalm the body. They were crying as they walked, wondering how they were going to move the large stone blocking the entrance to the tomb. Suddenly a violent earthquake shook the earth, but the earthquake did not roll back the stone sealing the tomb; an angel did. The angel of the Lord came down from heaven and "rolled back the stone and sat on it" (Matt 28:2). On that very first Easter there was no need for any added drama or man-made hype. Extravagant musical performances came much later. Earthquakes and angels marked the occasion. The Roman guards fled when the angels appeared.

The story of the first Easter spotlights Mary Magdalene as she stands outside the tomb weeping. A contrived narrative would not have highlighted women as the principal witnesses in the unfolding and unexpected Easter drama. In Mary's mind, the body of Jesus was stolen, desecrated, and unceremoniously dumped somewhere. There was no shortage of realism in Mary's imagination. She imagined the worst as she looked inside the tomb. She beheld two angels in white, "sitting where the body of Jesus had lain, one at the head and one at the feet" (John 20:12). "Woman, why are you weeping?" the angels asked. Mary sobbed, "They have taken away my Lord, and I do not know where they have laid him" (John 20:13). Her heartache was palpable.

Mary turned around to see the gardener. Through her tear-filled eyes she did not recognize Jesus. He asked, "Woman, why are you weeping? Whom are you seeking?" She said, "Sir, if you have carried him away, tell me where you have laid him, and I will take him away" (John 20:15). Each word in her insensible comment is burdened with weariness and perplexity. She was willing to do anything to assuage her grief. But Jesus only needed to speak her name, "Mary." She knew the voice of Jesus. Mary cried out, "Rabboni!" "Teacher!" Person-to-person with her risen Lord, Mary was confronted by a resurrection reality that no one imagined. Her resurrection faith was independent of religious aesthetics and homiletical drama.

One wonders whether our Easter efforts are not designed to cushion the blow of modern disbelief. The spectacle overshadows the underlying question, Does anyone really believe this stuff anymore? Probably not, unless you hear your name on the lips of Jesus, unless you have become convinced of the reality of the resurrection by the power of the Spirit of God.

The women ran to Peter and John to say, "They have taken the Lord out of the tomb, and we do not know where they have laid him" (John 20:2). When Peter and John ran to the tomb and discovered its emptiness along with the discarded grave clothes, they took note of the evidence. John saw and believed. Faith dawned in a troubled heart that was not predisposed to believe. Suddenly the tomb's emptiness filled John's mind with meaning, and reality shifted in his world.

The sadness of the two Marys gave way to fear as they hurried back to tell the disciples. Matthew says that they were afraid yet filled with "great joy" (Matt 28:8). The phrase captures our experience of Easter this year—every year. Like these two early disciples, we are afraid yet filled with great joy. In the throes of life's struggles we are afraid, but in the midst of our human frailty and vulnerability, we rest in the resurrection power of Jesus Christ. Mark ends his account of the resurrection with a description of the women. They "fled from the tomb, for trembling and astonishment had seized them, and they said nothing to anyone, for they were afraid" (Mark 16:8). The women ran back to tell the disciples, who were in lockdown for fear of a crackdown on Jesus's followers. We can identify with the disciples longing for the immediacy of Jesus's presence. The stark reality of faith in the bodily resurrection of Jesus will not be overshadowed by a musical extravaganza, spring fashions, and Easter dinner.

There is no humanistic explanation for the transition from grief's resignation to resurrection hope. The first Easter, and every other real Easter ever since, lies on the fault line between unbelief and belief. Easter does not celebrate the great assumptions shared by Christendom crowds. The tragedy of the fallen human condition, in all of its pain and sorrow, causes all Christians, not just preachers, to point to the reality of the risen Lord Jesus Christ. Easter celebrates the truth of the one who said, "I am the resurrection and the life. Whoever believes in me, though he die, yet shall he live, and everyone who lives and believes in me shall never die" (John 11:25–26). If we waited for the tragedy of our human frailty and vulnerability to run its course before celebrating Easter, we would be waiting for the second coming of Christ. Easter should always take us back to the grief and sorrow of the first Easter and fill us with resurrection hope. There is an answer to the stillness of a poised and anxious sorrow: Easter joy.

THE EMPTY TOMB

The empty tomb of Jesus is emblematic of *all* meaningfulness. It is the only emptiness that fills history and creation with meaning. The bodily resurrection of Jesus rolls away the stone of nihilism and materialism and opens the way to the beauty and mystery of life itself. Christ's death atones for our sins; Christ's life assures our salvation. Jesus Christ is the source and goal of all creation, and the source and goal of all redemption.[2]

Our natural tendency may be to reduce the gospel to human-interest stories that say more about us than they do about the Lord. Why settle for inspirational talks that feature a cameo appearance of Jesus when we can explore the whole counsel of God? We would never think of equating a television sitcom with the drama of real life. Why do we settle for anything less than in-depth thinking and preaching when it comes to the reality of the resurrection of Christ? We should want to explore the complexity of God's creation and revel in the mystery of God's resurrection power. Instead of dumbing down the gospel, we should be striving to understand its marvelous depth.

Paradoxically, as we become more sophisticated in our methods of communication, we seem to become more simplistic in our communication of the gospel. As the speed and accessibility of communications have increased, so has our apparent impatience with the meaning of the gospel itself. We expect physics and math to be complex—why not the truth of God's revelation? So, instead of reducing the gospel to sound bites, we ought to grasp the whole counsel of God and wrestle with "the manifold wisdom of God" (Eph 3:10).

Faith does not operate in a different realm from sight. Faith is the earnest expectation of sight. In the most real world, the two are inseparably linked and inherent in objective reality. "Without faith," writes the author of Hebrews, "it is impossible to please him, for whoever would draw near to God must believe that he exists and that he rewards those who seek him" (Heb 11:6). Sight does not create that which is seen, nor does faith create that which is believed. If seeing meant believing for the first disciples, then believing means seeing for today's disciples. The resurrection of Christ is a fact of science and history that is believed by faith. If the resurrection of Christ did not actually happen in real time and real history, the apostle Paul spelled out the verdict: our faith is useless, and we are guilty of bearing false witness. We are still in our sins, and we are lost, without hope in the world. "If only for this life we have hope in Christ, we are of all people most to be pitied" (1 Cor 15:19 NIV).

There is order, beauty, meaning, and joy woven into the very nature of creation. Everything points to a complexity that is neither random nor lucky. There is an inherent revelatory quality in all aspects of life. Creation is always beckoning for greater exploration, always inviting a deeper experience, always pointing beyond itself, and always bearing testimony not only to its many truths, but to the one and only singular truth. It is this truth that Jesus sums up when he says, "I am the way, the truth, and the life. No one comes to the Father except through me" (John 14:6). The empty tomb is a coherent testimony that the world is not the product of luck or magic. The world is called into existence by the will and word of God. "By faith we understand that the universe was created by the word of God, so that what is seen was not made out of things that are visible" (Heb 11:3).

IN HISTORY BUT NOT OF HISTORY

If the bones of Jesus disintegrated in a Palestinian tomb, then the Christian faith dissolves into dust. If the resurrection is reduced from historical fact to myth and metaphor, then the convergence between creation and redemption, and nature and grace, is canceled out. Since Jesus was "not abandoned to the realm of the dead, nor did his body see decay," the apostle Peter boldly affirms, "God has made this Jesus, whom you crucified, both Lord and Messiah" (Acts 2:31, 36 NIV).

New Testament scholar Rudolf Bultmann claimed that a literal, physical resurrection was impossible. In his judgment, "an historical fact which involves a resurrection from the dead is utterly inconceivable!"[3] Bultmann denied the resurrection of Jesus insofar as it meant the return of a dead human being to life, but he affirmed Jesus's resurrection as an existential experience of freedom and self-understanding in the present life. For many professing believers who pride themselves on a sophisticated grasp of metaphor, the resurrection stands for a positive outlook on life. They cannot embrace it as the promised reality that assures them of an everlasting life with God. To them the resurrection is more believable as a desupernatural-ized and dematerialized symbol for hope than the act of God that raised Jesus bodily from the dead.

The Bible reasons that "there can be no purely historical explanation for the rise of the resurrection faith. It is due to an act of God which happened in history but did not happen in terms of historical causality."[4] How could it be otherwise? Hence the explanation for the reality of the resurrection is found in God and believed by faith. But the Bible also asserts that resurrection faith is reasonable. It calls for an explanation. There is historical evidence for the wonder of the resurrection. The resurrection is a supernatural act without historical causality; nevertheless, it is a historical reality that helps explain the convictions and actions of the early Christians. There is an empirical, factual quality to the historical evidence for the resurrection.

If the resurrection did not happen, there is some explaining to do. How do we account for the empty tomb, knowing that the authorities would have made every attempt possible to produce the body of Jesus in order to discredit the preaching of Jesus's resurrection? Is there an explanation for the radical change in the discouraged and bewildered disciples? Would these same men, who failed so miserably to stand with Jesus during his trial, go on to face persecution and death for the sake of a lie? Why do the biblical accounts of the resurrection draw significantly on the witness of women, when Jewish principles of evidence judged women as invalid witnesses? If the disciples were concerned only with a symbolic resurrection, why did they go out of their way to claim the historicity of Jesus's resurrection? Why would they have documented his appearances and described their disbelief, if they wanted to say only that the spirit of Jesus's life survived his death and lived on in the proclamation of the gospel?

Christians have argued that the most reasonable answer to these questions is the reality of the bodily resurrection of

Jesus. It has never been easy to believe in the resurrection. The disciples had great difficulty coming to terms with this unexpected phenomenon. It was easier for them to believe that the body of Jesus had been stolen than to believe that Jesus had risen from the dead. There is no hint that the disciples were either intellectually or theologically prepared to believe in the resurrection of Jesus. It took them all by surprise. Contrary to their personal trauma, scriptural interpretation, and intellectual outlook, they came to believe in the reality of the resurrection. Something had to happen to make the risen Lord Jesus central to their powerful, dangerous preaching. Christians have believed that, in light of the whole history of Jesus, the most reasonable explanation for the empty tomb, the disciples' courage, and the biblical description of his appearances was in fact the resurrection of Jesus. Faith did not create the resurrection; the resurrection created faith.

Thomas's famous ultimatum was necessary. Of all the disciples, he was the one who refused to settle for anything less than empirical evidence. His insistence on a real resurrection was valid. He discounted what seemed to him to be strange and unfounded reports of Jesus's appearance first offered by women and then by the disciples behind locked doors. Thomas would have nothing to do with their wishful thinking. If he was going to believe in the resurrection, it had to be a real resurrection. If Jesus did not personally confront him with an actual body, he would reject any notion of resurrection. It is either a bodily resurrection or nothing at all.

BEYOND NATURAL CAUSES

The apostle Paul agreed with Thomas's insistence on a real resurrection. Without the bodily resurrection of Jesus, the apostle Paul admits that Christian preaching would be useless, faith in

Christ futile, and the burden of sin remaining. As far as Paul was concerned, Christianity without the resurrection had no credibility. If God did not raise Jesus from the dead, believers were false witnesses of God and without hope. Paul is clear: "If in this life only we have hope in Christ, we are of all people most to be pitied" (1 Cor 15:19 NIV). Without the reality of the resurrection, the gospel not only does not make sense but is in fact dishonest and deceptive. If there is no resurrection from the dead, then death ends all, and all are lost.

Biologists, astronomers, and physicists are familiar with the inconceivable becoming comprehensible. Much of what science knows to be true today about the cosmos and the cell was beyond imagining less than a hundred years ago. What we have learned about creation makes the resurrection credible. The universe itself has gone from a form we cannot understand to one we almost can. Cosmologists contemplate the process from nothingness to our space-time universe. Why do we believe scientists when they say that the core of a neutron star is so dense that a single spoonful of matter from it would weigh two hundred billion pounds? We accept without fainting the astronomer's claim that there are 140 billion galaxies in the visible universe. We believe in atoms, even though they measure one ten-millionth of a millimeter. That is to say that the width of one atom is to the width of a millimeter line as the thickness of a sheet of paper is to the height of the Empire State Building.[5]

Geologists tell us that Yellowstone is a supervolcano, sitting on top of an enormous reservoir of molten rock forty-five miles across, and we believe them. Biologist marvel at the inner universe of the cell. "Of the twenty-three main divisions of life, only three—plants, animals, and fungi—are large enough to be seen by the human eye." Microbes make up at least 80 percent of life on this planet. Your mattress is home to perhaps two million microscopic mites, but we were unaware of their intimate presence until 1965. We are all finding out that "life is infinitely more clever and adaptable than anyone had ever supposed."[6]

The validity of the bodily resurrection of Jesus rests in the sovereign will of God, who is more than able to create an imperishable body, the nature of which is beyond anything we could imagine. Ultimately, we believe that no natural explanation can account for either the first Adam or the second Adam. Humanly speaking, we are no closer to believing in God our Creator than we are to believing in God our Savior. The truth of creation is no easier to accept than the truth about salvation. In both cases we are face to face with the mystery of God and his work. There is a logical connection between creation and redemption, natural life and supernatural life, but not a causal connection. In both cases we are dependent on the revelation of God to bring home the truth of God and give us eyes to see and ears to hear what God has done for us and will do for us.

Paul's argument for the resurrection of the body draws on the science of nature. "What you sow does not come to life unless it dies. And what you sow is not the body that is to be, but a bare kernel, perhaps of wheat or some other grain. But God gives it a body as he has chosen, and to each kind of seed its own body" (1 Cor 15:36–38). Paul saw a pattern in nature that helped him understand the resurrection of the body. A tiny seed is buried in the ground, it germinates, its outer shell dries out and cracks, and it begins to sprout. Slowly the seed is transformed from a little, hard-shelled pebble into a flowering plant. If we did not know better, it would be hard to imagine the relationship between an acorn and an oak tree or a zygote and a human person. Like a wise biologist or a good theologian, Paul gives God the credit for this amazing natural transformation and drives home the point that no one can imagine what the resurrected body will be like. The nature of this new body is completely up to God and beyond our ability to conceive.

Paul also observes the differences between species: "For not all flesh is the same, but there is one kind for humans, another for animals, another for birds, and another for fish" (1 Cor 15:39).

Paul uses the term "flesh" in a variety of ways. Here he uses it to indicate the external, physical differences between humans, animals, birds, and fish. Today's scientific emphasis is usually on the relatedness of all living organisms, but it only takes a trip to the San Diego Zoo or Petco Park, where the San Diego Padres play, to be reminded of the amazing diversity of life. Instead of dwelling on the cell structure or the molecular nature of organisms, which he knew nothing about, Paul marveled at the seemingly infinite variety of living organisms, a truth no sensible person would deny. In the phenomenal diversity of life, Paul found logical support for the reality of the resurrected body. It was conceivable that the God of such a wonderfully diverse creation was fully capable of doing as he promised and creating a new, glorified, resurrected body. Paul's observations move out from the tiny seed to the immensity of space. "There are heavenly bodies and earthly bodies, but the glory of the heavenly is one kind, and the glory of the earthly is of another. There is one glory of the sun, and another glory of the moon, and another glory of the stars; for star differs from star in glory" (1 Cor 15:40–41). The planets and stars have their own unique splendor, which sets them apart from one another. They may share common elements, but they are studied and appreciated for their uniqueness. Wherever Paul looked he saw this amazing diversity in creation, bolstering his confidence in the reality of the resurrection. Nature's pattern of incredible transformation, phenomenal diversity, and amazing splendor made faith in the resurrection credible for Paul. Based on God's promise and these illustrations from nature, Paul concluded that it was reasonable to believe in the resurrection of the body.

However, the conclusions he drew from creation did not imply either natural continuity or a naturalistic explanation for the resurrection. There was nothing in nature itself that led to this new creation. Just the opposite was true. Paul stressed the difference between the perishable body and the imperishable body. He stressed the discontinuity between the natural body and the spiritual body. The old creation, with its tremendous diversity of bodies, illustrates the creative power of God but offers no clue as to the nature of the resurrection. The connection between the old creation and the new creation is neither natural nor physical, but relational. The link between them is in the mind of God, but make no mistake—they are two separate works. The reality of the natural realm does not exist as a platonic shadow or as a scientific prototype of the world to come, but as a testimony of the power and wisdom of God. "So is it with the resurrection of the dead. What is sown is perishable; what is raised is imperishable. It is sown in dishonor; it is raised in glory. It is sown in weakness; it is raised in power. It is sown a natural body; it is raised a spiritual body" (1 Cor 15:42–44).

Paul's description of the difference between these two bodies captures the pathos of the human condition and the expectation of the new creation. The contrast is not between bodily decay and a bodiless existence, but between a natural life of death and a spiritual life of living. On this side of eternity, bodily death is part and parcel of biological living. It factors in everywhere from reproduction to digestion to circulation. Apart from death, we would be unable to live. But in the new creation, bodily existence will be characterized by life, not death. Now life is characterized by death and dying, grief and humiliation, frailty and weakness, but a new day is coming when the key to life will not be death but life. The inevitability of decay, shame, and weakness will be eliminated by the life, glory, and power of the resurrection. This new, glorified, resurrected body will surpass the limitations of a natural body. It will embrace the fullness of personal identity and experience the richness of community life. This risen body will include the whole person and will be nothing like the Greek notion of a bodiless, immortal soul or the modern idea of the spirit of a person living on in people's memory. The spiritual body is no less real than the natural body, though at this point we cannot imagine what our spiritual bodies will be like.

That there are two types of bodily existence helps us put the struggle of human existence in perspective. If we have only this body to contend with, then cosmetic surgery and spare-no-expense pleasure seeking are eminently reasonable endeavors. The medical full-court press to extend life and forestall death also makes a lot of sense, as do elaborate funerals with expensive coffins and memorial headstones. If bodily existence is limited to the physical realm, then we ought to be thorough-going materialists. But the natural life, rooted as it is in death, is only part of the story. "If there is a natural body," Paul reasons, "there is also a spiritual body." For Paul this was not a huge leap, as it might be for some today, because he was convinced that the God of creation was also the God of redemption. Not only was humanity made in the image of God, but God became human in order to redeem humanity from sin and death. The resurrection of Jesus is the firstfruits of a whole new harvest; it is the key that unlocks the door to a whole new order. There are no humanistic resources that can transform the natural life into the spiritual life and triumph over death. "I declare to you, brothers and sisters, that flesh and blood cannot inherit the kingdom of God, nor does the perishable inherit the imperishable" (1 Cor 15:50 NIV).

Paul further understood the contrast between death-defining natural life and death-defying spiritual life by turning to salvation history. If the wonderful diversity of creation points to the power of God to create an entirely new mode of existence, then the message of salvation history declares that there is much more to life than the old Adam. The first Adam stands for sin and death; he represents the fallen human condition. The last Adam stands for salvation and life; he represents the firstfruits of the new creation. It does not take a genius to conclude that "the first Adam was of the dust of the earth," but it is tragic that some of our best minds stop there. Why do intellectuals become famous for observing a half-truth—and an illogical half-truth at that? If men and women are ultimately only dust, mere accidental freaks of nature, why does it take so much human ingenuity to make the case? The wisdom of this age believes in the first Adam's dust but not in the last Adam's life. But the apostle Paul linked the two together in the saving work of God. In the light of the revelation of God, it is illogical to insist on a half-truth at the expense of God's saving truth in Christ. Paul is able to move from dust to destiny, and from death to life, because of the last Adam, a life-giving spirit. "And just as we have borne the image of the man of dust, we shall also bear the image of the man of heaven" (1 Cor 15:49).

Paul concludes that it is only by the power of the cross that we can be free from sin and death. Only God can transform the natural life into the spiritual life and triumph over death. Paul's summation is not a rhetorical flourish but an earnest plea for the believers to come to their senses and put their trust in God. Having demonstrated the logic of the resurrection on the basis of God's work in creation and redemption, and having insisted that whatever is dying cannot achieve life, Paul brings his argument to a climax by emphasizing the final consummation. Neither creation nor history is best understood as an endless cycle of reoccurring patterns or a linear stream of events with no conclusion. Neither creation nor history is ruled by fate. Both are ruled by the sovereign Lord, and the ultimate transformation for which we yearn will not happen until God's appointed end.

The ultimate transformation we need and long for cannot be achieved gradually through any natural, flesh-and-blood means, but only through the work of God creating for us a new, glorified, resurrected body. When Paul says, "I tell you a mystery," he means "mystery." He is not offering a puzzle to test our ingenuity or a problem that requires speculation, but a promise that calls for trust because it is completely beyond our calculations and capacities.

There is no hidden knowledge waiting to be discovered by a self-styled spiritual elite who pride themselves on being in the know. The mystery lies in the nature and timing of a transformation that belongs absolutely to the Lord. We do not know how the perishable will clothe itself with the imperishable, nor do we have any idea how mortals will put on immortality. But by faith we believe "the dead will be raised imperishable, and we shall be changed" (1 Cor 15:52). For it is only then that Isaiah's prophecy will come true, "Death is swallowed up in victory" (1 Cor 15:55; see Isa 25:8).

Death itself will be swallowed up in victory. Death, the undeniable fact of life that looms larger than any other fear, will be consumed in a bite and a gulp. Death's end defies humanistic explanation. Only the God of creation and redemption can achieve the end of death. We react to the immensity and the inevitability of death with defiance and denial, contempt and fear. We throw everything we have in science and philosophy against death, but nothing brings it down to size. We may delay it, but we cannot stop it. We may numb its pain, but we cannot shrink its tragedy. All of our death-defying tactics are destined for defeat against an enemy so overwhelming that nothing can overcome it. Nothing, that is, but the risen Lord, who has the power to reduce the monster to a miserable morsel. That which threatens to engulf us is swallowed up. Praise God! "Death has been swallowed up in victory."

Emboldened by this truth, Paul talks back to death. It is not as if he is shaking his fist at death. It is more like he is standing over a defeated enemy. He draws on the prophet Hosea's personification of death in order to deliver his mocking taunt, "O death, where is your victory? O death, where is your sting?" (1 Cor 15:55; see Hos 13:14). Death has been rendered powerless to condemn; its poison is harmless. It no longer has the ultimate power to destroy us. Death is stingless because Christ absorbed the venom for us. On the cross he took on himself the consequences of our sin and evil. "The sting of death is sin, and the power of sin is the law." Paul has been careful to leave the climactic truth for the end. "But thanks be to God, who gives us the victory through our Lord Jesus Christ" (1 Cor 15:57).

INESCAPABLE WONDER

To my surprise, luck is a major concept pulled in by modern writers to make sense of life. Luck never shows up in their indexes, but it is offered as a major explanation for the origin of life and hope for the future. Richard Dawkins attributes both the origin of life and the origin of human consciousness to luck.

Two big ones, if you ask me! "Once that initial stroke of luck has been granted," argues Dawkins, we are off and running with evolution.[7]

Bill Bryson concludes his masterful work on the science of life by saying how "awfully lucky" we are to be here—"doubly lucky," in fact, because we have the singular ability to appreciate the privilege of existence. He credits our survival to "a nearly endless string of good fortune." We are only at the beginning of this "one planet, one experiment" experience, but we will "require a good deal more than lucky breaks" to "make sure we never find the end."[8]

If luck is the best explanation for the origin of life and hope for the future, if love is little more than a biological drive to pass along our genes, if meaning is entirely self-created, then wonder is best described as a strange mood that comes over us at odd times. Meaning and wisdom are only illusions. In an uncreated world of nature alone, joy is an individual stroke of good luck. Present-moment happiness is the key. Nobel laureate Francis Crick sums it up this way: "*You*, your joys and your sorrows, your memories and your ambitions, your sense of personal identity and free will, are in fact no more than the behavior of a vast assembly of nerve cells and their associated molecules."[9]

The thoroughgoing materialist handles death very differently from the apostle Paul. The materialist need neither defy nor fear death, because death is nothing at all. Before becoming a Christian, Lewis was comforted by the thought that death ended all. "The materialist's universe had the enormous attraction that ... death ended all. ... And if ever finite disasters proved greater than one wished to bear, suicide would always be possible. The horror of the Christian universe was that it had no door marked *Exit*."[10] For the materialist, the last thing to reduce to nothing is death. For the Christian, the last thing to triumph over is death. The empty tomb means that life has been emptied of nothingness and filled with meaning.

When I hold a newborn grandchild, I feel something of the glory of God. What is even more strange and wonderful is the experience of the glory of God at the bedside of a dying loved one. How, in the presence of death, is it possible for us to have a palpable sense that death does not end all? It is this unexpected surprise not of a wishful dream but of resurrection hope that lays hold not only of the heart but the mind. The incomprehensible becomes comprehensible. Ultimately the power of the explanation shifts. It is not we who explain the resurrection but the resurrection that explains us. We are not in control of the truth; the truth is in control of us.

"If the dead are not raised," Paul contends, then "Let us eat and drink, for tomorrow we die" (1 Cor 15:32). If there is no resurrection, or if the resurrection is only believed in a pious, symbolic way, then there is no reason to live for anything else but the self. There is nothing else to seek than present-moment happiness and nothing else to be gained but personal pleasure. If there is no resurrection, then a self-indulgent, me-first life-style is the way to go.

If, through the power of the Holy Spirit, we believe by faith in the resurrection of Christ, we will not think of Jesus as an inspirational memory but as the living Lord. Instead of funeral services that offer a generic celebration of life, our memorial services will witness to the power and hope of the risen Lord Jesus. Our investment strategy and giving will be guided by the hope of everlasting life rather than the anticipation of a long retirement. We will not think of Jesus as the founder of a religious tradition, but as the coming King who will rule and reign forever and ever. Like the apostle Paul, we will be willing to risk our careers, our resources, our reputations, even our lives, because of our hope of the resurrection.

Resurrection faith does not call for the sacrifice of a believer's intellect. However, unless there is a personal encounter with the risen Lord, eliciting the exclamation of worship, "My Lord and my God," the evidence ultimately matters little. Unquestionably, Thomas's situation was unique. He actually saw the body of Jesus. Consequently, the requirement of faith becomes the greater for those who follow after Thomas. As Jesus said, "Blessed are those who have not seen and yet have believed" (John 20:29). Easter is a big deal. How can it not be? How can we not celebrate the defeat of death and the hope of the resurrection? But may our preaching of the risen and ascended Lord be without fanfare and showmanship, and in the Spirit appeal to the marginalized, penetrate the agnostic, and build up the disciple.

*The business of the Christian is nothing else
than to be ever preparing for death.*

Irenaeus, "Fragment XI,"
Fragments from the Lost Writings of Irenaeus

*I want to know Christ—yes, to know the power of
his resurrection and participation in his sufferings,
becoming like him in his death, and so, somehow,
attaining to the resurrection from the dead.*

Philippians 3:10–11 NIV

10

Memorial Meditations

S ometimes when I am with a believer or praying for them, I wonder what I might say if I were asked to preach at their memorial service. Pastors think about these things. They are called to comfort the family and console the household of faith. In Christ, pastors frame grief and loss in terms of gospel truth and resurrection hope. No one is naturally well-suited to this task, and no one finds it easy. I meet seminary students who want to preach and teach God's word, but they wonder whether they have what it takes to come alongside a grieving family. There are more than a few seminarians who end up pursuing a PhD because they cannot imagine becoming a pastor and comforting people crushed by the loss of a loved one. I aim to encourage these students when I say, "No one is cut out for this ministry. All pastors have to grow into this responsibility." But make no mistake—this ministry of comfort goes hand in hand with proclaiming the gospel and teaching biblical theology. When you extend the comfort of the risen Lord to a grieving family, you know your theology has touched your heart.

Theology as head knowledge alone is not much help, but theology as life-giving truth is what pastor-theologians are all about. Those who trust in the Lord "and lean not on [their] own understanding" will find the redemptive trajectory of the gospel in their daily life and pastoral ministry. They will find their hope in the power of the resurrection and in the gospel promise of everlasting life. If our theology does not work in an emergency-room waiting room as we meet with grieving parents who just lost a daughter in a car accident, or if it is out of place at the graveside of a young father whose body was ravaged by cancer, then it deserves to remain in academic ivory tower. Only people who have a working pastoral theology ought to be teaching theology.

FUNDAMENTAL TRUTHS

When we stand with a grieving family and friends and say, "Let not your hearts be troubled," we do so on the basis of gospel truth. We discover in Jesus's upper-room discourse (John 13–17) that the soul's real comfort depends on the comings and goings of Jesus. Four distinct comings shape our understanding of Jesus's comfort. Christian hope is anchored in four gospel realities:

1. the *parousia*—Jesus's final coming

2. the *Paraclete*—Jesus's gift of the Holy Spirit

3. the *passion*—Jesus's death and resurrection

4. the *presence*—Jesus's abiding fellowship

These four comings are the ways in which Jesus makes himself real in our ordinary daily routine and in the midst of our life-and-death crises. These are the truths that comfort and give believers meaning and purpose at all times, but especially in moments of crisis and loss. The comfort we have to offer grieving spouses, distraught parents, and heartbroken friends is the comfort of the gospel. The apostle Paul praises the God of all comfort, "who comforts us in all our affliction, so that we may be able to comfort those who are in any affliction, with the comfort with which we ourselves are comforted by God" (2 Cor 1:4).

All of our crises, griefs, and deaths are framed by these four comings of Jesus:

1. Parousia: "And if I go and prepare a place for you, I will come again and will take you to myself, that where I am you may be also" (John 14:3).

2. Paraclete: "And I will ask the Father, and he will give you another Helper, to be with you forever, even the Spirit of truth" (John 14:16–17).

3. Passion: "Yet a little while and the world will see me no more, but you will see me. Because I live, you also will live" (John 14:19).

4. Presence: "Whoever abides in me and I in him, he it is that bears much fruit, for apart from me you can do nothing" (John 15:5).

The fourfold coming of Jesus encompasses God's holistic comfort and shapes the household of faith's perspective on life and death. These truths are reflected in the spiritual disciplines of the life of the church.

1. WE BELIEVE IN THE BREVITY OF LIFE

We know that on this side of eternity life is transitory and brief, and will soon be passed. This conviction is challenged in our day by the prevailing ethos of living in the moment. Left to ourselves and our own opinions, we may ignore the frailty of our human condition and neglect the love and mercy of God. We struggle to hold in tension the fleeting nature of mortal life and the promise of the Lord's everlasting love and life. Worship gives us a realistic and redemptive appraisal of our personal circumstances.

The brevity of life does not mean the futility of life. "The life of mortals is like grass, they flourish like a flower of the field; the wind blows over it and it is gone, and its place remembers it no more. But from everlasting to everlasting the LORD's love is with those who fear him" (Ps 103:15–17 NIV). In worship we are reminded that God redeems us from the pit. Our moral bodies take on immortality, as the apostle Paul says: "So it is with the resurrection of the dead. What is sown is perishable; what is raised is imperishable. It is sown in dishonor; it is raised in glory. It is sown in weakness; it is raised in power" (1 Cor 15:42–43).

2. WE PRAY WITH THE PSALMIST, "SO TEACH US TO NUMBER OUR DAYS, THAT WE MAY GET A HEART OF WISDOM" (PSALM 90:12)

Not only are we mortal, "earth to earth, dust to dust," but we are such frail creatures that life passes by like a dream. The newborn child makes us acutely aware of how fragile and tenuous life truly is. Yet our short life span is framed by God's sovereign purposes and infused with God's eternal meaning. Medical doctor Samuel Harrington sees "our society's emphasis on youth, celebrity, and consumerism coupled with the successful marketing of medical advances, health care products, and political promises" as contributing to unrealistic expectations of longevity. Remarkably, life expectancy between seventy years and eighty has remained fairly constant. Harrington uses the concept of "compression morbidity" to refer to the fact that we are "living longer healthier lives and dying quickly with less disability." Life expectancy is still about seventy-nine, with the maximum improvements in health occurring between ages fifty and seventy. In other words, "if seventy is the new fifty, then eighty-six is the new eighty-five."[1] We are living healthier for longer but still dying at about the same age.

We may like to think of ourselves as living at the zenith of evolutionary development, but the psalmist thinks of us as a wispy dream or a blade of grass. The psalmist did not use these metaphors to disparage humanity. He was simply being honest about the human condition. Our value lies not in our chemical constitution or in our longevity. The meaning of the person lies in our unique and wonderful relationship with our Creator, in whose image we are made. We are recipients of his wisdom, compassion, unfailing love, and favor.

3. THE PURITAN IDEAL OF PREPARING FOR A GOOD DEATH IS SET AGAINST THE PROMETHEAN SPIRIT OF THE AGE

In Greek mythology Prometheus took away humanity's sense of mortality, its sense of doom, and gave people technology (fire) to change their condition. The Promethean death-defying state of mind counters the Puritan commitment to preparing for a good death. The question before us is this: Which is more shocking, to be told you are already dead, since we are dead in our transgressions and sins (Eph 2:1), or to be told simply that death ends all? Christians ought to face death differently from those who believe physical death ends all. We sorrow not as those without hope. A Christian understanding encourages not the mere acceptance of death, but the over-coming of death (1 Thess 4:13). Martin Luther famously said, "He who fears death or is unwilling to die is not a Christian to a sufficient degree; for those who fear death still lack faith in the resurrection, since they love this life more than they love the life to come. ... He who does not die willingly should not be called a Christian."[2]

John Calvin believed that it was "monstrous ... that many who boast themselves Christians are gripped by such a great fear of death, rather than a desire for it, that they tremble at the least mention of it, as of something utterly dire and disastrous." If we believe in the resurrection, Calvin insisted that we really believe it. "For if we deem this unstable, defective, corruptible, fleeting, wasting, rotting tabernacle of our body to be so dissolved that it is soon renewed into a firm, perfect, incorruptible, and finally, heavenly glory, will not faith compel us ardently to seek what nature dreads?"[3]

4. ON "BANNER SUNDAY" WE KEEP THESE SALIENT TRUTHS FRONT AND CENTER

Every year on All Saints' Day we remember the saints who went to be with the Lord that year. We celebrate God's work in their lives, and we pray for their families. Our children make banners in children's church. Four or five symbols that represent their life are traced on felt, cut out, and glued to a colorful banner. At the end of the service, the banner is given to a family member. On Banner Sunday, the service opens with the congregation singing "For All the Saints," and the children process in carrying the banners of these saints who have gone before. The sermon on All Saints' Sunday reminds the church of the fundamental truths of the Lord's gifts: the gift of salvation, the gift of the Holy Spirit, the gift of his presence, and the gift of Christ's coming again. Through the years some of the biblical verses we focused on include:

Even though I walk through the valley of the shadow of death, I will fear no evil, for you are with me. (Ps 23:4)

For to me to live is Christ, and to die is gain. (Phil 1:21)

We live by faith, not by sight. (2 Cor 5:7 NIV)

To be absent from the body is to be present with the Lord. (based on 2 Cor 5:8)

Death has been swallowed up in victory. (1 Cor 15:54 NIV)

Who shall separate us from the love of Christ? ... For I am convinced that neither death nor life ... will be able to separate us from the love of God that is in Christ Jesus our Lord. (Rom 8:35, 38–39 NIV)

PASTORAL CONSIDERATIONS

Pastors who grow into the joyful burden of comforting those who grieve will keep a few practical concerns in mind.

1. Be present to the family. This usually means seeing them right away. The visit may be brief, but to be with them face to face is important. I never want to overstay my stay, but I want the family to know that the church cares, that I care. You may talk about the memorial service at another time, but these initial overtures of prayer and comfort are important even if the family seems hesitant to bother you. Many will say, "Oh, don't bother," but the visit will be greatly appreciated.

2. Communication is important. In a close-knit household of faith, you want the body of Christ to know what is going

on, so they can pray and encourage the family. Encourage the family to talk about their loved one. Are there biblical texts and hymns that were especially meaningful to the loved one? These might be used in the memorial service because of their special meaning.

3. Memorial services should be kept to about an hour in most cases. Asking a few people to share (if that is something done in your tradition) is better than inviting the whole assembly to share at an open mic. Someone has to assume leadership for every aspect of the service. That person is often the pastor, who is responsible for how the service goes from beginning to end.

4. Natural humor that arises from the character of the person may work well, but contrived humor to lighten the mood does not work and often feels inappropriate.

5. Memorial services take a lot out of pastors, as they should. But with that said, you cannot walk through the deepest, darkest valley every week, even though someone in your congregation is doing just that. Pastors need to learn how to point people to Christ, the great Shepherd, who alone can bear their burden and lead them home. Pastors have to work out how best to do that. Believers need to be trained as a household of faith to share one another's griefs and sorrows. If this is the burden of the pastor alone, it will not be a joyful burden for long. People grieve differently. It is helpful to be sensitive to that dynamic and allow people the freedom to grieve in their way.

6. We are always proclaiming Christ and his gospel, but we do so in a way that does not force the message on people. We want the Spirit of God to open people's minds and hearts. Pastors agree with the psalmist when he writes, "Precious in the sight of the LORD is the death of his faithful servants" (Ps 116:15

NIV), because like Abel, faithful saints still speak, even though dead (Heb 11:4).

Memorial services cause us to pray and serve in humility.

MEMORIAL SERVICE PROFILES

Over the years I have kept the worship bulletins and notes of my memorial service meditations. This thick file is a reminder to me of the Lord's sustaining grace. I have listed here some of the more challenging memorial services I have led. But I believe I was always following the Lord's lead in doing these worship services. We cannot do this work without the Lord's help and the fellowship of believers.

Scott, a thirty-eight-year-old opera singer, died quickly from AIDS. Scott was raised in the church but had been away from the church, living in New York City for several years. His parents were very involved in the church, and they were devastated. Scott was well known in our local community, and many came to his service from the university's music school. I was relatively new to the church, and I had never met Scott personally. My meditation was from the three voices in Isaiah 40:1–11, the voice of expectation, the voice of desperation, and the voice of celebration. The prophet begins with, "'Comfort, comfort my people,' says your God." I stressed that Jesus's first word of the gospel is, "Do not be afraid." No matter how great the grief, God's comfort is greater.

We acknowledged Scott's gifts, talents, joys, and successes as God's gifts. God speaks tenderly, introducing the voice of anticipation (Isa 40:3). The voice of desperation (Isa 40:6) articulates the fallen human condition, followed by the voice of celebration (Isa 40:9) introducing the caring Shepherd. The power of Scott's voice anticipated the powerful voice of the

Lord (Rev 5:11–14). At the end of the meditation, a recording of Scott singing *The Holy City* was played. The ambiguity surrounding this baptized son of the church whose own profession of faith had fallen silent in recent years was set in sharp contrast to the beauty and power of Scott's recorded rich baritone voice. He sang about the new Jerusalem, "The light of God was on its streets / The gates were open wide / And all who would, might enter / And no one was denied." The song ends, "Jerusalem! Jerusalem / Sing for the night is o'er / Hosanna in the highest / Hosanna for evermore!"

* * * * *

William was four months old when he died from SIDS. The family did not attend our church, but a relative did and called our church, asking for our help. I called the grieving family, and yes, they wanted me to come over. It was a painful visit. There is nothing in seminary that prepares a pastor for such a visit, nor can it. In Christ we must grow into the responsibility of caring for people in their deepest, darkest valley. I have noticed that at times of grief pastors need to bring to the situation a sense of peace and assurance. I cannot allow myself to crash emotionally. Like a doctor in an emergency, the pastor has to remain calm and attentive to the family. The pastor is there to listen, to pray, to reassure, and to support because he or she can in the Lord.

They asked if I would lead a graveside service. My texts were Matthew 18:1–5 and John 11:25–26. The service was one of the most painful and difficult services I have been involved in. Although raised in the church, William's parents expressed no faith in Christ. His father, a medical doctor, was not only crushed but angry. He was angry at the God he did not believe in and angry at me for saying things that he could not stomach. I felt like I represented all that he rejected and maybe even hated. I felt that he would be happy if he never saw me again.

In my prayer and meditation, I focused on our cry to the Lord for comfort. I thanked the Lord that Willie had been born into a loving and caring family. Willie's grandfather had recently passed away, and he had a strong testimony of faith in Christ. I based my meditation on what Willie's grandfather might have said to comfort his family. Willie's grandfather would have reassured us that Willie was now in the presence of God, that death does not end all, and that the last enemy to be destroyed is death. Willie's life brought new meaning to the sacrifice of God, who gave his one and only Son to redeem us and raised him from the dead, to give us the hope of the resurrection. It was hard.

* * * * *

Steven Peter Befus, a close and dearly loved friend, died from cancer at forty-eight after nearly twenty years of service as a medical missionary doctor in Liberia. I was the best man in his wedding to Sue and remained close friends through the years. I led the graveside service that followed the church memorial service. I began with the question the angels asked the women at Jesus's tomb, "Why do you look for the living among the dead? He is not here; he has risen!" (Luke 24:5–6 NIV). We affirmed that we do not grieve as those who have no hope (1 Thess 4:13). We affirmed that Steve would go right on glorifying God and enjoying him forever. My meditation was based on Psalm 116, focusing on its honesty, referring to the anguish of the grave and its brave confidence in the Lord's salvation.

We affirmed there is hope in the midst of our trouble, sorrow, tears, and affliction. We expressed fervent gratitude for the Lord's mercy. "Precious in the sight of the Lord is the death of his saints. O Lord, truly I am your servant; I am your servant, a faithful son; you have freed me from my chains. … I will fulfill my vows to the Lord in the presence of all his people" (Ps 116:15–16, 18). Steve's earthly life was highly valued, and his death was costly in the eyes of the Lord. "The sting of death is sin, and the power of sin is the law. But thanks be to God! He gives us the victory through our Lord Jesus Christ" (1 Cor 15:56–57 NIV). The bodily resurrection of Christ is the pivotal truth on which the meaning and purpose of our earthly lives depends and the fact guaranteeing our future bodily resurrection. This is what Job looked forward to when he said, "I know that my redeemer lives, and that in the end he will stand on the earth. And after my skin has been destroyed, yet in my flesh I will see God; I myself will see him with my own eyes—I, and not another. How my heart yearns within me!" (Job 19:25–27 NIV). Jesus said, "I am the resurrection and the life. Whoever believes in me, though he die, yet shall he live, and everyone who lives and believes in me shall never die" (John 11:25–26).

In the last days of his life, Steve chose 2 Corinthians 4:5–5:9, because he identified with the deep paradox of holding the treasure of the gospel in "jars of clay" and the "all-surpassing power of God." His body was wasting away, but his confidence in the Lord was strong. Steve characteristically refrained from quoting anything heroic and preferred to concentrate on the truth: "We always carry around in our body the death of Jesus, so that the life of Jesus may also be revealed in our body" (2 Cor 4:10 NIV). Steve could not bring himself to compare himself to Job or Paul, even though the parallels fit. His decision, along with

Sue, to give their lives sacrificially in humble service was made without fanfare and hype. They were always down-to-earth, life-embracing servants of Jesus Christ.

* * * * *

Daniel Deaton, a sixty-five-year-old Navy captain, Presbyterian pastor, and chaplain, died from a cancerous brain tumor. In the last year of his life, he clung to Christ and his promise: "We have this as a sure and steadfast anchor of the soul, a hope that enters into the inner place behind the curtain, where Jesus has gone as a forerunner on our behalf" (Heb 6:19–20). Like Hebrews, Dan was a tour de force for the person and work of Christ. He could not stop giving glory to his Lord and Savior Jesus Christ. For the last couple of years, it was not uncommon for Dan to speak of Jesus with tears. I knew Dan as a pastor and a preacher of God's word since 1993. I knew firsthand his life experiences—the good and the bad—that drove him to his Savior and made him totally and emphatically dependent on the mercy and grace of God. Even in his last earthly struggle, Dan and his wife, Barb, rejoiced together in their utter dependence on the grace of God.

Dan earnestly believed that God had "spoken to us by his Son, whom he appointed the heir of all things, through whom also he created the world" (Heb 1:2). That God has spoken and is speaking made all the difference in the world for Dan. God spoke into Dan's life with his compelling, convicting, and saving truth. Dan wanted everyone he met to share that experience.

Dan was marked by a passion for Christ. He believed that the truth of Jesus Christ deserved to be communicated with all the thought, skill, passion, and ability that he could summon.

He knew that the truth of God was too deep for humanistic consumption. Dan lived and preached with a passion for Christ, and with the help of the Holy Spirit he plunged into the ocean depth of God's truth. There was nothing manipulative or contrived about Dan. When I read Hebrews even now, I can hear Dan's voice: "Therefore we must pay much closer attention to what we have heard, lest we drift away from it ... [for] how shall we escape if we neglect such a great salvation" (Heb 2:1, 3). Dan embraced the fullness of God's great gift of salvation.

Dan's life was not all smooth sailing. He experienced the dark night of the soul. He knew the depths of a crisis of faith. He could say with the psalmist, "When my heart was grieved and my spirit embittered, I was senseless and ignorant; I was a brute beast before you" (Ps 73:21–22 NIV). Like his Lord, Dan learned obedience by the things he suffered. Jesus Christ knew no sin. He suffered for our sin, and Dan would be quick to say that Christ suffered for his sin. But that is why Dan literally wept when he contemplated the greatness of his Savior.

Dan experienced the arc of devotion in a beautiful way—and Barb did too. By the grace of God, Dan, Barb, and their girls demonstrated a faith in Christ tested by the fire of life, by the fallenness of the human condition. They embraced the end of religion and faithfulness to the end. Dan was a man after God's own heart, and he lived and breathed the words of David, "My sacrifice, O God, is a broken spirit; a broken and contrite heart you, God, will not despise" (Ps 51:17 NIV). Dan took God at his word. This career naval officer and chaplain claimed that Christ was the anchor of his soul, firm and secure. Pastors have the honor and responsibility of preaching a gospel meditation and shaping a worship service that celebrates the hope of the resurrection. Behind every meditation we preach and worship service that we lead is the conviction and the consolation that "for me to live is Christ and to die is gain" (Phil 1:21).

This is the day that the LORD has made;
let us rejoice and be glad in it.

Psalm 118:24

11

Wedding Meditations

Weddings are a joyous occasion and a great opportunity to worship the Lord. It is important for pastors to encourage a countercultural shift away from a self-indulgent event to a Christ-honoring witness. This chapter focuses on wedding meditations and the liturgy of a wedding worship service. The household of faith aims for a wedding to serve the marriage. "Weddings are easy," writes Eugene Peterson. "Marriages are difficult. The couple wants to plan a wedding; I want to plan a marriage." Weddings are important, but relatively easy compared to marriages. "The event of the wedding without the life of the marriage doesn't amount to much."[1]

Pastors who take marriage seriously invest in couples. They pray for them and counsel them. I usually meet with couples several times for conversation about their lives. We begin with how they met and their relationship to Christ. I ask them to share about their families, their parents' marriages, their relationship with siblings. These conversations always include biblical insights into Christian discipleship and marriage. We talk about a range of issues from work and finances to suffering and commitment. We plan a Christ-honoring wedding worship service and a Christ-centered marriage.

Weddings ought to be deeply moving experiences, not just for the couple getting married but for everyone attending the wedding. Heidi and Todd were a fun couple to counsel. They talked freely and openly about their lives and their love for one another and for Christ. To give you a picture, Heidi was a petite, articulate blonde, and Todd was a big strapping firefighter who drove a Harley. On our last session together, we talked about the meaning of the vows. Sometimes I lead the couple in an informal recital of the vows just so we all get a feel for the cadence and phrasing of the exchange of vows. Heidi went first, but I hardly got a line out before she started crying. In the moment, she was overwhelmed by the meaning of their vowed commitment. She and Todd were actually, finally doing this! Todd shifted uncomfortably in his chair as Heidi cried. He was a little taken aback by her show of emotion. So, I shifted to Todd, who rattled the vows off like they were no big deal. Heidi never did get through the vows that afternoon, but before we were through, we were all laughing about the whole thing.

On their wedding day, Heidi was not only radiant, but she was in full command of her emotions. She seized the moment in a beautiful way. Grooms usually impress me as a bit shellshocked, but brides tend to be fully present on their wedding day. When we got to the vows, Todd, who was looking into the eyes of his bride, became completely undone. Much to his shock, he was overcome with emotion. He cried so hard through the vows that we were reduced to *a word-for-word* recitation. But through it all, a totally composed Heidi looked upon Todd adoringly. She affirmed her vows in a clear, steady voice. Their wedding was a beautiful experience.

A wedding meditation may only be about ten or fifteen minutes in length but its value for defining the meaning of the vows is important. I encourage couples to focus on what is actually being said in the meditation, because if they are able to focus, the time goes by quickly. Eye contact is crucial. Grooms or brides who let their minds wonder at this point may end up in *neverland*. This makes it all that much more important for the pastor to focus on the gospel of Jesus Christ, which ought to center everything about the wedding, from the processional and call to worship, to the benediction and presentation of the couple.

INVITING JESUS

When Jesus showed up at the wedding in Cana of Galilee, he turned water into wine. He "revealed his glory," and "his disciples put their faith in him." The unsuspecting bride and groom never dreamed that their invitation to Jesus would change everything. I am afraid many of today's Christian weddings forget to invite Jesus. The bride and groom have thought of everything else. They reserved the banquet hall for their wedding reception six months in advance, ordered their engraved invitations, lined up a photographer and a videographer, set a date with a pastor, picked out a special place for the wedding, purchased a wedding dress, decided on a florist, selected a menu, booked their honeymoon, asked their closest friends to be in the wedding, hired a disc jockey for their reception, debated whether to have an open bar at the reception, and arranged for an organist or a guitarist to play for the wedding service. The list of things to do for a modern wedding is actually much longer. I know one church that has a one-hundred-page manual on how weddings should be done at their church. Everything from the color of tablecloths to no smoking on the premises is meticulously detailed. But nothing is said about inviting Jesus to the wedding.

The invitation to Jesus and his disciples was not without its practical problems. Who do you think drank up all the wine?

We read, "When the wine was gone, Jesus's mother said to him, 'They have no more wine.'" The implication is clear. The invitation to Jesus and his cohort had unintended consequences. No more wine was no small problem, and in that culture, it was a major embarrassment. That is how it is when you invite Jesus to your wedding. There is an embarrassing downside. The presence of Jesus puts a certain strain on the wedding. You can pretend otherwise, but if you have invited Jesus to your wedding, be prepared to face the unavoidable challenges of his presence. To begin with, Jesus shifts attention away from you to him, just as he did at Cana. The bride and groom need to ask themselves whether they can handle this. Brides especially cherish the dream of everything going just as they had imagined, but when Jesus shows up, the wedding is no longer about her wishes and dreams.

Weddings are often expensive, extravagant affairs, with a dollar value affixed to a couple's worth and parental love. But in the presence of Jesus, the bride awakens to a stunning realization: "It's not about me." Instead of being queen for a day in a Cinderella wedding, she is a disciple awaiting Jesus's next move. Like all disciples, the bride and groom are called to salvation, service, sacrifice, and simplicity. That is as true on their wedding day as any other day. Her radiance reflects Christ's love and light. His character rests in God.

The need of the hour was for more wine, so Mary turned to Jesus. The need of the hour in today's Christian wedding is for new wine. More than ever before, weddings intersect at the mess of the human condition and the mystery of God. The pain and brokenness of divorce intrudes on just about everyone's wedding. Exes who have avoided all contact with one another put on a happy face and brave the occasion. Unmarried Christian couples who are sleeping together proudly attend.

Friends from school and work who like you in spite of your Christian commitment smirk their way through the prayers, hymns, and the pastor's meditation.

Sadly, the tipping point in many weddings favors nominal Christians and non-Christians, causing some Christian couples to change the venue for their wedding and downplay the Christian aspects of the ceremony. They do not want their guests to feel awkward or uncomfortable, so they dilute and diminish their Christian witness. Sometimes they want to move the wedding ceremony outside the church context, and often the change of venue affects the ability of the couple and the congregation to worship because the setting is strange.

At the wedding in Cana, when Mary turned to Jesus and said, "They have no more wine," she had the good sense to look to Jesus to solve the wedding dilemma, and so should we. Instead of shifting attention away from Christ, we ought to draw attention to Christ. Instead of dropping the hymns, let the congregation sing "Great Is Thy Faithfulness" or "In Christ Alone" or "Come Thou Fount of Every Blessing." Let doxology and prayer inspire the worship. Let the bride come in on "Be Thou My Vision" and the soloist sing "How Deep the Father's Love." Let Scripture be read boldly and unapologetically. Instead of a five-minute, awkward homily, let the pastor offer a ten-minute, gospel-centered meditation. From beginning to end, make the service God-honoring, Christ-centered, and Spirit-filled. Do not be embarrassed. You invited Jesus to your wedding. Look to him the way Mary did. Let your friends experience the pulse and joy of authentic worship.

Jesus's response to Mary was telling. "Woman, what does this have to do with me? My hour has not yet come" (John 2:4). With his response Jesus underscored two truths: First, Jesus is King, and he is never at our disposal to be used for our purposes; we are at his disposal to be used for his purposes. Second, the revelation of Jesus always points to the cross. His hour refers to the reason the Incarnate One came. Christ's atoning sacrifice on the cross, his saving grace, his gift of forgiveness, and his promise of eternal life are foundational to everything Jesus does. The principle of the cross, "my life for yours," lies at the heart of the covenant commitment made by a man and a woman in holy marriage. The vows they exchange are grandly inclusive of all that they are or will be, but no sacrifice they will make for each other will ever come close to the sacrifice Jesus Christ made for them. This truth ought to be honored, and the crucified and risen Christ ought to be worshiped in the wedding worship service.

Mary told the servants to do whatever Jesus told them to do. The six stone water jars that stood nearby were used for ceremonial cleansing. They represented a tradition that was passing away because of Jesus's better cleansing. These stone jars symbolized an old religion of works and rules and rituals. Jesus said to the servants, "Fill the jars with water," so they filled them to the brim. Then Jesus said, "Now draw some out and take it to the master of the feast." They did as they were told, and when the master of the banquet tasted the new wine, he called the bridegroom aside and praised him for saving the best wine for last. The master of the banquet did not know that Jesus had performed a miracle. He was simply impressed by the quality of the wine. But wine signifies a deeper meaning. It symbolizes God's gracious provision. The miracle of changing water into wine was a sign of Jesus's identity, revealing his glory. Only God in Christ can provide this new wine, the wine that exceeds all expectations.

Nothing is said about the master of the banquet glorifying God or putting his faith in Jesus, but he commended the bridegroom for saving the best wine until the end. This wedding was special. It was not your typical wedding. The bridegroom and the bride did their wedding differently from everyone else, because Jesus was present. Christian weddings that copy the culture and dilute the gospel end up changing wine to water, but Christians who invite Jesus to their wedding and look to him to solve the wedding dilemma will see water turned to wine. Even pagan friends will be impressed.

A WEDDING LITURGY
AND MEDITATION

Following the musical prelude and the bridal processional the pastor welcomes family and friends and offers a prayer.

> In recognition of the part that family and friends have had in their lives and in affirmation of their desire publicly to declare their mutual commitment to marriage, Dan Blanchard and Jennifer Neely have invited you to this ceremony. We are more than observers. We are participants in a worship service before the presence of God. And we share in the responsibility of supporting, enriching and encouraging Dan and Jennifer in this vowed commitment they are about to make. It is our solemn responsibility to pray and uphold Dan and Jennifer in their relationship with the Lord and each other.

Hymns are sung and Scripture is read before the pastor begins the meditation.

Together in Christ

In this worship service we celebrate two great loves. These two loves, marital love and divine love, romantic love and redemptive love, are meant to support and illuminate each other. The lesser love, the love between husband and wife, is meant to help us grasp more completely the personal intimacy and earnestness of God's love for us. The greater love, God's sacrificial, saving love, is meant to be the source and strength for human love. The power and intensity of the oneness experienced between a man and a woman points to the greater mystery of our oneness with God in Christ.

These Two Loves shape the covenant you are about to make. It is this First Love that has brought you here this afternoon and it is this Costly Love that empowers you to make this commitment to each other. The oneness you are about to create depends upon the wholeness you have received in Christ. Before you give yourselves to each other in the bond of holy marriage, God has given to you the gift of forgiveness and everlasting life.

The greater love—God's love for you, God's redemptive love—makes your marital love possible. To insist on finding the ultimate soul-saving love in one's spouse is to drain the energy and joy right out of marriage. No matter how real and beautiful the oneness of the marriage relationship may be, we are reminded of our need for the greater love.

Augustine's prayer says it so well: "You have made us for yourself, and our heart is restless until it rests in you."[2] The ultimate oneness that satisfies the soul is found in loving and obeying the Lord God. Making marriage the thing that matters in a wedding is a spiritual discipline worth every ounce of energy a couple can give. Colossians 3:12–17 is an especially meaningful wedding text. It begins, "Therefore, as God's chosen people, holy and dearly loved ..." (NIV).

Dan and Jennifer, you begin this marriage with God's great salvation remaking and transforming you into his image. In Christ, you are a new creation, and we are confident "that he who began a good work in you will carry it on to completion until the day of Christ Jesus" (Phil 1:6 NIV). This marriage will not make your life. Your marriage issues from that great and enduring relationship you have with God.

"Clothe yourselves with compassion, kindness, humility, gentleness and patience" (Col 3:12 NIV). Marriage depends on your personal relationship with God and your covenant commitment to one another. Today you pledge yourselves to one another—the language of your vows is grandly inclusive of all you are and will be. This comprehensive commitment is also a timeless commitment. "As long as our lives shall last" is the bottom line of a costly vow. Though all things change—and there is uncertainty in the world—this commitment before God and between yourselves shall persist to comfort you. Your God and this vow shall be a stay against the confusion and uncertainties of life.

Your vowed commitment will lead you into the work of marriage. The work of marriage involves a putting on of compassion, kindness, humility, gentleness, and patience. We are properly attentive to what we wear for a wedding, so Dan and Jennifer, give attention, and I know you will, to what you put on for your marriage. Dressed in compassion and patience, you will put off selfishness. Clothed in kindness and humility, you will put off pride and a harsh spirit. Sin will be disrobed and exposed for what it is. The work of marriage requires that you give yourselves to the work of forgiveness.

"Bear with each other and forgive one another if any of you has a grievance against one someone. Forgive as the Lord forgave you" (Col 3:13 NIV). Communication is so important. Your marriage will be a burden without it, but not just any communication will do. Let the thing communicated be forgiveness. This is the single most significant tool you have for meeting and for healing the troubles that marriage will surely breed between you.

"Over all these virtues put on love, which binds them all together in perfect unity" (Col 3:14 NIV). Realism speaks not only of forgiveness but also of perfect unity. In the same paragraph Paul speaks not only of how to deal with grievances but how to have perfect unity. Christians should not sell marriage short. The vows you offer are vows of love, and the life you share together has not only the promise but the power of a great unity. Develop the habits of the soul that will nurture everyday love expressed in compassion, humility, kindness, gentleness, and patience. Your vows are a burden, perhaps an impossible burden, to fulfill apart from the word of Christ and the peace of Christ.

The mystery of a mature and loving marriage is not a secret, but it is a revelation. Paul expresses it as a twofold exhortation: "Let the peace of Christ rule in your hearts, since as members of one body you were called to peace. And be thankful. Let the message of Christ dwell in you richly" (Col 3:15–16 NIV). This is really a single challenge to pay special attention to the one who preserves your life, love, and relationship together. There is so much that threatens to rule our hearts: anxiety, insecurity, and pride. But the mystery of a beautiful marriage is found in the peace of Christ ruling our hearts and the word of Christ dwelling in us abundantly.

Spiritual discipline and Christian community are necessary for your marriage. You will need the challenge and the growth that other Christians offer. And the result of such a marriage founded in Christ and sustained by Christ is ministry: the ministry of teaching yourselves and others, the ministry of praise and gratitude in your heart and before others, the ministry of service to one another and others in need.

The marriage union is signified publicly in several ways: the wedding ceremony, the pledge of vows, the exchange of rings, and the giving and changing of a name. "And whatever you do, whether in word or deed, do it all in the name of the Lord Jesus, giving thanks to God the Father through him" (Col 3:17 NIV). The language of your vows is grandly inclusive of all you are and will be. Your comprehensive commitment is a covenant, not a contract; an enduring promise, not a hope-it-works-out proposal. It is real work, but it is the kind of work we are called to do. As the apostle said, "Work out your own salvation with fear and trembling, for it is God who works in you, both to will and to work for his good pleasure" (Phil 2:12–13). Your marriage may be your greatest testimony to the love of Christ.

When the apostle thought of the shared work of marriage and the oneness of the marriage relationship, he drew on the principle of the cross, "my life for yours," and the principle of creation, "and the two will become one flesh." By divine design, marriage was created to point beyond itself to our union with God in Christ. May your love for one another be a reflection of even the greater reality of God's love. To this end, "Let the peace of Christ rule in your hearts … [and] let the word of Christ dwell in you richly, teaching and admonishing one another in all wisdom, singing psalms and hymns and spiritual songs, with thankfulness in your hearts to God. And whatever you do, in word or deed, do everything all in the name of the Lord Jesus, giving thanks to God the Father through him."

Exchange of Vows

As an expression of your willingness to engage in these obligations and as a seal of the holy vows you are about to make, will you face one another and join your hands.

Pastor: Dan, do you take Jennifer to be your wife and to live together after God's command in holy marriage? Do you promise to be her considerate, faithful, and loving husband and to submit your life to the authority of God's word? Do you covenant to love her, support and serve her, guide and cherish her in prosperity and in adversity; in sorrow and in happiness; in sickness and in health; and forsaking all others, be united to her so long as you both shall live?

Dan: Jennifer, I take you to be my wife. I love you and give myself and all I am to you. With deepest joy I join my life with yours. I promise to cherish and uphold you from this day forward as long as our lives shall last. And as a symbol of my promise, I give you this ring, a celebration of our union in Christ, in the name of the Father, and the Son, and the Holy Spirit. Amen.

Pastor: Jennifer, do you take Dan to be your husband and to live together after God's command in holy marriage? Do you promise to be his considerate, faithful, and loving wife and to submit your life to the authority of God's word? Do you covenant to love him, support and serve him, guide and cherish him in prosperity and in adversity; in sorrow and in happiness; in sickness and in health; and forsaking all others, be united to him so long as you both shall live?

Jennifer: Dan, I take you to be my husband. I love you and give myself and all I am to you. With deepest joy I join my life with yours. I promise to cherish and uphold you from this day forward as long as our lives shall last. And as a symbol of my promise, I give you this ring, a celebration of our union in Christ, in the name of the Father, and the Son, and the Holy Spirit. Amen.

Pastoral Prayer: God of love and faithfulness, you have witnessed this vow of commitment. May you give Dan and Jennifer the grace they need to fulfill their vows. May they know your wisdom and insight. May the strength and endurance of your Holy Spirit guard and protect them and give to them all that is required in their daily pursuit of love, faithfulness, and service.

Holy Father, help them surrender to the authority of your word. Grant to them the qualities of compassion, kindness, humility, gentleness, patience, and love in their relationship with each other and with all others. May your grace, mercy, and peace be on their marriage from this day forward, through Jesus Christ our Lord. Amen.

Prayer and Responsive Reading

Leader: Eternal God, creator and preserver of all life, author of salvation, and giver of all grace: Look with favor upon the world you have made, and for which your Son gave his life, and especially upon Dan and Jennifer whom you have made one in holy marriage.[3]

Congregation: Give them wisdom and devotion in the ordering of their common life, that each may be to the other a strength in need, a counselor in confusion, a comfort in sorrow, and a companion in joy.

Leader: Grant that their wills may be so knit together in your will, and their spirits in your Spirit, that they may grow in love and peace with you and one another all the days of their life.

Congregation: Give them grace, when they hurt each other, to recognize and acknowledge their fault, and to seek each other's forgiveness and yours.

Leader: Make their life together a sign of Christ's love to this sinful and broken world, that unity may overcome estrangement, forgiveness heal guilt, and joy conquer despair.

Congregation: Bestow on them, if it is your will, the gift and heritage of children, and the grace to bring them up to know you, to love you, and to serve you.

Leader: Give them such fulfillment of their mutual affection that they may reach out in love and concern for others.

Congregation: Grant that all who have witnessed these vows may find their devotion to Christ deepened, their lives strengthened, and their commitments confirmed.

Leader: Grant that the bonds of our common humanity may be so transformed by your grace, that your will may be done on earth as it is in heaven; where you live and reign in perfect unity, now and forever, O Father, Son and Holy Spirit. Amen.

Declaration and Benediction

Pastor: We acknowledge, Dan and Jennifer, that you have given your marriage vows in the presence of God and before this company. Therefore, I declare you to be husband and wife, in the name of the Father, Son and Holy Spirit. Those whom God has joined together, let no one separate. Amen.

"May the Lord bless and protect you; May the Peace of Christ rule in your hearts and may the Word of Christ dwell in you richly. And through the power of the Holy Spirit, may whatever you do, whether in word or deed, be done in the name of the Lord Jesus Christ, giving thanks to God the Father through Him. Amen."

May I present to you: Dan and Jennifer Blanchard.

Pastors who are inspired by weddings and value spiritual formation refuse to take them as just another thing on the schedule. Yes, weddings take a lot of prayer, energy, and thought, but the value of centering a couple and the work of marriage in Christ is invaluable.

How firm a foundation, ye saints of the Lord,
is laid for our faith in his excellent word!
What more can he say than to you he hath said,
to you who for refuge to Jesus have fled?

Fear not, I am with thee, O be not dismayed,
for I am thy God, and will still give thee aid;
I'll strengthen thee, help thee, and cause thee to stand,
upheld by my righteous, omnipotent hand.

"How Firm a Foundation"

12

Preaching Crisis Sermons

One of the assignments in my preaching class is to prepare and deliver a "crisis sermon." For this exercise we distinguish between a personal crisis that affects individuals and a public, national, or international crisis that affects most everyone. It may be a terrorist attack or a pandemic or some large-scale national or global disaster, but everyone coming to church on Sunday is longing for insight into the crisis and an understanding grounded in God's word.

Some of my students choose a biblical text from the lectionary to prepare their sermon. They show how the assigned Old Testament reading or the psalm or the New Testament passage relates to the crisis and offers an essential perspective for Christ's followers. Other students select a biblical text that is especially well-suited for preaching the gospel in the midst of a congregation facing a public crisis of some magnitude.

The purpose of these crisis sermons is to prepare students for the possibility of changing or rewriting their sermon even at the last minute in order to address *biblically* the concerns and fears of the household of faith. It would be a shame for pastors to forfeit the opportunity to address what is on everyone's mind. Besides, not to address a pressing concern suggests that the church is situationally unaware and spiritually tone-deaf. Before offering an example of a biblical response to a public crisis, I would like to offer a pastoral perspective on personal crises.

PERSONAL CRISES

On any given Sunday, someone in the church is in their deepest, darkest valley. Mature believers are sensitive to the needs of the body of believers, and pastors play a significant role in encouraging a ministry of comfort and compassion. Personal crises in the household of faith are never ending. They are a constant challenge and very much part of the weekly workload. If we are hoping for a break from the unrelenting experience of human suffering and brokenness, we will be forever disappointed. Martin Luther's line is true: "Our Helper He amid the flood of mortal ills prevailing." The "flood of mortal ills" is unrelenting.[1] Divorce, cancer, unexpected deaths, job loss, heart attacks, teenage rebellion, infertility, and persecution in some form for Christ's sake—there is an endless list of troubles afflicting sincere Christians.

If pastors absorb all that pain and suffering as if it were their own, they will not last long in pastoral work. We all share in the burden of living through the mess of the human condition. But the people of God cannot afford to live vicariously through pastors, and pastors cannot live vicariously through individual believers. With that said, it is helpful for someone to say to a brother or sister who is going through the deepest, darkest valley, "The Lord is our comfort, we will fear no evil." And oftentimes it is the pastor who is called on to say these very words, but we must not forget the essential truth of the priesthood of all believers. The resources of comfort in the body of Christ are great theologically and relationally. We remind each other that God's grace is sufficient, for God's power is made perfect in weakness (2 Cor 12:9).

The Sunday morning pastoral prayer is an important opportunity to bring before the Lord and the household of faith those individuals who are facing acute concerns and special needs. It is also helpful to establish a solid group of trained caregivers who have the gift of wisdom and comfort. This is usually best done by identifying men and women who are "fully mature" in Christ and asking them personally to prayerfully consider sharing in this important ministry (Col 1:28).

When a personal crisis affects pastors and their families directly, such as when a spouse suffers a heart attack or a child is diagnosed with cancer, it is important to strike a balance between openness and overexposure. The temptation is either to hide one's personal life or to overshare one's pain. Wise pastors know that every family in the congregation struggles at some time or another with serious health issues and painful losses. The pastor's family ought to be treated like any other person or family in the household of faith.

PUBLIC CRISES

I was driving to our church in San Diego around 6:30 a.m. on Tuesday, September 11, 2001, listening to NPR, when I first heard that a plane crashed into the World Trade Center. First reports speculated that it was a tragic accident involving a small plane, but the early reports quickly changed as the magnitude of the terrorist attack became apparent. More than two decades have passed since that fateful day on September 11, 2001, but if you preached that Sunday, you probably remember what you said.

On the Sunday following the worst terrorist attack in US history, churches were crowded with people trying to cope and make sense out of a horrendous, evil attack. The sheer magnitude of the disaster and the loss of life was overwhelming. The entire nation mourned. Churches were filled with people seeking comfort and support in the weeks following 9/11. The nation rallied, and we have been fighting a war against terrorism ever since. Few would have imagined that twenty years later domestic terrorism from fringe white supremacist groups would pose a greater threat to national security than foreign terrorists. The post-9/11 spiritual hunger and longing for comfort quickly subsided, and the churches returned to normal. However, a sense of pending doom remains, made worse by the global pandemic and the geopolitical tension between autocratic nations and democratic nations. Global climate change only adds to a deep sense of vulnerability and loss.

Terror struck again on December 26, 2004, when a 9.0 earthquake in the Indian Ocean buckled the ocean floor and produced a devastating tsunami. This time, instead of three thousand deaths, there were more than 230,000 dead from fourteen countries. But there were no terrorists to blame. Without warning, beautiful tropical beaches suddenly became scenes of horror and catastrophic devastation. The forces of nature governed by laws absolutely objective in application unleashed unimaginable destruction. News of the disaster spread around the world faster than it did to some who were in the path of the tsunami. Mountainous waves obliterated whole villages, killing poor fishermen and wealthy tourists, kids playing on the beach and the elderly looking on. Instead of humanity's inhumanity to humanity, a natural disaster of apocalyptic proportions was unleashed on unsuspecting humanity.

On both of these occasions, the 9/11 terrorist attack and the Indian Ocean tsunami, I preached on Psalm 46. There are aspects of the sermon below that reflect the New Year's timing of the devastating late December tsunami disaster.

GOD IS OUR REFUGE

God is our refuge and strength,
> a very present help in trouble.
Therefore we will not fear though the earth gives way,
> though the mountains be moved
>> into the heart of the sea,
though its waters roar and foam,
> though the mountains tremble at its swelling.

> > > > (Ps 46:1–3)

This is where we must begin in a crisis. "God is our refuge and strength, a very present help in trouble." God with us is the single most important truth for confronting our fears. When we are shaken to the core, we return to this bedrock truth. When we are painfully aware of our depravity and vulnerability, we begin here: God is our refuge and strength, whether we are up against terrorists or natural disasters or our own depravity. Our souls are anchored in the enduring truth that God is our sure defense, our inner strength, our means of salvation, and our eternal hope.

"God is our refuge" takes on an even greater meaning in the light of Christ. Psalm 46 is prayed today in the light of the far-reaching impact of the gospel of Jesus Christ. When we sing "Joy to the World!" we can hardly imagine the great reversal described in the third stanza: "No more let sin and sorrow grow / Nor thorns infest the ground. / He comes to make his blessings flow / Far as the curse is found, Far as the curse is found, Far as the curse is found."[2] To speak of Jesus Christ as "an ever-present help in trouble" causes us to grasp the unique and specific ways that God helps us. We are helped through his passion (his life, death, and resurrection), his parousia (his second coming), his Paraclete (the gift of the Holy Spirit), and his abiding presence (the gift of union with him in the body of Christ). The help we need in this world and the next is salvation through Jesus Christ.

Psalm 46 and Psalm 2 can be prayed together. The nations rage and plot in vain, but, "The One enthroned in heaven laughs; the Lord scoffs at them. He rebukes them in his anger and terrifies them in his wrath" (Ps 2:4–5 NIV). We do not "see everything in subjection to him" (Heb 2:8), but we look forward to the day when "the kingdom of the world has become the kingdom of our Lord and of his Christ, and he shall reign forever and ever" (Rev 11:15).

The magnitude of the devastating Indian Ocean earthquake and tsunami is hard to grasp. Throughout the history of the church, extreme catastrophes have been understood as a reminder of the ultimate spiritual struggle between God and his creation. The apostle Paul writes, "For the creation was subjected to futility, not willingly, but because of him who subjected it, in hope that the creation itself will be set free from its bondage to decay and obtain the freedom of the glory of the children of God" (Rom 8:20–21).

Christians through the ages have seen terrorism and tsunamis as a *wake-up call*, calling people to turn to God and receive his grace and mercy. The psalmist does not dwell on evil. He deftly describes the cataclysmic and apocalyptic extent of evil, but he refuses to be overwhelmed by it.

French philosopher Voltaire used the devastating Lisbon earthquake of 1755 to refute the existence of a good and just God. According to Voltaire, all was not well with the world, and he defied biblical revelation to make sense of it. His poem was a tour de force against the biblical worldview. It reads in part:

> Unhappy mortals! Dark and mourning earth!
> Affrighted gathering of humankind!
> Eternal lingering of useless pain!
> Come, ye philosophers, who cry, "All's well,"
> And contemplate this ruin of a world.
> Behold these shreds and cinders of your race,
> This child and mother heaped in common wreck,
> These scattered limbs beneath the marble shafts—
> A hundred thousand whom the earth devours,
> Who, torn and bloody, palpitating yet,
> Entombed beneath their hospitable roofs,
> In racking torment end their stricken lives.

Voltaire questioned the moral order of the universe: "Did fallen Lisbon deeper drink of vice / Than London, Paris, or sunlit Madrid?" He challenged the idea that there was a sovereign God in control of the universe. Voltaire reasoned that if "a God came down to lift our stricken race," he left it in the same mess that he found it. "He visited the earth, and changed it not!" Voltaire was right; we do not live in *the best of all possible worlds*, but he was wrong to think that the Bible claimed we did. His moral indignation against evil was right and a sign that he himself was made in God's image, but he was wrong to reject God's "very present help in trouble" (Ps 46:1).

In 1755 John Wesley also wrote about the Lisbon earthquake. Unlike Voltaire, he saw the devastating tragedy as an event that ought to drive men and women to God, because it proved that we have no defenses sufficient to withstand the forces of evil or the judgment of God.

Wesley saw all humanity inherently fallen and subject to the judgment of God. "The earth threatens to swallow you up. Where is your protection now?" "Money offers no defense, and you cannot fly away. Wisdom and titles offer no protection. And if an earthquake doesn't threaten you, maybe a comet will!"

Wesley cut through the philosophy of blame and the psychology of despair and concluded that if

> our own wisdom and strength be not sufficient to defend us, let us not be ashamed to seek farther help. Let us even dare to own that we believe there is a God. ... Let us secure him on our side; let us make this wise, this powerful, this gracious God our friend. Then need we not fear, *though the earth give way and the mountains fall into the heart of the sea*; no, not even if the heavens being on fire are dissolved, and the very elements melt with fervent heat. It is enough that the Lord of hosts is with us, the God of love is our everlasting refuge.

Wesley used the Lisbon earthquake to prove we cannot protect ourselves. Suppose you are not crushed in an earthquake, he reasoned, or swept away in a flood, or struck by a comet; the sad truth is that we all must face death. The consequence of sin is death, and there is no avoiding it, but the gift of God is eternal life in Christ Jesus (Rom 6:23). For Wesley the question was this: "How shall we secure the favor of this great God?"

> If you love God, then you are happy in God; if you love God, riches, honors, and the pleasures of sense are no more to you than bubbles on the water. ... If you love God, God is in all your thoughts, and your whole life is a sacrifice to him. And if you love humankind, it is your one design, desire, and endeavor, to spread virtue and

happiness all around you, to lessen the present sorrows, and increase the joys, of every child of humanity; and if possible to bring them with you to the rivers of pleasure that are at God's right hand for evermore.

Voltaire's poem on the Lisbon earthquake ends in resignation and despair. Wesley's sermon ends with hope and benediction. "May the Father of your spirit, and the Father of our Lord Jesus Christ, make you such a Christian! May He work in your soul a divine conviction of things not discerned by eyes of flesh and blood! May He give you eyes to see Him that is invisible, and to taste of the powers of the world to come! May He fill you with all peace and joy in believing, that you may be happy in life, in death, in eternity!"[3]

THE CITY OF GOD

> There is a river whose streams make glad the city of God,
>   the holy inhabitants of the Most High.
> God is in the midst of her; she shall not be moved;
>   God will help her when morning dawns.
> The nations rage, the kingdoms totter;
>   he utters his voice, the earth melts.
> The LORD of hosts is with us;
>   the God of Jacob is our fortress. (Ps 46:4–7)

The stability and security of the city of God are set in contrast to the earth giving way and the mountains falling into the heart of the sea. Psalm 46 insists that no matter what happens on earth, the Lord is sovereign. In a violent and chaotic world, "the city of God is set down as a simple matter of fact."[4] Violence in all its forms—in nature (Ps 46:2–3), in politics (Ps 46:6), and in war (Ps 46:9)—is no match for the indwelling presence of God, the promise of God's help, and the proclamation of God's voice.

The river running through the city of God is symbolic of God's sustaining help. Instead of chaotic seas that menace and threaten, there is a life-giving river that runs as clear as crystal "down the middle of the great street of the city" (see Ezek 47:1–9; Zech 14:8; Joel 3:18). This river flows from the throne of God and of the Lamb, and on either side of the river there is the fruit-bearing tree of life (Rev 22:1–2). We sing the hymn: "Like a river glorious is God's perfect peace, over all victorious in its bright increase: perfect, yet it floweth fuller every day, perfect, yet it groweth deeper all the way. Stayed upon Jehovah, hearts are fully blest, finding as he promised, perfect peace and rest."[5]

Nations are in an uproar, and kingdoms fall. The earth gives way, and mountains fall into the sea, but the city of God is secure, stable, and immovable. Its safety and permanency comes from God's holiness. His holy presence establishes her. God's help is constant day to day and from beginning to end. The world is filled with disorder and confusion, but in God's presence we find peace and righteousness. The praying poet uses the word "earth" to link the bedrock reality of God to our earthy lives:

> The nations rage, the kingdoms totter; he utters his voice, the earth melts. (Ps 46:6)

> Come, behold the works of the LORD, how he has brought desolations on the earth. (Ps 46:8)

> He makes wars cease to the end of the earth. (Ps 46:9)

> I will be exalted among the nations, I will be exalted in the earth! (Ps 46:10)

God's presence is our bedrock foundation and our true vantage point. The earth can give way and the nations can rage, but God is stronger than the evil. The psalmist calls for real-world, real-time confidence and trust in Yahweh. "The LORD Almighty is with us; the God of Jacob is our fortress" (Ps 46:7 NIV). Wesley speaks of the "unspeakable advantage" a believer has over an unbeliever: "a continual serenity of mind, a constant evenness and composure of temper, 'a peace which passes all understanding,' contentment with life, a continual attitude of gratitude to the living God, and tender compassion toward all people."[6]

CEASE AND DESIST

Come, behold the works of the LORD,
> how he has brought desolations on the earth.
He makes wars cease to the end of the earth;
> he breaks the bow and shatters the spear;
> he burns the chariots with fire.
"Be still, and know that I am God.
> I will be exalted among the nations,
> I will be exalted in the earth!"
The LORD of hosts is with us;
> the God of Jacob is our fortress. (Ps 46:8–11)

Four imperatives bring Psalm 46 to a powerful conclusion: "come," "see," "stop," and "know." In worship the people of God are projected into the future to see the desolations wrought by God on the earth. These desolations are good news because they bring evil to a decisive and definitive end.[7] The global mission of the gospel could not be more political, but it is political in a way entirely different from worldly politics. The psalmist offers to the world the first word of the gospel, "Come and see." The announcement of the kingdom of God is open to all. The gospel is inviting, not intimidating. But the day will come when the war to end all wars will be waged by the Lamb of God, the Heavenly Warrior who is Faithful and True (Rev 19:11–21). No literal military battle will be fought, because as Luther said in his famous hymn, "one little word shall fell him." The metaphoric broken bow and shattered spear stand for the end of evil. Every sin, every crime, every disease, every form of deviancy and perversion will come to an end. The apostle John joins the psalmist in announcing this end and plays it out live on the stage of our praying imagination so we can feel the drama of the cataclysmic end of evil.[8]

The second imperative couplet, "Stop and know," is addressed to the nations. It "is not in the first place comfort for the harassed but a rebuke to a restless and turbulent world: 'Quiet!'—in fact, 'Leave off!'" Derek Kidner continues, "It resembles the command to another sea: 'Peace! Be still!'" (Mark 4:39).[9] The Sovereign Lord announces, "Cease and desist," to the world's superpowers and rebel factions. The nations are exhorted to "be still" and know that the Lord is God. The verb "be still" conveys the idea of "stand down" or "relax." God is commanding the nations: "Stop fighting," "Cease your resistance." Alan Ross explains, "The imperative is a warning for the turbulent world to stop what they are trying to do."[10]

"Be still, and know that I am God" is a familiar challenge to restless believers who are encouraged to trust the Lord and rest in his sovereign care. The Lord's rebuke to the nations is taken personally and transposed as a sought-after discipline of Christian spirituality. Although the psalmist did not have this specific meaning in mind, John Goldingay offers the following insight: "Spirit-inspired interpretation often works by making the words of Scripture mean something quite different from what they actually meant, because new situations make it necessary for God to say new things."[11]

The psalm ends by repeating the refrain and emphasizing the abiding truth of the Lord's presence. Those who resonate with the fearless hope of Psalm 46 share Wesley's last words, "The best of all is, God is with us." Psalm 46 inspired Martin Luther's famous hymn "A Mighty Fortress Is Our God." The hymn, like the psalm, testifies to the sovereign strength of God: "Our helper he amid the flood of mortal ills prevailing." Luther boldly proclaimed that "God is our refuge" because "the right man" is on our side, "the man of God's own choosing ... Christ Jesus it is he." Luther wrote the hymn in 1527 after learning that Leonhard Kaiser, a close friend, had been burned at the stake in the Netherlands for refusing to recant his Christian convictions. A resilient Luther wrote the fourth stanza in tears of faith:

> That word above all earthly powers, no thanks to them,
>   abideth;
> the Spirit and the gifts are ours through him who with
>   us sideth:
> let goods and kindred go, this mortal life also; the body
>   they may kill:
> God's truth abideth still, his kingdom is forever.

Crises are anything but routine, but crises that shake us to our core are inevitable, and only pastors grounded in God's word and rooted in the gospel are able to offer a true message of salvation. We will learn to pray the praise and pain of the Psalms and lean into the power of biblical hope and justice. We will long for Christ's kingdom to come in all of its joy and peace.

*The gospel of Jesus Christ is more political than
anyone imagines, but in a way that no one guesses.*

Eugene Peterson, *Reversed Thunder*

13

Preaching with Social Impact

Preachers who embrace the rock-and-reed challenge are situationally aware. We are tasked with addressing pressing political and ethical issues in a way that depends on the whole counsel of God. Early pastor-theologians such as Tertullian (155–220), Augustine (354–430), and John Chrysostom (349–407) felt it was their duty to apply God's word to the social, economic, and political issues of their day. During the global Covid-19 pandemic, very few pastors felt it was appropriate to openly and publicly encourage their brothers and sisters in Christ to get vaccinated. Our reluctance to weigh in on important social issues such as pandemics and racial reconciliation suggests that preaching is focused mainly on individualistic spiritual concerns. Apart from a few notably important issues such as abortion and gay marriage, pastors seem to practice self-censorship. Pastors are silent on many issues that affect their congregations, such as public health, economics, poverty, politics, creation care, climate change, and guns.

There is a significant difference between a New Testament understanding of the salt-and-light, countercultural household of faith and a Christendom model of the church as the moral majority fighting for power in a secular culture. The challenge before us is how to live for Christ in a culture that is more like first-century Rome or Corinth than Billy Graham's 1950s America. The myth of a Christian nation has run its course. Christendom's "God and country" agenda has betrayed the meaning and the mission of the kingdom of God.

Today's polarized political scene provides a unique challenge for Christians to reexamine their biblical convictions and develop a biblical political theology regardless of their political party affiliation. It is reasonable to conclude that living under the rule of Christ should affect the way Christians view politics and culture. We need to retrace our steps and return to the political theology of the early church. The twenty-first-century church is living in a secular age. Christendom is receding. Nominal Christian culture is fast fading in significance. The church is returning to the New Testament reality of becoming *resident aliens*. Instead of being *against* culture or *of* culture, we are a church *for*-culture in a distinctly Christ-centered way. The social and political wisdom of the New Testament has never been more relevant.

IDENTITY POLITICS

When Jesus asked his disciples, "Who do people say the Son of Man is?" he meant not only to distinguish between popular opinion and their personal conviction, but to define their identity. He asked the question in the region of Caesarea Philippi, which is located at the base of Mount Hermon (modern-day Banias). This region is the northernmost border of Israel and the furthest point of Jesus's journey from Jerusalem. Jesus and his disciples walked along a deep gorge, the headwaters for the Jordan River. As Jesus and the disciples ascended the mountain, they encountered pilgrims on their way to worship at shrines to the Syrian god Baal, the Greek god Pan, and the Roman godhead of Caesar. They saw a deep cavern and shrines embedded in the rocky slopes of Mount Hermon. In the vicinity of Zeus's temple and a shrine to Pan, Jesus asked the question. Symbolically, Jesus had left his home culture and entered into the world at large. He did not ask the question in the temple courts in Jerusalem but in the context of foreign gods and pagan religious pilgrims. It is as if Jesus deliberately set himself against the background of the world's religions and imperial powers in all their history and splendor and demanded to be compared to them.[1]

The disciples responded with high praise. In the mind of the first-century Jew there was no greater tribute than to compare Jesus to Elijah or Jeremiah. "But what about you?" Jesus asked. "Who do you say I am?" Peter spoke first, "You are the Christ, the Son of the living God" (Matt 16:16). Peter's confession is not just a higher view of Jesus; it is a radically different view of Jesus. As Scot McKnight says, "Peter is the first to penetrate into one of the mysteries of the kingdom: the identity of the true king (Jesus)."[2]

Jesus is not one of the many key figures in Jewish history, no matter how commendable and congratulatory it is to be ranked with the prophets. Jesus is the culmination and climax of salvation history. He is the one all the prophets proclaimed and yearned to see. Understanding Jesus's true identity was and is a matter of supernatural revelation. The power of persuasion lies not in human ingenuity and creativity, nor in techniques and methods, but in God's communication. There is an all-or-nothing character to Peter's confession. Being positively attracted to Jesus is not the same thing as confessing Jesus is King. It is critical that we understand that the church is built on the confession—the conviction—that Jesus is the Christ, the Son of the living God. This is a conceptual conviction as well as a relational commitment. It is both intellectual and emotional. This belief is an assertion, a conviction, and a confession that is either altogether true or altogether false. There is no in-between, no middle ground, and its truth transforms us personally and politically. It shapes us profoundly spiritually and socially.

What follows is the most remarkable call to individuality *and community* that the world has ever heard: "You are Peter, and on this rock, I will build my church, and the gates of Hades will not prevail against it" (Matt 16:18). In Christ, Peter is the rock on whom the church is built. First Peter underscores that relationship. "As you come to him, the living Stone ... you also, like living stones are being built into a spiritual house" (1 Pet 2:4–5). Christ's followers (living stones) are being built by God into a spiritual household, a house of the Spirit, to be a holy priesthood offering sacrifices "controlled and animated by God's sanctifying Spirit."[3] Peter offers this remarkable description of King Jesus's subjects: "But you are a chosen race, a royal priesthood, a holy nation, a people for his own possession, that you may proclaim the excellencies of him who called you out of darkness into his marvelous light. Once you were not a people, but now you are God's people; once you had not received mercy, but now you have received mercy" (1 Pet 2:9–10).

Peter affirms that the followers of Christ are a new race. They are a set-apart, holy people redeemed by "the precious blood of Christ, like that of a lamb without blemish or spot" (1 Pet 1:19). Church was not a mixed gathering of Christians and non-Christians who assembled weekly to hear an introduction to the gospel. Church was the priestly community meeting for worship and fellowship. Non-Christians were graciously welcomed, but when they walked through the door they entered into a radically different culture, one that was not designed to cater to their felt needs, much less entertain them. They experienced a noncompetitive counterculture that shared together a no-shame identity and a no-fear solidarity. They were befriended in a clearly defined and welcoming community dedicated to engaging the world for Christ and his kingdom.

Evangelism in the early church was largely dependent on the edification of the believing community. The New Testament letters are a strong indication that the apostles preached to the individual *through their edification of the household of faith.* The seeker was not the focus of attention as it often is in our individualistic preaching. The seeker was an observer of the church's worship, witness, fellowship, and service. The community of believers exemplified and illustrated what it meant to follow the Lord Jesus. The witness of the church was organic, holistic, relational, and participatory. Tim Keller encourages pastors when he writes,

> If you solve Christians' problems with the gospel every week, secular people are not only hearing it a little differently each time, and so getting a more comprehensive view of it, but also seeing how faith in Christ actually works and brings about life change. That is crucial for them to see. They are being evangelized very effectively, not superficially, even as Christians are being built up.[4]

The keys of the kingdom redefine the Christian's political identity. Jesus is King, and he has entrusted to his disciples the responsibility of showing the world what it means to obey King Jesus. The kingdom of God is a people under the reign of Christ, submissive to the Lord. The keys of the kingdom signify both access and exclusion. McKnight describes the indissoluble connection between church and kingdom and its impact on politics:

The kingdom is the people under King Jesus who fellowship with one another and form churches. These churches are the politics of Jesus in this world. That is, a local church embodies—or is designed by God to embody—the kingdom vision of Jesus in such a way that it tells the kingdom story. That is a politic, a witness to the world of a new worship, a new law, a new king, a new social order, a new peace, a new justice, a new economics, and a new way of life.[5]

RESIDENT ALIENS

The radical divergence of perspectives found among sincere believers depends on a variety of factors including region, education, age, race, and denomination. This cultural and religious diversity leads to ideological convictions that lie outside out the Bible. Indifference to what the Bible has to say coupled with ideological indoctrination cripples a Christian understanding of politics and government and distorts the witness of the church. Sincere Christians may differ on how government should be run, but Jesus's kingdom goals ought to be the foundation for our political thinking. We are not at liberty to write off the Sermon on the Mount as teaching that applies to us *personally*, but not *politically*. There may be alternative views on how the poor should be helped, the nation defended, moral convictions upheld, and Wall Street regulated, but these positions must look to the Bible for their understanding and rationale. Christians who believe that the Bible is the inspired word of God engage life in the light of the Scriptures, whether personal or political, spiritual or social.

Many believers have either lost or never knew the New Testament perspective on being resident aliens in their home culture. By virtue of their conversion and baptism, the followers of Jesus Christ become strangers in their own homeland. Without moving from one country to another and without crossing any political or regional boundaries, Christians become resident aliens. Believers are no longer defined primarily by their ethnicity and nationality but by the rule and reign of Christ. They are citizens of the kingdom of heaven both now and for eternity. This new identity leads inevitably to a clash with both secular and religious cultures.

God's chosen outsiders and resident aliens form a noncompetitive, holy community. They have not been called of God to flee the world or fight the world. They have not been called to withdraw into their own tight-knit culture. They are not separatists, narrow-minded, and opinionated. They do not impress the world as hostile and rigid and angry. Their form of offense, the offense of the cross, is the most winsome and attractive "offensiveness" that human culture has ever known. They understand in themselves their own sinfulness and the fallen human condition. But by God's grace they have experienced the power of God's sacrificial love and the responsibility of the ministry of reconciliation.

Christians are identified as "a chosen race, a royal priesthood, a holy nation, a people for [God's] own possession" (1 Pet 2:9). This is not only a spiritual identity but a political identity. The people of God are drawn from every nation, tribe, people, and language (Rev 7:9). Christ's redemption destroys ethnic privilege and pride of race. No person, group, race, tribe, nation, or nations have the right to feel morally superior to others. The identity, calling, solidarity, and significance of the people of God is not based on ethnicity, family, heritage, or merit, but on Christ's atoning once-and-for-all sacrifice. The one new humanity formed in Christ is not part Jewish and part gentile, nor is it part Black and part white. This new race is an act of creation, not a mixture of Asian and Arab, Latin and European. God's chosen people were not meant to divide along ethnic, cultural, racial, social, gender, and generational lines. Since the Christian community is founded solely on Jesus Christ, it is a spiritual reality. This solidarity transcends sociological and psychological compatibility. It is the house of the Spirit, built by the Father on the cornerstone of the Son.

Many American Christians assume that America is a Christian nation that has been exceptionally blessed by God above all other nations and is in danger of losing or has lost that blessing because of the growing influence of a secular/liberal agenda. They apply 2 Chronicles 7:14 as the perceived antidote to the political crisis. They see themselves as part of a moral majority fighting for marriage between a man and woman and defending the right to life for the unborn. Their strategy is to gain the power of the majority and to legislate these biblical moral principles.

Proponents of American exceptionalism are for a strong military, strict immigration rules, lower taxes, and reduced government regulations. They are opposed to welfare for the poor, universal health-care coverage, and environmental regulations. They resist the notion of a global free-trade economy even though they have been the beneficiaries of the developing nations' cheap labor for generations. They believe that God has ordained American superiority for the world's sake. Sadly, this political persuasion identifies more with the American dream than with the kingdom of God. However, thoughtful Christians who identify with a conservative approach to government distance themselves from this nationalistic rhetoric of superiority and resentment.

Another form of political ideology that flies under the banner of Christendom identifies itself as progressive and celebrates conformity to the spirit of the times. They advocate gay rights, abortion on demand, and radical pluralism. They pride themselves on being open minded and tolerant, but they are in fact radically intolerant of biblical truth. They represent a secular agenda that freely diminishes biblical authority on virtually all matters that run counter to the prevailing cultural ethos.

Neither form of popular cultural Christianity can identify with the apostle Peter's description of the resident alien. The alienation fostered by the conservative and progressive extremes of Christendom is radically different from the social alienation addressed by the apostle Peter. Both the right's alien alienation and the left's progressive conformity are worldly strategies. Discerning the difference between cultural conformity and true alienation is critical to understanding Christ's *for*-culture strategy. "We have a story to live and to tell," writes McKnight, "and that story is the kingdom story. The culture war story is not the kingdom story, and it is idolatrous when Christians equate the two."[6]

Fidelity to Christ and the holiness he commands invariably leads to cultural conflict and social estrangement, not because Christians are revolutionaries or separatists, but because their holiness is perceived as a social and political threat. Their life together as the people of God rests in Christ and his mission, but sadly Christ's convictions and compassion invariably produce social alienation. The early Christians knew that their hope was not in Rome, nor in the local tribal gods, nor in the idols sponsored by the local professional guilds. The Christian's hope is not in politics or the economy. Some Christians talk as if their primary identity or loyalty were to the nation, and when things do not go their way politically, they are filled with anger and fear.

Pastor Tim Keller writes, "This may be a reason why so many people now respond to U.S. political trends in such an extreme way. ... They become agitated and fearful for the future. They have put the kind of hope in their political leaders and policies that once was reserved for God and the work of the gospel."[7] The vitriolic rhetoric and slander expressed by Christians against politicians is an indication not of strength and boldness, but of fear and hate. Frustrated Christians feel that their culture is slipping away from them in spite of their best efforts to "bring back America" and "change the world for Christ." For many, the American dream stands for the pursuit of happiness, individual rights, and democratic rule.

Jesus never assumed that he would reform the system and remake Rome into the new Israel, but neither did he ever stop resisting evil, showing compassion, and doing kingdom work. The Christian before the world is like Jesus before Pilate. Believers need to hear these words over and over again to stay on mission: "My kingdom is not of this world. If my kingdom were of this world, my servants would have been fighting, that I might not be delivered over to the Jews. But my kingdom is not from the world" (John 18:36). Jesus accepted that the national ideology was materialistic, militaristic, hedonistic, and pluralistic. He knew that the culture was dedicated to a form of tolerance that was categorically intolerant of absolute truth.

What was true for the early Christians is true for all believers everywhere. If we have any hope of redeeming our witness, we will have "to disentangle the life and identity of the church from the life and identity of American society." Sociologist James Hunter continues,

> For conservatives and progressives alike, Christianity far too comfortably legitimates the dominant political

> ideologies and far too uncritically justifies the prevailing macroeconomic structures and practices of our time. ... The moral life and everyday social practices of the church are also far too entwined with the prevailing normative assumptions of American culture ... Christianity has uncritically assimilated to the dominant ways of life in a manner dubious at the least. Even more, these assimilations arguably compromise the fundamental integrity of its witness to the world.[8]

The legacy of Christendom continues to shape the political imagination of many sincere Christians who have trouble letting go of their "God and country" vision of America. Instead of embracing the New Testament experience of being resident aliens and citizens of heaven, they still look to politics to preserve their Christian morality. It is painful for them to admit that they live in a post-Christian era. They cannot accept the moral relativism and pluralism promoted by our secular age. It is hard for them to face that America can no longer live up to their moral vision of a Christian nation, even if conservative Supreme Court Justices overturn precedent-setting laws that enshrine individual rights. Many sincere Christians fear that they are losing their country, but I am afraid they will eventually realize that their power tactics and shrewd efforts have caused serious harm to the Christian witness.

The big picture of our cultural situation today should cause Christians to reconsider their place in culture and in the world. America today is like first-century Rome, and the followers of Jesus Christ ought to be encouraged to make the most of their "chosen exile" status. They are strangers in their home culture, missionaries in a familiar but foreign land. Now is not the time for Christians to bemoan the loss of religious clout and resent the power and influence of our secular age. The god of American civil religion is dead, and the Triune God, Father, Son, and Holy Spirit, is the only God who lives. There is no generic deity around which we can gather as a nation and pay our respects, but eventually every knee will bow and every tongue confess that Jesus Christ is Lord.

Christians are not called to change the world, but to be faithful in the world. They are called to bear witness to the gospel. Jesus's intercessory prayer in John 17 challenges the triumphal dreaming and guilt-inducing blame that claims the world is as bad as it is because Christians have failed to grasp the reins of power. The world is the world, and the world will be the world until Christ comes again. As Don Carson writes, "The world can be prayed for only to the end that some who now belong to it might abandon it and join with others who have been chosen out of the world."[9] Jesus is not calling Christians to aspire for cultural greatness or join the ranks of the elite or take back America in a groundswell of populist support. Jesus's humble prayer for protection is humiliating to the misguided soul who seeks to impose his or her worldly vision on the church and turn the gospel into a great crusade or a grand cause. Jesus did not set his sights too low; he set his sights on the Holy Father.

SITUATIONAL AWARENESS

Jesus told his followers to be as wise as serpents and as harmless as doves (Matt 10:16). He modeled this strategy when the Pharisees and Herodians set a trap and tried to trick him into speaking against Rome. The exchange between Jesus and his enemies illustrates the positive tension between conviction and strategic thinking. A full and transparent disclosure of Jesus's perspective on Rome would have ended his ministry right there and then. Suppose Jesus had said, "Caesar is a despicable and oppressive ruler, whose reign of terror and evil will be condemned by the Lord God, who will one day raise up his Anointed One, King of kings and Lord of lords, to rule and reign with justice and righteousness." Carson asks,

> Shall we tell Christians in southern Sudan to adopt a different paradigm of Christ-and-culture relations than Christians in Washington, D.C., and vice versa? Shall we tell them that the Bible sets forth several discrete patterns, and they can choose the pattern that seems best to them? Or do we seek to work out a more comprehensive vision, a canon-stipulated vision, of what such relations should be (recognizing, of course, how imperfect all syntheses are), while insisting that the outworking of that comprehensive vision is sufficiently rich and flexible to warrant appropriate diversity in outworking in these two very different cultural contexts?[10]

When Jesus said, "Give back to Caesar what is Caesar's, and to God what is God's," he was underscoring the tension between respect for God-ordained civil authority and obedience for God's all-encompassing authority (Matt 22:21; Mark 12:17; Luke 20:25). The coin stamped with Caesar's image symbolized the power of the civil authority. Christians should pay their taxes and submit to their rulers. But the authority of the state and the authority of God are not two parallel authorities that deserve equal respect. Jesus made that clear when he said to Pilate, "You would have no authority over me at all unless it had been given to you from above" (John 19:11). The authority of the state is subsumed under God's authority and deserves support and compliance only up to a point. Of course, that point may lead all the way to the cross. When Jesus was arrested, he asked a rhetorical question with an obvious answer: "Have you come out as against a robber, with swords and clubs?" (Luke 22:52). He rejected rebellion for the sake of redemption, which proved to be far more revolutionary than anyone ever imagined.

Jesus's whole ministry was politically subversive from its inception down to the present. Herod's massacre of innocents greeted his birth, and in the decades following his resurrection, countless Christians died because they would not bend the knee to Caesar. True Christians make good citizens. They are dependable, law-abiding, trustworthy, and hardworking, but invariably the culture wants some kind of loyalty oath that the Christian is not willing to give because of devotion to the Lord Jesus. In a variety of ways, the culture at large finds it infuriating that the followers of Jesus actually believe that "Salvation is found in no one else, for there is no other name under heaven given to mankind by which we must be saved" (Acts 4:12 NIV).

The best way to phrase this comprehensive and integrative approach to Christ and culture may be to use the little yet flexible preposition "for." Christ *for* culture includes what Christ opposes in our sinful, broken, and fallen human culture, not for the sake of opposition, but for the sake of redemption and reconciliation. Christ *for* culture underscores the love and compassion that Christ and his followers demonstrate on behalf of culture. "Greater love has no one than this: to lay down one's life for one's friends" (John 15:13 NIV). If Christ is *for* culture, who can be against it? The ultimate victory of the risen Lord Jesus Christ is assured, having conquered sin and death and overcome the devil and his forces. No one has the power to raise culture up and transform its members but Christ alone. Christ is *for* culture, as Creator, Savior, reigning Lord, and coming King.

MARKED BY THE CROSS

Peter saw in Jesus what the world could not see: "You are the Christ, the Son of the living God." But his Spirit-inspired confession required a Spirit-inspired commitment, a commitment marked by the cross. It was a commitment that Peter could not fathom, much less accept. It was a commitment he resisted emphatically. "Never, Lord! This shall never happen to you."

When Jesus began to explain how "he must go to Jerusalem and suffer many things at the hands of the elders, the chief priests and the teachers of the law, and that he must be killed and on the third day be raised to life," Peter objected in no uncertain terms (Matt 16:21). Jesus rebuked Peter, saying, "Get behind me, Satan! You are a stumbling block to me; you do not have in mind the concerns of God, but merely human concerns" (Matt 16:23). Then Jesus launched into the meaning of discipleship. "If anyone would come after me, let him deny himself and take up his cross and follow me. For whoever would save his life will lose it, but whoever loses his life for my sake will find it" (Matt 16:24–25).

The only church built by Jesus is a confessing church. This is the only church that needs divine protection, and the only church empowered by God to engage the world with eternal direction and the keys of the kingdom. Any hint of triumphalism is removed by Jesus. The church has always failed miserably spiritually and politically when she has thought otherwise. The confessing church will always be a church from below, an incarnational body, a community marked by the cross and the fellowship of Jesus. The world will never see the household of God as a success.

If we are going to let God's word dwell within us the way the Living Word dwelled among us (John 1:14), we will have to reexamine the way we preach the Bible. We will have to read it and preach it the way Jesus did. The Incarnate One is the preaching paradigm par excellence. He embodied the truth: "The Word became flesh and dwelt among us, and we have seen his glory, glory as of the only Son from the Father, full of grace and truth" (John 1:14). The Incarnate One moves into our neighborhood. There is nothing abstract and theoretical about this. Belief is not a cognitive assent to ideas, but a living, grace-based relationship of faithful obedience. We take up our cross daily and follow the crucified and risen Messiah.

Meekness fits God's modus operandi. God's self-revelation is slow, personal, counterintuitive, and characterized by great reserve. The climax of God's great salvation history is reached in the Incarnate One at the point of God's greatest humility and vulnerability. But the clarity and the victory of God's redemptive love is never in doubt. Inherent in salvation history is the humility of God, whose costly love and divine forgiveness is the free gift of grace.

The meekness of God is revealed in the Father's reserve, in the Son's reticence, and in the Spirit's selflessness. Divine meekness has no parallel in the history of man-made gods and in the religions of human origin and invention. It is the meekness of the Father that wills to redeem humankind through love and grace. It is the meekness of the Son that proves the Father's will and preserves the integrity of the incarnation. And it is the meekness of the Spirit, who was sent not to speak on his own behalf, but to bear witness to Jesus Christ (John 16:13–15).

Preaching is a labor of love that demands great insight, intense prayer, and behind-the-scenes energy. All good preachers seek to point people to Christ, not themselves. Instead of basking in the limelight, they want to shine the light on Jesus. Good preachers cultivate a humility that causes them to resist being the center of attention. There is a sense of urgency and immediacy in good preaching that defies the flippant and casual air of today's seriously unserious culture. Preachers extend themselves as Jesus did. They issue a loving appeal, a call to reason, a desire for dialogue. They echo the prophet Isaiah when he says, "Come now, let us reason together, says the LORD: though your sins are like scarlet, they shall be as white as snow; though they are red like crimson, they shall become like wool" (Isa 1:18). Like Jesus, good preachers proclaim without the presumption of agreement and the cockiness of success. In short, they refuse to diminish their listeners.

THE NEW TESTAMENT CHALLENGE

The New Testament stands for the sanctity of human life and upholds a biblical sexual ethic. The church's pro-life stance is for the unborn, the poor, the victims of injustice, the disabled, the addict, the refugee, the abused, and the exploited. The household of faith practices sexual purity outside marriage and fidelity between a man and woman in marriage. The church is centered in Jesus Christ, who alone offers personal and social salvation. Redemption and reconciliation are foundational to the life and ministry of the church. The impact of Jesus's kingdom ethic and his call to make disciples of all nations replaces the American dream of the good life with a gospel life marked by the cross. Jesus challenges American exceptionalism and global superiority with the Great Commandment and the Great Commission.

The apostle Peter refused to focus on how bad the world was. Instead, he focused on how good the Christian should be. He asks,

Now who is there to harm you if you are zealous for what is good? But even if you should suffer for righteousness' sake, you will be blessed. Have no fear of them, nor be troubled, but in your hearts honor Christ the Lord as holy, always being prepared to make a defense to anyone who asks you for a reason for the hope that is in you; yet do it with gentleness and respect, having a good conscience, so that, when you are slandered, those who revile your good behavior in Christ may be put to shame. For it is better to suffer for doing good, if that should be God's will, than for doing evil.

For Christ also suffered once for sins, the righteous for the unrighteous, that he might bring us to God, being put to death in the flesh but made alive in the spirit. (1 Pet 3:13–18)

What the world needs more than anything else is the gospel of Jesus Christ. Wherever possible, the people of God advocate for social justice and humanitarian benefits, but we keep two realities always in focus in the process. First, only Christ can bring about the justice and shalom the human heart longs for. No amount of cooperation and contribution with the world will achieve God's will apart from the cross and the hope of the resurrection. Second, the complexity and depravity of the human condition means that unintended negative consequences inevitably trail behind the pursuit of social and political justice.

Seven Theses on Good Preaching

I conclude with the following key truths that comfort and challenge pastors who preach and all Christ's followers who love God's word.

1. Good preaching is dependent in every way on the Bible.

2. Good preaching preaches the whole counsel of God.

3. Good preaching brings to bear the whole counsel of God in our life situation.

4. Good preaching understands that God's word is central to everything pastors are called to do—everything Christ's disciples are called to do.

5. Good preaching is challenging spiritually because we are compelled to live in tension with the fallen human condition and God's redemptive provision.

6. Good preaching stirs the heart and mind with a passion for Christ and his kingdom.

7. Good preaching helps believers think for themselves so that they are no longer "conformed to this world" but "transformed by the renewal of [their] mind" (Rom 12:2).

1. Good Preaching Is Dependent
in Every Way on the Bible

Christian preaching is always and only biblical preaching. The sermon's content, shape, style, tone, and impact are derived from the biblical text. Disciples know that the power of God's word to achieve its purposes is not in doubt (Heb 4:12). The challenge comes with our ability to eat the word—ingesting, digesting, and metabolizing God's life-giving word. We engage the biblical text prayerfully, theologically, linguistically, personally, politically, sociologically, and emotionally to the end that we might proclaim Christ, "admonishing and teaching everyone with all wisdom, so that we may present everyone fully mature in Christ" (Col 1:28 NIV). Good preaching is prophetic and priestly, speaking to the individual and the community, evangelizing the lost, edifying the believer, witnessing to all, and building up the body of Christ.

2. Good Preaching Preaches
the Whole Counsel of God

The whole Bible undivided is the Christian book, and it is equally Christian at every point. As Dale Bruner says, "Every Old and New Testament text must be brought to kneel before the Messiah, Scripture's Center and Power, before it can be preached as Word of God."[1] The church calendar and the seasonal rhythms of the year provide opportunity to preach Christ from the whole counsel of God. We not only want to begin in the biblical story, but we want to remain in the gospel story throughout our pastoral ministry. Over time expository preaching develops a congregation's ability to approach and understand the Bible as an organic whole. Each book of the Bible has its own essence or thesis. The substance of revelation is explainable, and it is up to preachers to articulate that message in a clear and compelling way. The purpose of preaching is not to focus on the self, but on God's word. If the existential self is the preacher's text, rather than God's word, faithful and fruitful preaching is subverted. Preachers who care about the listener are preachers who draw out the passion of the passage for the sake of the listener. The preacher does not set out to impress the listener with the preacher's ability to read their hopes and fears. Whatever therapy a hearer receives ought to come from the theology of the text. The most powerful way to bring lasting value to the listener is to faithfully preach the biblical text in the power of the Holy Spirit. The goal of the gospel is the transformation of the person and the building up of the body of Christ.

3. Good Preaching Brings to Bear the Whole Counsel of God in Our Life Situation

Faithful biblical interpretation not only leads to a deeper understanding of the biblical text in its original context, but it impacts the life of the church today. Careful exegesis requires practical and pastoral application. If our intellectual efforts neglect this essential pastoral task, then the impact of the Bible is cut off from its true purpose and where it is needed most. We do not have the luxury of leaving the truth in the ancient world. The Spirit deepens our situational awareness to bring the truth of the text to bear on the real situation facing Christ's followers. The avoidance of applicable biblical meaning and action is not an option. Good preaching requires discernment, challenging work, and prayer. We want to pay attention prayerfully and thoughtfully to God's overarching salvation history, the original intention of the passage, the context of the text, and the people to whom one is preaching. You know good preaching when you hear it. Your heart is stirred, and your mind is moved. "Were not our hearts burning within us while he talked with us on the road, while he opened to us the Scriptures?" (Luke 24:32).

4. Good Preaching Understands That God's Word Is Central to Everything Pastors Are Called to Do—Everything Christ's Disciples Are Called to Do

The first duty of pastoral ministry is to teach the word of God, and everything else flows from this responsibility. As Martin Luther puts it:

> The first and foremost of all on which everything else depends, is the teaching of the Word of God. For we teach with the Word, we consecrate with the Word, we bind and absolve sins by the Word, we baptize with the Word, we sacrifice with the Word, we judge all things by the Word. Therefore when we grant the Word to anyone, we cannot deny anything to him pertaining to the exercise of his priesthood. This Word is the same for all, as Isaiah says, "All your sons shall be taught by the Lord."[2]

Luther envisioned every believer wielding the double-edged sword and every believer sharing the apostle's conviction, "Lord, to whom shall we go? You have the words of eternal life. We have come to believe and to know that you are the Holy One of God" (John 6:68–69 NIV).

5. Good Preaching Is Challenging Spiritually because We Are Compelled to Live in Tension with the Fallen Human Condition and God's Redemptive Provision

It is provocative intellectually because we embrace a worldview and a metanarrative that counters our secular age. It is unsettling socially because thinking Christianly runs contrary to the way the world works relationally, sexually, politically, economically, and globally. It is convicting ethically because Jesus's kingdom ethic calls for conduct that at times opposes the world. It is disconcerting pastorally because the demand for true discernment and pastoral leadership in the household of faith never lets up.

Good preaching is fulfilling *personally* because giving one's life for the sake of understanding and proclaiming God's word is preeminently worthwhile, deeply satisfying, and lifesaving. It is coherent *intellectually* because the same eternal word that created the heavens and established the earth is the enduring word that saves us and directs our steps. It is meaningful *socially* because the word of God centers the person and the community in Christ. There is no greater relational guide for facing the complexities of life together than God's word. It is enduring *ethically* because the Lord has shown us what is required of us, "to act justly and to love mercy and to walk humbly with [our] God" (Mic 6:8). By God's grace, we have clear moral guidance and empowerment to live in the way God designed us to live. It is life-affirming *pastorally* because if we let the word of Christ dwell in us richly, we will be able to teach and admonish our brothers and sisters in Christ with all wisdom (Col 3:16).

6. Good Preaching Stirs the Heart
and Mind with a Passion for
Christ and His Kingdom

Before we parse a verb, outline a passage, or read a commentary, we know the gospel shapes character. It is divine revelation delivered through the life experience of Christ's disciples. We preach who we are, but we do not preach ourselves. God takes our childhood experiences, our relationships, our loneliness, our education, our suffering, our brokenness, our successes, and all our strengths and weaknesses and forms a pastor who lives into the gospel. "For what we proclaim is not ourselves, but Jesus Christ as Lord" (2 Cor 4:5). Good preaching is authentic speech, voiced out of the integrity of the disciple, stripped of empty jargon, and free of cliché. It is a message that issues from the preacher's heart, mind, and soul. Those who live to proclaim the gospel depend on God's power "to destroy strongholds ... arguments and every lofty opinion raised against the knowledge of God, and [to] take every thought captive to obey Christ" (2 Cor 10:4–5). And we know the *divine weakness* rooted in the sufficiency of God's grace; God's power "is made perfect in weakness" (2 Cor 12:9). Good preaching issues out of the holistic character of the preacher, who combines gift and responsibility, style and substance, text and context into a sermon that evangelizes and edifies to the glory of God.

7. Good Preaching Helps Believers Think
for Themselves, So That They Are No
Longer "Conformed to This World"
but "Transformed by the Renewal
of [Their] Mind" (Rom 12:2)

Preachers preach so the people of God can preach.[3] Faithful preaching equips the saints for works of righteousness by offering "the sound instruction of our Lord Jesus Christ" and "godly teaching" (1 Tim 6:3 NIV). Faithfulness and fruitfulness combine when we correctly handle the word of truth (2 Tim 2:15). Every biblical passage deals with the clash between the mystery of God and the mess of the human condition. To the degree that we identify with Jesus, his person, and his work, we live in that tension. Every sermon runs along a fault line between the fallen human condition, in all its personal and social complexity, and God's redemptive provision, in all its grace and mercy. This tension in the text leads to the passion of the passage. Good exegesis discovers the tension in the text, and good preaching brings out the passion of the passage. We seek to preach the gospel of Jesus Christ with clarity and honesty to the religious and the irreligious.

Good preachers cultivate a humility that causes them to resist drawing attention to themselves. There is a sense of urgency and immediacy in good preaching that defies the flippant and casual air of seriously unserious late modern culture. Preachers extend themselves as Jesus did. They issue a loving appeal, a call to reason, and a desire for gospel resolution. They echo the prophet Isaiah when he writes, "'Come now, let us settle the matter,' says the LORD. 'Though your sins are like scarlet, they shall be as white as snow; though they are red as crimson, they shall be like wool'" (Isa 1:18 NIV).

Bibliography

Alcántara, Jared E. *Crossover Preaching: Intercultural-Improvisational Homiletics in Conversation with Gardner C. Taylor*. Downers Grove, IL: InterVarsity Press, 2015.

———. *The Practices of Christian Preaching*. Grand Rapids: Baker, 2019.

Allen, Leslie C. *Psalms 101–150*. Word Biblical Commentary 21. Waco, TX: Word Books, 1983.

Allen, Michael R., and Scott R. Swain. "In Defense of Proof-Texting." *Journal of the Evangelical Theological Society* 54.3 (Sept 2011), 589–606.

Arnett, Jeffrey. *Emerging Adulthood: The Winding Road from the Late Teens through the Twenties*. Oxford: Oxford University Press, 2014.

Augsburger, David. *Dissident Discipleship*. Grand Rapids: Baker, 2006.

Augustine. *Confessions*. Oxford: Oxford University Press, 2008.

———. "Homilies on the Gospel of John." In vol. 7 of *Nicene and Post-Nicene Fathers*, edited by Philip Schaff. Peabody, MA: Hendrickson, 1995.

———. "On Christian Doctrine." In vol. 2 of *Nicene and Post-Nicene Fathers*, edited by Philip Schaff, 519–97.Peabody, MA: Henderickson, 1995.

Bandy, Thomas. "This Is the Christ Postmodern People Need to Hear About." *NETResults* (Nov/Dec 2000): 13–14.

Barth, Markus. *Ephesians*. Anchor Bible 34. New York: Doubleday, 1974.

Baxter, J. Sidlow. *Awake My Heart*. Grand Rapids: Zondervan, 1960.

Beasley-Murray, George R. *John*. Word Biblical Commentary 36. Waco, TX: Word Books, 1987.

Bonhoeffer, Dietrich. *Meditating on the Word*. New York: Ballantine, 1986.

———. *Spiritual Care*. Translated by Jay C. Rochelle. Minneapolis: Fortress, 1985.

Brown, Raymond. *The Message of Hebrews*. The Bible Speaks Today. Downers Grove, IL: InterVarsity, 1984.

Bruce, F. F. *Commentary on the Epistles to the Ephesians and the Colossians*. New International Commentary on the New Testament. Grand Rapids: Eerdmans, 1957.

———. *Paul: Apostle of the Heart Set Free*. Grand Rapids: Eerdmans, 1977.

Brueggemann, Walter. *Genesis*. Interpretation. Atlanta: John Knox, 1982.

Bruner, Frederick Dale. *The Churchbook: Matthew*. 2 vols. Grand Rapids: Eerdmans, 2004.

———. *The Gospel of John*. Grand Rapids: Eerdmans, 2012.

Bryson, Bill. *A Short History of Nearly Everything*. New York: Broadway, 2004.

Bultmann, Rudolf. *Kergyma and Myth*. Edited by Hans Werner Bartsch. New York: Harper & Row, 1961.

Calvin, John. *Institutes of the Christian Religion*. 2 vols. Edited by John T. McNeill. Translated by Ford Lewis Battles. Louisville: Westminster John Knox, 2006.

Carson, D. A. *Christ and Culture Revisited*. Grand Rapids: Eerdmans, 2008.

———. *The Gospel according to John*. Grand Rapids: Eerdmans, 1991.

———. *Matthew*. Expositors Bible Commentary. Grand Rapids: Zondervan, 2010.

Chambers, Oswald. *My Utmost for His Hightest*. New York: Dodd, Mead, 1935.

Chapell, Bryan. *Christ-Centered Preaching: Redeeming the Expository Sermon*. 2nd ed. Grand Rapids: Baker, 2005.

Craigie, Peter. *Psalms 1–50*. Word Biblical Commentary 19. Waco,
        TX: Word Books, 1983.

Crick, Francis. *The Astonishing Hypothesis: The Scientific Search for
        the Soul*. New York: Simon & Schuster, 1994.

Dawkins, Richard. *The God Delusion*. Boston: Houghton Mifflin,
        2006.

Dinwiddie, Richard D. "Messiah: Behind the Scenes of Handel's
        Masterpiece." *Christianity Today*, Dec 17, 1982, 12–20.

Edwards, William D., Wesley J. Gabel, and Floyd E. Hosmer. "On
        the Physical Death of Jesus Christ." *Journal of the American
        Medical Association* 255.11 (1986): 1455–63.

Gillquist, Peter. "A Marathon We Are Meant to Win." *Christianity
        Today* Oct 1981, 22–23.

Goldingay, John. *Psalms 42–89*. Grand Rapids: Baker, 2007.

Gregory the Great. *The Book of Pastoral Rule*. Translated by George
        Demacopoulos. Crestwood, NY: St. Vladimir's Seminary
        Press, 2007.

Guthrie, George H. "Hebrews." In *Commentary on the New
        Testament Use of the Old Testament*, edited by G. K. Beale
        and D. A. Carson, 919–95. Grand Rapids: Baker, 2007.

Haidt, Jonathan. *The Righteous Mind*. New York: Pantheon, 2012.

Harrington, Samuel. *At Peace: Choosing a Good Death after a Long
        life*. New York: Grand Central Life and Style, 2018.

Hunter, James Davison. *To Change the World: The Irony, Tragedy,
        and Possibility of Christianity in the Late Modern World*. New
        York: Oxford University Press, 2010.

Hurtado, Larry W. *Mark*. Understanding the Bible Commentary
        Series. Grand Rapids: Baker, 1989.

Hustad, Donald P. *The Worshiping Church: A Hymnal*. Carol Stream,
        IL: Hope, 1990.

John Chrysostom. *On the Priesthood: Six Books*. Translated by
        Graham Neville. Crestwood, NY: St. Vladimir's Seminary
        Press, 1964.

Johnson, Dennis. *Him We Proclaim: Preaching Christ from All the Scriptures*. Phillipsburg, NJ: P&R, 2007.

Keener, Craig S. *Matthew*. Downers Grove, IL: InterVarsity Press, 1997.

Keller, Timothy. *Counterfeit Gods: The Empty Promises of Money, Sex, and Power, and the Only Hope That Matters*. New York: Dutton, 2009.

———. *Preaching: Communicating Faith in an Age of Skepticism*. New York: Viking, 2015.

Kidner, Derek. *Psalms 1–72*. Downers Grove, IL: InterVarsity Press, 1975.

———. *Psalms 73–150*. Downers Grove, IL: InterVarsity Press, 1975.

Kierkegaard, Søren. *Attack upon "Christendom."* Translated by Walter Lowrie. Princeton: Princeton University Press, 1968.

———. *Concluding Unscientific Postscript*. Translated by David F. Swenson and Walter Lowrie. Princeton: Princeton University Press, 1968.

———. *Purity of Heart Is to Will One Thing*. Translated by Douglas V. Steere. New York: Harper & Row, 1956.

———. *Training in Christianity*. Translated by Walter Lowrie. Princeton: Princeton University Press, 1957.

King, Martin Luther, Jr. "Letter from a Birmingham Jail." In *Letters to a Birmingham Jail: A Response to the Words and Dreams of Dr. Martin Luther King, Jr.*, edited by Bryan Loritts, 19–39. Chicago: Moody, 2014.

Lewis, C. S. *A Grief Observed*. New York: Bantam Books, 1976.

———. *Mere Christianity*. San Francisco: HarperCollins, 2001.

———. *Miracles*. New York: Collins, 1978.

———. *Surprised by Joy*. London: Fontana, 1955.

Litfin, A. Duane. "The Perils of Persuasive Preaching." *Christianity Today*, Feb 4, 1977, 14–17.

———. *St. Paul's Theology of Proclamation: 1 Corinthians 1–4 and Greco-Roman Rhetoric*. Cambridge: Cambridge University Press, 1994.

———. "Swallowing Our Pride: An Essay on the Foolishness of
      Preaching." In *Preach the Word: Essays on Expository
      Preaching*, edited by Leland Ryken and Todd Wilson,
      109–26.

Lloyd-Jones, Martyn. *Preaching and Preachers*. Grand Rapids:
      Zondervan, 1971.

Luther, Martin. "Concerning the Ministry, 1523." In vol. 40 of
      Luther's Works, edited by Conrad Bergendoff, 5–44.
      Philadelphia: Fortress, 1958.

———. "Preface to the Old Testament." In vol. 35 of *Luther's Works*,
      edited by E. Theodore Bachmann, 235–36.Philadelphia:
      Muhlenberg, 1960.

Mackie, Tim. *Read Scripture: Illustrated Summaries of Biblical Books*.
      Portland, OR: Bible Project, 2018.

Marshall, I. Howard. *Luke: Historian and Theologian*. Grand
      Rapids: Zondervan, 1982.

———. *Luke*. New International Greek Testament Commentary.
      Grand Rapids: Eerdmans, 1978.

Martin, Ralph P. *2 Corinthians*. Word Biblical Commentary 40.
      Waco, TX: Word Books, 1986.

McCaulley, Esau. *Reading while Black: African American Biblical
      Interpretation as an Exercise in Hope*. Downers Grove, IL:
      InterVarsity Press, 2020.

McKnight, Scot. *Kingdom Conspiracy: Returning to the Radical
      Mission of the Local Church*. Grand Rapids: Brazos, 2014.

Melville, Herman. *White Jacket*. North Hollywood, CA: Aegypan,
      2006.

Millar, Gary, and Phil Campbell. *Saving Eutychus: How to Preach
      God's Word and Keep People Awake*. MatthiasMedia, 2013.

Motyer, J. Alec. *The Prophecy of Isaiah: An Introduction and
      Commentary*. Downers Grove, IL: InterVarsity Press, 1993.

Mounce, Robert. *The Book of Revelation*. Rev. ed. New International
      Commentary on the New Testament. Grand Rapids:
      Eerdmans, 1997.

O'Brien, Peter. *Colossians, Philemon*. Word Biblical Commentary 44. Waco, TX: Word Books, 1982.

O'Conner, Flannery. "The Catholic Novelist in the Protestant South." In *Collected Works*, 853–64. New York: Library of America, 1988.

Oden, Thomas C. *Pastoral Theology: The Essentials of Ministry*. New York: HarperOne, 1983.

Palmer, Parker J. *The Courage to Teach: Exploring the Inner Landscape of a Teacher's Life*. San Francisco: Jossey-Bass, 1998.

Patrick, Tim, and Andrew Reid. *The Whole Counsel of God: Why and How to Preach the Entire Bible*. Wheaton, IL: Crossway, 2020.

Peterson, Eugene H. *Christ Plays in Ten Thousand Places*. Grand Rapids: Eerdmans, 2005.

———. *Earth and Altar: The Community of Prayer in a Self-Bound Society*. Downers Grove, IL: InterVarsity Press, 1985.

———. *Eat This Book*. Grand Rapids: Eerdmans, 2006.

———. *Run with the Horses*. Downers Grove, IL: InterVarsity Press, 1983.

Pink, Arthur. *The Seven Sayings of the Savior on the Cross*. Louisville: GLH, 2019.

Ross, Allen P. *The Psalms*. 3 vols. Grand Rapids: Kregel, 2011–2016.

Smith, Christian. *Lost in Transition: The Dark Side of Emerging Adulthood*. Oxford: Oxford University Press, 2011.

Smith, Robert, Jr. *Doctrine That Dances: Bringing Doctrinal Preaching and Teaching to Life*. Nashville: B&H, 2008.

Spurgeon, Charles H. *Christ's Words from the Cross*. Grand Rapids: Baker, 1997.

Stott, John R. W. *Between Two Worlds: The Art of Preaching in the Twentieth Century*. Grand Rapids: Eerdmans, 1982.

———. *The Message of 1 & 2 Thessalonians: The Gospel and the End of Time*. Downers Grove, IL: InterVarsity Press, 1991.

———. *The Message of Ephesians: God's New Society.* Downers Grove, IL: InterVarsity Press, 1979.

———. *The Message of the Sermon on the Mount.* Downers Grove, IL: InterVarsity Press, 1978.

———. *Romans.* Downers Grove, IL: InterVarsity Press, 1994.

———. *The Spirit, the Church, and the World.* Downers Grove, IL: InterVarsity Press, 1990.

Thielicke, Helmut. *Encounter with Spurgeon.* Translated by John W. Doberstein. Philadelphia: Fortress, 1963.

Thielman, Frank. *Philippians.* NIV Application Commentary. Grand Rapids: Zondervan, 1995.

Thiselton, Anthony. *The First Epistle to the Corinthians.* Grand Rapids: Eerdmans, 2000.

Walker, Vicky. "An Interview with Sir David Suchet: The Bible Cannot Be Silenced." *Church Times,* Apr 16, 2021. https://www.churchtimes.co.uk/articles/2021/16-april/features/features/an-interview-with-sir-david-suchet-the-bible-cannot-be-silenced.

Waltke, Bruce K. "The Fear of the Lord: The Foundation for a Relationship with God." In *Alive to God: Studies in Spirituality Presented to James Houston,* edited by J. I. Packer and Loren Wilkinson, 17–33. Downers Grove, IL: InterVarsity Press, 1996.

———. *An Old Testament Theology.* Grand Rapid: Zondervan, 2007.

Waltke, Bruce K., and James M. Houston. *The Psalms as Christian Worship: A Historical Commentary.* Grand Rapids: Eerdmans, 2010.

Webster, Douglas D. *A Christmas Journey.* Toronto: Clements, 2007.

———. *The Easy Yoke.* Colorado Springs: NavPress, 1995.

———. *Follow the Lamb: A Pastoral Approach to the Revelation.* Eugene, OR: Cascade, 2014.

———. *Living in Tension: A Theology of Ministry.* 2 vols. Eugene, OR: Cascade, 2012.

———. *The Living Word: Ten Life-Changing Ways to Experience the Bible*. Chicago: Moody, 2003.

———. *Preaching Hebrews: The End of Religion and Faithfulness to the End*. Eugene, OR: Cascade Books, 2017.

———. *Second Thoughts for Skeptics*. Toronto: Regent College Publishing, 2010.

———. *Text Messaging: A Conversation on Preaching*. Toronto: Clements, 2010.

Wesley, John. "Serious Thoughts Occasioned by the Late Earthquake at Lisbon." In vol. 11 of *The Works of John Wesley*, 1–13. New York: J. Emory & Waugh, 1818.

Willimon, William H. *Pastor: The Theology and Practice of Ordained Ministry*. Nashville: Abingdon, 2016.

Wright, N. T. *Paul: A Biography*. New York: HarperOne, 2018.

Notes

CHAPTER 1

1. Douglas D. Webster, *Preaching Hebrews: The End of Religion and Faithfulness to the End* (Eugene, OR: Cascade Books, 2017), 98.

2. Jared E. Alcántara, *The Practices of Christian Preaching* (Grand Rapids: Baker, 2019), 43, 51–59.

3. Robert Smith Jr., *Doctrine That Dances: Bringing Doctrinal Preaching and Teaching to Life* (Nashville: B&H, 2008), 44.

4. Parker J. Palmer, *The Courage to Teach: Exploring the Inner Landscape of a Teacher's Life* (San Francisco: Jossey-Bass, 1998), 2, 11, 33.

5. Palmer, *Courage to Teach*, 10.

6. N. T. Wright, *Paul: A Biography* (New York: HarperOne, 2018), 58.

7. F. F. Bruce, *Paul: Apostle of the Heart Set Free* (Grand Rapids: Eerdmans, 1977), 81.

8. Wright, *Paul*, 65.

9. Wright, *Paul*, 69.

10. Jared Alcántara, *Crossover Preaching: Intercultural-Improvisational Homiletics in Conversation with Gardner C. Taylor* (Downers Grove, IL: InterVarsity Press, 2015), 28, 34. Preaching with *intercultural competence* involves "the cultivation of knowledge, skills, and habits for effectively negotiating cultural, racial, ethnic, and ecclesial difference."

11. Eugene Peterson, *Eat This Book* (Grand Rapids: Eerdmans, 2006), 51.

12. Esau McCaulley, *Reading while Black: African American Biblical Interpretation as an Exercise in Hope* (Downers Grove, IL: InterVarsity Press, 2020), 12 (emphasis added).

13. I. Howard Marshall, *Luke*, New International Greek Testament Commentary (Grand Rapids: Eerdmans, 1978), 16.

14. Dennis Johnson, *Him We Proclaim: Preaching Christ from All the Scriptures* (Phillipsburg, NJ: P&R, 2007), 13.

15. Alcántara, *Practices of Christian Preaching*, 36.

16. Flannery O'Conner, "The Catholic Novelist in the Protestant South," in *Collected Works* (New York: Library of America, 1988), 858–59.

17. Eugene H. Peterson, *Christ Plays in Ten Thousand Places* (Grand Rapids: Eerdmans, 2005), 182.

18. Douglas D. Webster, *Text Messaging: A Conversation on Preaching* (Toronto: Clements, 2010), 58.

19. On my shelf I have a number of John Stott's pastoral commentaries, including *Romans* (Downers Grove, IL: InterVarsity Press, 1994); *The Message of Ephesians: God's New Society* (Downers Grove, IL: InterVarsity Press, 1979); *The Message of 1 & 2 Thessalonians: The Gospel and the End of Time* (Downers Grove, IL: InterVarsity Press, 1991); and *The Message of the Sermon on the Mount* (Downers Grove, IL: InterVarsity Press, 1978).

20. John Stott, *The Spirit, the Church, and the World* (Downers Grove, IL: InterVarsity Press, 1990), 7.

21. Frank Thielman, *Philippians*, NIV Application Commentary (Grand Rapids: Zondervan, 1995), 13.

22. Douglas D. Webster, *Follow the Lamb: A Pastoral Approach to the Revelation* (Eugene, OR: Cascade, 2014), 10.

23. Bryan Chapell, *Christ-Centered Preaching: Redeeming the Expository Sermon*, 2nd ed. (Grand Rapids: Baker, 2005), 103.

24. Chapell, *Christ-Centered Preaching*, 103, 110.

25. Webster, *Text Messaging*, 13.

26. Søren Kierkegaard, *Training in Christianity*, trans. Walter Lowrie (Princeton: Princeton University Press, 1957), 109.

27. Thomas C. Oden, *Pastoral Theology: The Essentials of Ministry* (New York: HarperOne, 1983), 139.

CHAPTER 2

1. Augustine, *On Christian Doctrine* 4.6, in *Nicene and Post-Nicene Fathers*, vol. 2, ed. Philip Schaff (Peabody, MA: Hendrickson, 1995), 577–78, 581.

2. Augustine, *Confessions* (Oxford: Oxford University Press, 2008), 78.

3. Douglas D. Webster, *The Living Word: Ten Life-Changing Ways to Experience the Bible* (Chicago: Moody, 2003), 172–74.

4. Augustine, *Confessions*, 88.

5.   Augustine, *Confessions*, 88, 96.

6.   Palmer, *Courage to Teach*, 10.

7.   Martin Luther King Jr., *Letters to a Birmingham Jail: A Response to the Words and Dreams of Dr. Martin Luther King, Jr.*, ed. Bryan Loritts (Chicago: Moody, 2014), 35. The book begins with King's "Letter from a Birmingham Jail," Apr 16, 1963, 19–39.

8.   Webster, *Follow the Lamb*, 5.

9.   Søren Kierkegaard, *Concluding Unscientific Postscript*, trans. David F. Swenson and Walter Lowrie (Princeton: Princeton University Press, 1968), 164–66.

10. Kierkegaard, *Training in Christianity*, 108.

11. Kierkegaard, *Training in Christianity*, 114.

12. Søren Kierkegaard, *Attack upon "Christendom,"* trans. Walter Lowrie (Princeton: Princeton University Press, 1968), 19.

13. Kierkegaard, *Attack upon "Christendom,"* 8.

14. Kierkegaard, *Attack upon "Christendom,"* 13–15.

15. Kierkegaard, *Attack upon "Christendom,"* 17.

16. Kierkegaard, *Attack upon "Christendom,"* 29, 35.

17. Kierkegaard, *Concluding Unscientific Postscript*, 166.

18. Douglas D. Webster, *The Easy Yoke* (Colorado Springs: NavPress, 1995), 14.

19. Douglas D. Webster, *Living in Tension: A Theology of Ministry* (Eugene, OR: Cascade, 2012), 1:64.

20. Webster, *Follow the Lamb*, 44–45.

21. St. John Chrysostom, *On the Priesthood: Six Books*, trans. Graham Neville (Crestwood, NY: St. Vladimir's Seminary Press, 1964), 130.

22. Used with permission.

23. John R. W. Stott, *Between Two Worlds: The Art of Preaching in the Twentieth Century* (Grand Rapids: Eerdmans, 1982), 140–41.

24. St. Gregory the Great, *The Book of Pastoral Rule*, trans. George Demacopoulos (Crestwood, NY: St. Vladimir's Seminary Press, 2007), 57.

25. Kierkegaard, *Training in Christianity*, 134, 139.

26. Dietrich Bonhoeffer, *Spiritual Care*, trans. Jay C. Rochelle (Minneapolis: Fortress, 1985), 31.

27. John Calvin, *Institutes of the Christian Religion*, vol. 2, ed. John T. McNeill, trans. Ford Lewis Battles (Louisville: Westminster John Knox, 2006), IV.7.1132.

CHAPTER 3

1. Martyn Lloyd-Jones, *Preaching and Preachers* (Grand Rapids: Zondervan, 1971), 87–88.

2. Quoted in Webster, *Easy Yoke*, 33.

3. Herman Melville, *White Jacket* (North Hollywood, CA: Aegypan, 2006), 210–18.

4. Palmer, *Courage to Teach*, 5.

5. Webster, *Living Word*, 10.

6. Duane Litfin, "Swallowing Our Pride: An Essay on the Foolishness of Preaching," in *Preach the Word: Essays on Expository Preaching*, ed. Leland Ryken and Todd Wilson (Wheaton, IL: Crossway, 2007), 120.

7. Litfin, "Swallowing Our Pride," 121.

8. Litfin, "Swallowing Our Pride," 127.

9. Anthony Thiselton, *The First Epistle to the Corinthians* (Grand Rapids: Eerdmans, 2000), 214, 219 (emphasis original).

10. Thiselton, *First Epistle to the Corinthians*, 220.

11. Duane Litfin, *St. Paul's Theology of Proclamation: 1 Corinthians 1–4 and Greco-Roman Rhetoric* (Cambridge: Cambridge University Press, 1994), 212.

12. A. Duane Litfin, "The Perils of Persuasive Preaching," *Christianity Today*, Feb 4, 1977, 16.

13. Litfin, "Perils of Persuasive Preaching," 17.

14. Bruce Waltke, "The Fear of the Lord: The Foundation for a Relationship with God," in *Alive to God: Studies in Spirituality Presented to James Houston*, ed. J. I. Packer and Loren Wilkinson (Downers Grove, IL: InterVarsity Press, 1996), 17–33.

15. Ralph P. Martin, *2 Corinthians*, Word Biblical Commentary 40 (Waco, TX: Word Books, 1986), 121.

16. Westminster Confession 5.3.

17. Alcántara, *Practices of Christian Preaching*, 85.

18. Gary Millar and Phil Campbell, *Saving Eutychus: How to Preach God's Word and Keep People Awake* (MatthiasMedia, 2013), 17–24.

19. Chapell, *Christ-Centered Preaching*, 84. Chapell defines an expository sermon as "a message whose structure and thought are derived from the biblical text, that covers the scope of the text, and that explains the features and context of the text in order to disclose the enduring principles for faithful thinking, living, and worship intended by the Holy Spirit, who inspired the text" (31).

20. Millar and Campbell, *Saving Eutychus*, 49.

21. Millar and Campbell, *Saving Eutychus*, 63–75.

22. Millar and Campbell, *Saving Eutychus*, 99, 101–110.

23. Augustine, *On Christian Doctrine*, 119–20.

24. Augustine, *On Christian Doctrine*, 7.

25. Augustine, *On Christian Doctrine*, 30.

26. Augustine, *On Christian Doctrine*, 39.

27. Augustine, *On Christian Doctrine*, 118.

28. Augustine, *On Christian Doctrine*, 119.

29. Augustine, *On Christian Doctrine*, 121.

CHAPTER 4

1. Tim Mackie, *Read Scripture: Illustrated Summaries of Biblical Books* (Portland, OR: Bible Project, 2018), v.

2. Webster, *Text Messaging*, 46.

3. Webster, *Text Messaging*, 43–58.

4. Webster, *Living in Tension*, 2:46–49.

5. Palmer, *Courage to Teach*, 145, 151.

6. Christian Smith, *Lost in Transition: The Dark Side of Emerging Adulthood* (Oxford: Oxford University Press, 2011), 15.

7. Jeffrey Arnett, *Emerging Adulthood: The Winding Road from the Late Teens through the Twenties* (Oxford: Oxford University Press, 2014), 224.

8. Kierkegaard, *Training in Christianity*, 232, 239.

9. C. S. Lewis, *A Grief Observed* (New York: Bantam Books, 1976), 41.

CHAPTER 5

1. Helmut Thielicke, *Encounter with Spurgeon*, trans. John W. Doberstein (Philadelphia: Fortress, 1963), 3.

2. Tim Patrick and Andrew Reid, *The Whole Counsel of God: Why and How to Preach the Entire Bible* (Wheaton, IL: Crossway, 2020), 81.

3. Patrick and Reid, *Whole Counsel of God*, 140, 149. The authors' thirty-five-year whole-Bible preaching plan means that the preacher only preaches a particular text once over the course of a long-term pastoral tenure. "We must remember that whatever we plan to preach now we will not plan to preach again." On the subject of the Psalms, the authors state, "Every time we pick an ideal psalm to contribute to a bigger point, we remove the option of preaching that psalm in the future." I cannot imagine serving a congregation for many years and only preaching Jesus's Sermon on the Mount or David's Psalm 1 or Paul's Letter to the Ephesians once!

4. Chapell, *Christ-Centered Preaching*, 122, 106.

5. Chapell, *Christ-Centered Preaching*, 122.

6. Waltke, *An Old Testament Theology* (Grand Rapids: Zondervan, 2007), 881. "Narrative or storytelling psalms aim to instruct Israel from its sacred history." Waltke identifies the following psalms in this category: 78, 105, 106, 135, 136.

7. Michael R. Allen and Scott R. Swain, "In Defense of Proof-Texting," *Journal of the Evangelical Theological Society* 54.3 (Sept 2011): 606.

8. Quoted in Bruce K. Waltke and James M. Houston, *The Psalms as Christian Worship: A Historical Commentary* (Grand Rapids: Eerdmans, 2010), 492.

9. Waltke and Houston, *Psalms as Christian Worship*, 488.

10. George H. Guthrie, "Hebrews," in *Commentary on the New Testament Use of the Old Testament*, ed. G. K. Beale and D. A. Carson (Grand Rapids: Baker, 2007), 939.

CHAPTER 6

1. William H. Willimon, *Pastor: The Theology and Practice of Ordained Ministry* (Nashville: Abingdon, 2016), 284. Willimon writes, "One of the greatest weaknesses in many of my moves from the biblical text to the preached sermon is that I neglect the communal, corporate intentions of scripture, turning a text that addresses the whole congregation into existential, subjective therapy. Yet scripture tends to be communally concerned before it is individually so."

2. Frederick Dale Bruner, *The Churchbook: Matthew* (Grand Rapids: Eerdmans, 2004), 2:816.

3. Stott, *The Spirit, the Church*, 323.

4.   Wright, *Paul*, 346.

5.   Oden, *Pastoral Theology*, 131–32, 135.

6.   Søren Kierkegaard, *Purity of Heart Is to Will One Thing*, trans. Douglas V. Steere (New York: Harper & Row, 1956), 125.

7.   Kierkegaard, *Purity of Heart*, 132.

8.   Kierkegaard, *Purity of Heart*, 136, 138.

9.   Kierkegaard, *Purity of Heart*, 160.

10. Kierkegaard, *Purity of Heart*, 31.

11. Calvin, *Institutes of the Christian Religion*, IV.1.5.

12. Calvin, *Institutes of the Christian Religion*, IV.3.1.

13. Markus Barth, *Ephesians*, Anchor Bible 34 (New York: Doubleday, 1974), 479.

14. F. F. Bruce, *Commentary on the Epistles to the Ephesians and the Colossians*, New International Commentary on the New Testament (Grand Rapids: Eerdmans, 1957), 219.

15. Peter O'Brien, *Colossians, Philemon*, Word Biblical Commentary 44 (Waco, TX: Word Books, 1982), 90.

16. Allen P. Ross, *The Psalms* (Grand Rapids: Kregel, 2011–2016), 3:460.

17. Derek Kidner, *Psalms 73–150* (Downers Grove, IL: InterVarsity Press, 1973), 419.

18. Leslie C. Allen, *Psalms 101–150*, Word Biblical Commentary 21 (Waco, TX: Word Books, 1983), 140, 142.

19. Dietrich Bonhoeffer, *Meditating on the Word* (New York: Ballantine, 1986), 93.

20. Bruner, *Churchbook*, 1:23–24.

21. Bruner, *Churchbook*, 1:24.

22. Peter Gillquist, "A Marathon We Are Meant to Win," *Christianity Today*, Oct 1981: 22.

CHAPTER 7

1.   Thomas Bandy, "This Is the Christ Postmodern People Need to Hear About," *NETResults* (Nov/Dec 2000): 13–15. Bandy is critical of "modern Christendom clergy" who think that they have the four Sundays of Advent to tell the Christmas story from "obscure lectionary texts vaguely describing a coming Messiah in metaphors nobody really understands." If we expect to evangelize the "spiritually hungry, institutionally alienated public," Bandy advises dropping the lectionary texts and preaching

only the truth of Col 1:19–20 throughout December and especially Christmas Eve. Bandy believes Christmas Eve is the "pivotal moment of the year" evangelistically. Wise pastors know that on Christmas Eve they are preaching to many people unfamiliar with Old Testament prophecies of the coming of the Messiah, but that does not remove the responsibility of preaching the deep story of Christ to the people of God through Advent.

2. Douglas D. Webster, *A Christmas Journey* (Toronto: Clements, 2007), 36.

3. Jonathan Haidt, *The Righteous Mind* (New York: Pantheon, 2012), 281.

4. Vicky Walker, "An Interview with Sir David Suchet: The Bible Cannot Be Silenced," *Church Times*, Apr 16, 2021, https://www.churchtimes.co.uk/articles/2021/16-april/features/features/an-interview-with-sir-david-suchet-the-bible-cannot-be-silenced.

5. Quoted in Richard Dinwiddie, "Messiah: Behind the Scenes of Handel's Masterpiece," *Christianity Today*, Dec 17, 1982, 14.

6. Dinwiddie, "Messiah," 16.

7. J. Alec Motyer, *The Prophecy of Isaiah: An Introduction and Commentary* (Downers Grove, IL: InterVarsity Press, 1993), 299.

8. Dietrich Bonhoeffer, *Letters and Papers from Prison* (New York: Macmillan, 1971), 135.

9. Bruner, *Churchbook* 1:16, 22.

10. Walter Brueggemann, *Genesis: Interpretation* (Atlanta: John Knox, 1982), 12–13.

11. Craig S. Keener, *Matthew* (Downers Grove, IL: InterVarsity Press, 1997), 54.

12. Bruner, *Churchbook,* 1:12.

13. Bruner, *Churchbook,* 1:12.

14. Bruner, *Churchbook,* 1:14.

15. Bruner, *Churchbook,* 1:22.

16. Bruner, *Churchbook,* 1:20.

17. C. S. Lewis, *Mere Christianity* (San Francisco: HarperCollins, 2001), 46.

18. Bruner, *Churchbook,* 1:68.

19. David Augsburger, *Dissident Discipleship* (Grand Rapids: Baker, 2006), 149.

20. J. Sidlow Baxter, *Awake My Heart* (Grand Rapids: Zondervan, 1960), 371.

21. Robert Mounce, *The Book of Revelation,* rev. ed., New International Commentary on the New Testament (Grand Rapids: Eerdmans, 1997), 232.

22. Martin Luther, "Preface to the Old Testament," vol. 35, *Luther's Works*, ed. E. Theodore Bachmann (Philadelphia: Muhlenberg, 1960), 235–36.

23. Webster, *Christmas Journey*, back cover.

CHAPTER 8

1. Lewis, *Mere Christianity*, 52–53.

2. Arthur Pink, *The Seven Sayings of the Savior on the Cross* (Louisville: GLH, 2019), 61.

3. Augustine, "Homilies on the Gospel of John," in *Nicene and Post-Nicene Fathers*, vol. 7, ed. Philip Schaff (Peabody, MA: Hendrickson, 1995), CXIX.19:24–30.

4. Charles H. Spurgeon, *Christ's Words from the Cross* (Grand Rapids: Baker, 1997), 51.

5. Spurgeon, *Christ's Words from the Cross*, 53.

6. Spurgeon, *Christ's Words from the Cross*, 53–54.

7. D. A. Carson, *Matthew*, Expositors Bible Commentary (Grand Rapids: Zondervan, 2010), 647.

8. Larry W. Hurtado, *Mark*, Understanding the Bible Commentary Series (Grand Rapids: Baker, 1989), 269.

9. Spurgeon, *Christ's Words from the Cross*, 52.

10. William D. Edwards, Wesley J. Gabel, and Floyd E. Hosmer, "On the Physical Death of Jesus Christ," *Journal of the American Medical Association* 255.11 (1986): 1455–63.

11. Edwards, Gabel, and Hosmer, "On the Physical Death," 1461.

12. Gregory of Nazianzen, "Letter to Cledonius," Epistle 101 in *Nicene and Post-Nicene Fathers*, vol. 7, second series, edited by Philip Schaff and Henry Wace (Peabody, MA: Hendrickson, 1995), 440.

13. Lewis, *Mere Christianity*, 145.

14. George R. Beasley-Murray, *John*, Word Biblical Commentary 36 (Waco, TX: Word Books, 1987), 352. Murray quotes A. Dauer, *De Passionsgeschichte im Johannesevangelium* (Munich: Kösel, 1972).

15. Oswald Chambers, *My Utmost for His Highest* (New York: Dodd, Mead, 1935), 11/21.

16. C. S. Lewis, *Miracles* (New York: Collins, 1978), 115.

17. Lewis, *Mere Christianity*, 58.

18. Spurgeon, *Christ's Words from the Cross*, 100.

19. Spurgeon, *Christ's Words from the Cross*, 101, 103.

20. Peter Craigie, *Psalms 1–50*, Word Biblical Commentary 19 (Waco, TX: Word Books, 1983), 260.

CHAPTER 9

1. Timothy Keller, *Preaching: Communicating Faith in an Age of Skepticism* (New York: Viking, 2015), 10–11.

2. Douglas D. Webster, *Second Thoughts for Skeptics* (Toronto: Regent College Publishing, 2010), 125–44.

3. Rudolf Bultmann, *Kerygma and Myth*, ed. Hans Werner Bartsch (New York: Harper & Row, 1961), 39.

4. I. Howard Marshall, *Luke: Historian and Theologian* (Grand Rapids: Zondervan, 1982), 48.

5. Bill Bryson, *A Short History of Nearly Everything* (New York: Broadway, 2004), 32, 129, 135.

6. Bryson, *Short History*, 235, 311, 365.

7. Richard Dawkins, *The God Delusion* (Boston: Houghton Mifflin, 2006), 140–41.

8. Bryson, *Short History*, 478.

9. Francis Crick, *The Astonishing Hypothesis: The Scientific Search for the Soul* (New York: Simon & Schuster, 1994), 3.

10. C. S. Lewis, *Surprised by Joy* (London: Fontana, 1955), 139.

CHAPTER 10

1. Samuel Harrington, *At Peace: Choosing a Good Death after a Long Life* (New York: Grand Central Life and Style, 2018), 30.

2. Martin Luther, as quoted in Raymond Brown, *The Message of Hebrews*, The Bible Speaks Today (Downers Grove, IL: InterVarsity Press, 1984), 71.

3. Calvin, *Institutes of the Christian Religion*, III.9.5.

CHAPTER 11

1. Eugene H. Peterson, *Run with the Horses* (Downers Grove, IL: InterVarsity Press, 1983), 68.

2. Augustine, *Confessions*, trans. Henry Chadwick (Oxford: Oxford University Press, 1993), 3.

3. This section follows *The Book of Common Prayer* (New York: Church Publishing, 1979), 429–30.

CHAPTER 12

1.   Martin Luther, "A Mighty Fortress Is Our God," in *The Worshiping Church: A Hymnal,* ed. Donald P. Hustad (Carol Stream, IL: Hope, 1990), 42.

2.   Isaac Watts, "Joy to the World! The Lord Is Come," in *Worshiping Church,* 146.

3.   John Wesley, "Serious Thoughts Occasioned by the Late Earthquake at Lisbon," in *The Works of John Wesley,* vol. 11 (New York: J. Emory & Waugh, 1818), 1–13.

4.   Eugene H. Peterson, *Earth and Altar: The Community of Prayer in a Self-Bound Society* (Downers Grove, IL: InterVarsity Press, 1985), 73.

5.   Frances R. Havergal, "Like a River Glorious," in *Worshiping Church,* 594.

6.   Wesley, "Serious Thoughts."

7.   John Goldingay, *Psalms 42–89* (Grand Rapids: Baker, 2007), 2:71.

8.   Webster, *Follow the Lamb,* 222–23.

9.   Derek Kidner, *Psalms 1–72* (Downers Grove, IL: InterVarsity Press, 1975), 176.

10. Ross, *Psalms,* 2:98.

11. Goldingay, *Psalms,* 2:73. Goldingay comments, "At the same time, we have to be wary of missing what the text actually did say. Here it issues an important challenge to the superpower to stand still and recognize that God is God and that the superpower is not."

CHAPTER 13

1.   Bruner, *Churchbook,* 2:119.

2.   Scot McKnight, *Kingdom Conspiracy: Returning to the Radical Mission of the Local Church* (Grand Rapids: Brazos, 2014), 86.

3.   John H. Elliot, *1 Peter: The Anchor Yale Bible.* New Haven, CT: Yale University Press, 2000, 418.

4.   Keller, *Preaching,* 120.

5.   McKnight, *Kingdom Conspiracy,* 101.

6.   McKnight, *Kingdom Conspiracy,* 102.

7.   Timothy Keller, *Counterfeit Gods: The Empty Promises of Money, Sex, and Power, and the Only Hope That Matters* (New York: Dutton, 2009), 99.

8.   James Davison Hunter, *To Change the World: The Irony, Tragedy, and Possibility of Christianity in the Late Modern World* (New York: Oxford University Press, 2010), 184–85.

9. D. A. Carson, *The Gospel according to John* (Grand Rapids: Eerdmans, 1991), 561.

10. D. A. Carson, *Christ and Culture Revisited* (Grand Rapids: Eerdmans, 2008), 43.

SEVEN THESES ON GOOD PREACHING

1. Frederick Dale Bruner, *The Gospel of John* (Grand Rapids: Eerdmans, 2012), 341.

2. Martin Luther, "Concerning the Ministry" (1523), *Luther's Works*, vol. 40, ed. Conrad Bergendoff (Philadelphia: Fortress, 1999), 21.

3. Smith, *Doctrine That Dances*, 44.

Subject & Name Index

Scripture Index

Old Testament

New Testament

PASTORS CARE FOR A SOUL IN THE WAY A DOCTOR CARES FOR A BODY.

In a time when many churches have lost sight of the real purpose of the church, *The Care of Souls* invites a new generation of pastors to form the godly habits and practical wisdom needed to minister to the hearts and souls of those committed to their care.

"Pastoral theology at its best. Every pastor, and everyone who wants to be a pastor, should read this book."
—Timothy George, Founding Dean, Beeson Divinity School, Samford University; General Editor, Reformation Commentary on Scripture

LEXHAM PRESS

For more information, visit
LexhamPress.com/Care-of-Souls